# The Child in Question

## Other books by Diana Gittins

**Non-fiction**

*Fair Sex: Family Size and Structure 1900–1939*

*The Family in Question: Changing Households and Familiar Ideologies* (second edition)

**Poetry**

*Dance of the Sheet*

# The Child in Question

## Diana Gittins

Consultant Editor: Jo Campling

First published 1998 by
MACMILLAN PRESS LTD
Houndmills, Basingstoke, Hampshire RG21 6XS
and London
Companies and representatives throughout the world

ISBN 0-333-51108-5 hardcover
ISBN 0-333-51109-3 paperback

A catalogue record for this book is available from the British Library.

This book is printed on paper suitable for recycling and made from fully
managed and sustained forest sources.

10   9   8   7   6   5   4   3   2   1
07   06   05   04   03   02   01   00   99   98

Printed in Hong Kong

*For Emily, Giovanni and their children*
*with love*

# CONTENTS

List of Illustrations     ix
Foreword     x
Preface     xi
Acknowledgements     xviii

**Introduction**     1
    Theory? What Theory?     12

**1   Is Childhood Socially Constructed?**     21
    History and Childhood     26
    Different Children, Different Lives     32
    Children and Nature     38
    If it's all Constructed, is it all Just a Story?     43

**2   Who Owns Children?**     46
    Slavery     49
    Illegitimacy     53
    Work     57
    Education     69
    In Whose Best Interests?     74

**3   Is there a Child Within?**     80
    The Child and Interiority     81
    The Unconscious     84
    Projection     90
    Poisonous Pedagogy?     94
    Memories, Violence, Mothers     99

**4  What do Children Represent?**                              109
    Paintings                                                   117
    Family Photographs                                          131
    Myths, Stories and Fairy Tales                              135
    A Story of the Nation?                                      143

**5  Are Children Innocent?**                                   145
    Original Sin, *Tabula Rasa* or Naturally Good?              146
    Representations of Innocence in Literature                  153

**6  Children's Sexuality: Why do Adults Panic?**               173
    What is Sexuality?                                          175
    The Cleveland Crisis                                        180
    Body/Mind                                                   185
    The Great Masturbation Debate                               191
    Desire for Children                                         197

**Conclusion**                                                  202

Notes                                                           208
Bibliography                                                    213
Index                                                           227

# LIST OF ILLUSTRATIONS

Figure 1    Hogarth, *The Graham Children*                              114
Figure 2    Cambodian boys cool off in Tonle Sap river                 115
Figure 3    Hans Memlinc, *The Virgin and Child*                       120
Figure 4    Frans Hals, *Catharina Hooft with her Nurse*               122
Figure 5    Lebanese girl and apple                                    124
Figure 6    Goya, *The Family of the Duke of Osuna*                     126
Figure 7    Gainsborough, *The Painter's Daughters*
            *Chasing a Butterfly*                                       129
Figure 8    Millais, *Sweetest Eyes were Ever Seen*                     130
Figure 9    Family photograph: Repulsive II (i)                        134
Figure 10   Family photograph: Repulsive II (ii)                       134
Figure 11   Family photograph: mother and daughters                    134

# FOREWORD

In might well be thought, in the final decade of the twentieth century, given the frequency of international horror stories involving children, that the status of childhood has improved little, if at all, since the world of Dickens, Lamb or Alcott. Neither the plethora of legislation, the good intentions of the welfare professionals nor the vigilance of investigative jornalists have proved to be the guarantee of empowerment or fulfilment for children as a group.

In writing this book Diana Gittins has simultaneously attempted to wrestle back the theory and practice of childhood from the grasp of the 'experts' whoever they be – sociologists psychologists, social workers, politicians – and to give them back in return a genuinely child-centred account of what it means, or what it *might* mean, to be a child. In doing so she illuminates the path for adults, including students and practitioners, to bodies of knowledge which might simultaneously enhance our understanding of children, childhood, and our own experiences. She reunites the personal and political in a way that ought to provide new incentives for grappling with the systems without imposing yet another straight-jacket on a group to which we've all belonged.

*Professor Jane Tunstill*
*University of Keele*

# PREFACE

It was the trees that set me off: the wild orange, red and gold of them. I could smell dank piles of raked leaves, wood smoke, pine needles, the vapour rising from damp dirt roads. I could hear the crack of a baseball bat spinning a ball into crisp blue sky, the sound of laughter, the song of the chickadees. I could taste ice-cold apple cider from a flagon bought at a roadside stand. I could feel the slime of stringy pumpkin flesh entwined with hundreds of viscous seeds that my sister and I scooped out ready for mother to carve the macabre face on a jack-o-lantern.

I was sitting in a cinema in Oxford Street, London watching *A League of their Own*. Neither the narrative nor the acting moved me, but the landscape and the colours of upstate New York in the 1940s brought back, like Proust's notorious madeleine, a rush of memories. I felt euphoric. I wanted to go back there, to return to the place of my childhood. Suddenly I felt I *had* to go back, back to the land I'd left 35 years ago. I had to go back to that ecstasy of childhood bliss.

What was peculiar, however, was that I had spent much of the past few years in therapy and in groups exploring and abreacting the horrors and pains of childhood. I had scooped out much of the twisted and viscous mass of negative emotions that had come from the jack-o-lantern of disturbed parents, sexual abuse and betrayal. The face of it was hideous; etchings of rape and leering psychosis were in the orange secrecy that now shone eerily in my front window, scaring away all but the most intrepid of trick-or-treaters.

So where had all these ecstatic memories come from so suddenly, so unexpectedly? Of course, I always knew there had been good times: going by sled through the snow with my father to cut down a Christmas tree; long, hot summers on the Rhode Island coast. After we left upstate New York there were years spent at a progressive school in the hills of Vermont, where we grew up among interesting intellectuals and artists, many seeking a haven from the horrors of the McCarthy witch hunts. I remembered my mother leading the Harvest Festival on a motorbike, then cartwheeling across fields in the September sun. I remembered Fernando Gerassi, friend of Sartre and de Beauvoir, standing on his bald head at my request in the school entrance. I remembered meeting Eleanor Roosevelt. I remembered my friend's parents who, deeply committed to the theories of Wilhelm Reich, used to sit naked in a kind of shower cubicle – the 'orgone box' – in the middle of their kitchen, chaotic with cats, children, old-fashioned milk cans and freshly picked apples. I remembered the freedom of roaming dirt roads, totally without adult supervision, exploring the pleasures of woods and streams and what seemed to be an endless, timeless scope for imaginative play.

All this contrasted so markedly with memories of being made to pose for pornographic photographs by my father. It contrasted with memories of my mother taking me to bed with her lover. It contrasted with my sister's intense, pathological hatred of me. It seemed so far removed from the all-pervasive terror I remembered – terror that kept me from school; terror that, after being raped when I was seven, left me with epileptic fits. And so I began to wonder, who was this child? Were there, in fact, two children, two childhoods? What does it mean to have been two children, two girls? It seems that the public face of my childhood, the sense of self built up by family narratives and photographic albums (there were no pornographic photos stuck in *there*) contradicted the painful memories hidden, so long unacknowledged and unexpressed in my unconscious. And yet, long before I went into therapy, I had an uneasy sense that there were other things more painful, that something had gone terribly wrong.

These questions led to more general ones. Is this, I wondered, how other children experienced childhood(s)? Could my own childhood have been in any way typical, or was I indeed some kind of freak outside of childhood altogether? What *is* this strange being we call 'the child' that seems to be everywhere – inside my mind, my memory, my photograph album – but co-exists with, and often contradicts, images and narratives in films, advertisements, television, books and articles? Who is this that seems both familiar and alien, puzzlingly both adored and feared? How does my own sense of having had a double child-hood correspond to broader cultural notions of childhood? How typical had been my experience of cruelty and abuse juxtaposed with the delights of a privileged middle-class upbringing in beautiful environments? How do all these questions relate to the material situation of other children worldwide: girls, boys, African, Asian, Muslim, Jewish, poor, ill, rich, hungry, homeless? When is a child not a child, and if a child is not a child, who makes such pronouncements?

As I reflected on these questions, so the apparently simple concept of 'the child' became increasingly complex and contra-dictory. There seemed to be so many children, so many child-hoods. 'The child', I concluded, exists at a number of levels: the personal level (both conscious and unconscious, memoried and forgotten); the material level, both in relation to embodiment, and in relation to access to various material resources; and at a cul-tural and representational level in art, photography, narratives of all sorts, and advertisements. As a result of these insights, how-ever, I came to realise that, for me, 'the child' could only be studied in a diverse, eclectic and interdisciplinary way. This may be considered by some to be an unconventional approach, and warrants an account of how I came to arrive at it.

Soon after I finished writing *The Family in Question* – in that ominous year, 1984 – I resigned an academic post as Lecturer in Sociology. Interested in social history, historical demography and the history of the family, my academic work until then had been greatly informed and influenced by Marxism and feminism. My primary focus was on material inequalities and injustices between social classes, and between women and men. Theories of social class, however, seemed woefully inadequate in explain-ing gender inequalities. The concept of patriarchy, though problematic, attracted me at this time, because it offered some insights into these. I was also influenced by Foucault and post-structuralist theories that brought attention to the importance of power, power relations and resistance. These I saw, and continue to see, as crucial determinants of inequalities affecting women, men and children. My second book, *The Family in Question*, was a result of these influences, in conjunction with many years of having to teach 'the family' using texts that I regarded as hopelessly outdated, based as they were on 1950s functionalist theory.

After writing it, however, something shifted for me. A series of tragedies in my own family led me into questioning the importance of more subjective and emotional aspects of families, living conditions and, indeed, 'the self'. I went into therapy and immediately began to confront a tidal wave of emotions and memories long hidden and denied. Neither sociology nor social history offered me any insights or explanations to these. Nor did Marxism or Foucauldianism. Emotion did not seem to be on the agenda of social science.

The world of emotions, transference and painful recall of my personal past jarred my 'sociological self' to the core. It has never fully recovered, though it has been part of the development of a more eclectic self. As I began to understand some of the reasons why I was who (I thought) I had become, old patterns started to fall apart. I read and re-read Freud, delved into Jung, Klein and Irigaray. I became fascinated by the workings and manifestations of the unconscious, both in theoretical writings and in my own experiences in therapy and dreaming. I also became acutely aware of how important 'the child' that (I thought) I had once been remained to who (I thought) I might be(come).

Six months after beginning therapy I gave up smoking (80 cigarettes a day!), gave up drinking two litres of black coffee a day, and stopped taking barbiturates, which I had been prescribed for over 27 years. I began to dream for the first time since I was nine years old (barbiturates suppress dreaming). During this time I also began to write – and read and re-read – poetry. I grew to realise how important images and imagery are, not just in poetry and dreams but in culture generally. I became fascinated with metaphor, symbolism and myth. All these 'irrational' phenomena seemed to offer insights and understanding in a way social science had never done. They helped me to understand my feelings, other people's feelings, my childhood memories, and offered insights into the irrational aspects of my thought processes and behaviour. The *aesthetic* aspect of them seemed vital; not just images, but the sounds and rhythm of words were part of a growing pleasure in language itself.

I began to value, appreciate and explore my own imagination, my creativity, and indeed the whole subjective 'irrational' aspect of my self which I had so long suppressed and denied, but which had also been denied, it seemed to me, by sociological theory. The ways in which things stood for other things – ways in which things were represented by imagery, metaphor and metonymy in language, dreams, and poetry – seemed to me to be an incredibly important aspect of self, culture, living. A healthier body, a body that felt as if it was melting after being frozen in ice for most of my life, made me increasingly aware of the importance of my own embodiment, a supreme material reality that Marxism had never, as it were, touched.

For several years I could not see how these discoveries could in any way be reconciled with my earlier beliefs and experiences. My own material poverty during this time seemed irrelevant in contrast to the revelations and insights I felt I was achieving. Although the childhood memories tapped in therapy were often excruciatingly painful, the release of them, the relief of bringing them into the light contributed to what I can only describe as a feeling of rebirth, or perhaps renovation would be more apt. It eventually led to the publication of a collection of my poetry, *Dance of the Sheet*.

Poverty, however, began to take its toll; proof, I suppose, of the validity of many of the theories I had recently been rejecting. I started working for the Open University as a consultant to the Women's Studies course team. Here I realised social science had not stood still during the time I had been spiralling into my psyche. Feminism and social science had joined hands with postmodernism, it seemed, to tackle some of the issues I had been confronting at a purely personal level. Postmodernist theory, for instance, raised important issues about subjectivity and identity and the construction of these through discourse and culture. For someone who felt deeply divided as a result of therapy and confrontation with a traumatic, hidden past, the discovery that postmodernist theory propounded the idea that we are all fragmented was deeply satisfying!

History, poetry/representation, psychoanalysis, postmodern-ism, feminism, Marxism – these have been the bodies of ideas that have most influenced me and which I draw on in this book around the theme of 'the child'. There are aspects of all of them that relate directly to the theme, yet I cannot, and will not, single out one perspective as the appropriate way in which to approach the subject. Perhaps such an eclectic approach weakens the possibility of formulating a neat, rational and logical argument or theory. I do believe, nevertheless, that it is imperative to understand 'the child' at different levels, because all these levels in the end are interrelated and affect one another.

Our own memoried and unconscious child and childhood affect what we think the child, children, childhood and childrearing are and should be. Our beliefs and memories are partly determined by wider cultural discourses, but they also feed into and contribute to these. Discourses, meanings and beliefs do not just float aimlessly in air. They are used to justify, rationalise and implement behaviours, policies and legislation. These inform and construct, and are in turn informed and constructed by, power relations of all sorts. These then affect children – and adults – in material ways and discursive ways which we experience as embodied beings.

If we try to understand 'the child' without acknowledging the centrality of our own experiences we stand in danger of making one-sided judgements and taking one-dimensional actions that deny a vital aspect of the meanings of 'the child' and 'childhood' in humanity and culture. I argue here that this is exactly what tends to happen; by denying the darker more shadowy and unconscious side of our selves, we end up denying its existence in everyone, including children. If we define children as angels, we also create a need for devils, because those aspects of children and of ourselves that we cannot accept as good must be directed, projected somewhere else. By doing this we project unwanted aspects of our selves on to others who are then stereotyped and scapegoated as Other.

Much of this book, therefore, focuses on the darker, more negative aspects concerning 'the child' and what it means to adults. I do not mean to neglect or ignore the more positive and happy aspects of 'the child' and 'childhood', which undoubtedly mean an enormous amount to all of us. Rather, I am interested in the contradictions between the positive ideas and hopes for 'the child', and the irrational, apparently dark and negative ways in which adults frequently act towards children, and, indeed, how children themselves can behave in ways adults regard as unacceptable and transgressive. Crucial to my argument overall is that only by trying to take on board the more negative and unaccept-able aspects both of ourselves and of children are we likely to be able to move towards change.

*Diana Gittins*

# Acknowledgements

This book has been a long time in the making. I would like to thank, therefore, both Frances Arnold and Catherine Gray, my editors at Macmillan, for their patience. Jo Campling has given me much help and advice throughout this protracted process and I would also like to thank her. I am very grateful to the staff of the Totnes Library, who diligently dealt with an endless succession of inter-library loan requests during a period when I had no access to academic library facilities. I would also like to thank my students on the freshman seminar 'What is a Child?' at Colgate University, who contributed to many lively discussions and were very kind to me during a difficult time. Most of all, however, it has been my dear and good friends who have given me no end of support and helped me to believe that eventually I would be able to finish this book. To them I owe the greatest debt and would like to thank them all, especially Joan Busfield, Isabel Cabot, John Daniel, Yasmin David, Leonore Davidoff, Felicity Edholm, Frankie Finn and Sarah Hopkins.

The author and publishers would like to thank the following illustration sources:

The Guardian pp. 115 (photographer Richard Vogl), 124; Museo del Prado, Madrid p. 126; The National Gallery, London pp. 114, 120, 129; The National Gallery of Scotland, Edinburgh p. 130; Staatliche Museen Preussischer Kulturbesitz Gemaldegalerie p. 122.

The photographs on p. 134 were supplied by the author.

Every effort has been made to trace all copyright holders but if any have been inadvertently overlooked the publishers will be pleased to make the necessary arrangements at the first opportunity.

# INTRODUCTION

Children delight us. They are beautiful. We celebrate their births and marvel at their growth. Women who cannot conceive often go to extreme lengths to try and obtain children by other means: *in vitro* fertilisation, surrogacy, adoption, abduction, purchase. Children are often central figures in films, television programmes, books and advertising. Our walls and shelves burst with photographs of them. We mourn their loss like no other loss. We see in them qualities of innocence, purity, trust, beauty and joy, which we see in virtually no other phenomena – qualities which we feel, by becoming adult, we have lost. Governments attempt to protect them and provide for them when nobody else can. Children in the past were worshipped as saints and martyrs. Because they are apparently so special in contemporary culture, it seems we, too, view them as almost divine. They are our future, a new beginning, our hope of regeneration.

Why, then, do a large proportion of adults abuse children physically, sexually and emotionally? Why do men like Thomas Hamilton, who claimed to love children, end up massacring a whole class of schoolchildren?[1] If children are so welcome, why have parents for so long set about chastising them, often quite severely, from an early age? Why do priests, social workers, teachers who purport to 'care' for children – many of whom have been professionally trained to do so – sometimes abuse the children they are employed to protect? Why do an increasing number of children, even in western countries, live in poverty? If we venerate children as we claim to do, why are they disenfranchised, not allowed to earn money or make decisions about their own lives? Why do we find children's violence so shocking

1

and transgressive, given that violence is rife in society and constantly represented in the media? In other words, what does 'the child' mean to us as adults, and why are these meanings so contradictory?

'The child' is a myth, a fiction, an adult construction. So is 'childhood'. Both, however, have become symbolically central to our culture and psychologically crucial to our sense of self. 'The child' exists in imagery that pervades our conscious, and indeed our unconscious, worlds; images of children are everywhere. They are not, however, children we know, but are representations of 'the child' designed and constructed by advertisers, television producers, photographers. In the past children filled the streets, parks and pavements in a way they no longer do. Declining fertility has resulted in fewer children; increased fear about children's safety has meant that we see 'real' children less, and when we do see them they are usually under adult supervision. Instead we are constantly confronted with images of children, images that are used to sell consumer products or to elicit donations to charity. What are the repercussions of such images and the associations they make in our minds?

Our minds are a crucial area where children lurk and linger. We sometimes dream of them. Memories of our own childhoods inform our ideas about who we think we are, who we think we once were, what we believe children are, and what, therefore, we believe 'the child' and 'childhood' should be. Memory, however, exists at different levels, conscious and unconscious, and early memories can be affected by images, narratives and experiences we subsequently encounter. Arguably, the most powerful memories exist and fester at an unconscious level we rarely know or acknowledge, yet which still influence our behaviour. Such hidden memories are by definition irrational. Yet we like to think we are rational, logical beings who behave consistently and coherently. Increasingly, however, it is becoming apparent that we are no such thing. Instead we are fragmented, contradictory, complex beings. Social workers, judges, government ministers, child killers, paedophiles, psychiatrists and parents all were children once. Each and every one of us consequently carries our own, usually well-hidden and frequently denied, emotional and irrational baggage relating to our own subjective experiences of having once been a child.

The term 'the child' denies these contradictions and complexities within us, just as it denies the very different life chances that exist between children born of different genders, classes, ethnic groups, family-households, religions and nations. Yet the term is used almost constantly by legislators, administrators and the media as if there really were *one* child, *one* childhood. The year 1994, for instance, was proclaimed the Year of the Child. But *which* child, *whose* child, and was it a girl or a boy, black or white, healthy, diseased, or maimed? Was it living in a five-bedroom house in Chicago, a children's home in rural Italy, or on the streets of Rio?

The notion of 'the child' is more complicated than it seems. It embraces, like so many words, many different layers of meaning. In Old English *cild* was related to the Gothic *kilpei*, meaning 'womb', and it denotes 'foetus' and 'infant' as well as 'boy' or 'girl'. Clearly at one level it relates to embodiment and biology. In the Bible it referred to youths entering manhood (Daniel 1:17) as well as to a lad in service or page. Dependency, then, is also one layer of its meaning. In Middle English it indicated a (male) chorister. It has also been, then, a gendered concept. Moreover, it was, and continues to be, used as a general expression for descendants, disciples, origin, extraction and offspring. Some expression of kinship or intimacy is thus another layer of meaning. Dictionary definitions, however, give few clues and little insight to some of the issues raised by personal experiences.

We tend to think of 'child' as having a clear chronological meaning directly related to biological development, but there is no universal agreement as to when a child ceases to be a child and becomes an adult; indeed, there are many different and conflicting definitions within our own culture. In Britain, both sexes may have (hetero)sexual relationships when they are 16, but males may not have homosexual relationships until they are 18. Sexual maturity thus apparently depends on what kind of sexual preference you have, or perhaps boys are deemed as warranting greater protection from predatory males than are girls. Marriage in western countries is often seen as a boundary, especially for women, between childhood and adulthood. In some countries, however, 'child brides' marry as young as eight or nine years old. Among the Nyinbas in Nepal, for example, some 50 per cent of marriages are polyandrous, and a woman may have several brothers as husbands, some of whom may be only six or seven years old.

In western countries a child may become economically active at the age of 15 or 16, although in the past children often worked from the age of four or five, a situation that still remains in many Third World countries. In Britain, a child may drink alcohol at home from the age of five, but not in a public house until 18. Muslims – women and men, children and adults – are not allowed to drink alcohol at all. In most western countries enfranchisement is now at 18; politically a person ceases to be a child at this age. Yet the age of criminal responsibility varies significantly from country to country. In Spain, for example, it is now 16, while it is 15 in Norway and 14 in Germany.

In Britain before 1933 it was only seven years old, and then it stood at eight until 1963. Yet in the Middle Ages – a time we usually imagine as brutal and cruel – the age of criminal responsibility in Britain was 14; children between the ages of seven and 14 could be placed on trial, but the customary punishment for all crimes was a whipping (Shahar, 1994, p. 255). Today the age of criminal responsibility in Britain stands at ten years old, so that in the legal system a ten-year-old can be treated as an adult, which is what happened to the boys who murdered James Bulger. Jon Venables and Robert Thompson, both aged ten, abducted James Bulger, aged two, from a shopping precinct in Bootle, Merseyside on 12 February, 1993. They beat him up and murdered him on a railway line. Though little of this was made in the trial, they also interfered sexually with him before he died. Many passers-by saw the older boys taking James and treating him roughly. Only one person tried to stop them, but they told her they had found a 'lost child'. At Preston crown court Venables and Thompson were sentenced to be detained at Her Majesty's Pleasure, the equivalent of a mandatory life sentence for murder. Eight years was the sentence recommended by the judge. But the Home Secretary, after receiving a petition from the Bulger family and 21 281 coupons from readers of the *Sun* newspaper, changed this sentence to at least 15 years. This has since been overruled by the European Court for Human Rights. There was a great deal of debate during the trial as to whether the boys understood adult morality and, implicitly, when they effectively ceased to be children.

There is no single definition of when childhood ends. The problem is further complicated by the fact that we are all in the rather peculiar situation of having been a child ourselves. Because of this we tend to assume we know what a child is. Yet as adults we are not embodied children any more and never will be again. Children are thus *transitory*. Having said that, however, it is important to realise that some social groups continue to be treated as children because in one way or another they are *defined* as non-adult. Slaves and servants have been treated this way, as symbolised by the use of the term 'boy' to signify their situation of dependency and subservience. In France the word *garçon* is still occasionally used to address waiters, who are often middle-aged men:

> Even as late as the eighteenth century, the French and German words *garçon* and *Knabe* referred to boys as young as six and as old as thirty or forty. In part, such confusions stemmed from the fact that such terms also denoted status or function . . . among Irish peasants it is still common to call unmarried, propertyless men 'boys', regardless of their age, because this denotes their low status in a community where marriage and inheritance mark one of the most important social boundaries. (Gillis, 1981, p. 1)

Women have often been treated as children and are still arguably seen by some as childlike. Legislation existed in most western countries until quite recently that forbade women to own property: everything she had was her father's or, if she were married, her husband's. This also applied to 'ownership' of children. Only widows could own property.[2] Political enfranchisement for women has been in existence for less than a century.[3] Use of the term 'girl' to refer to often middle-aged women in subservient positions, such as secretaries, typists, and shop assistants, reinforces this. Not all children, it seems, are necessarily transitory beings. Colonisers treated those they colonised as inferior, animal-like and childlike. Indeed, these associations were enshrined in Haeckel's theory of recapitulation, which argued that the development of the individual human recapitulates the development of the species.[4] *Dependency* is thus arguably the term that correlates most closely with a definition of 'the child'.

Dependency alone, however, is not an adequate definition of 'the child', although other defining characteristics are arguably linked to it. The child, for instance, is often treated as *Other*, in the sense of being anything (or something) that is non-adult. Yet we all have been a child and we all therefore have a sense of having been something we no longer feel we are. At an individual level the child is thus always Other, and yet, paradoxically, our memories of having been a child seem to remain a central part of our sense of subjectivity, our sense of who we are and who we think we have been. Memories are thus crucial, and arguably memories, both conscious and unconscious, affect our behaviour and beliefs as adults far more than we even realise. Some memories manifest themselves more reluctantly than others, yet if we accept Freud's theory of the unconscious, they continue none the less to affect our patterns of behaviour.

A memoried child and child as Other, however, make uneasy bedfellows. As Jordanova argues:

> The peculiarity of the otherness we assign to children is paradoxical in that we have all experienced childhood – hence to make the child other to our adult selves we must split off a part of our past, a piece of ourselves. This accounts for the profound ambivalence which informs our attitudes to children and which is relived when we become parents ourselves. (Jordanova, 1989, p. 6)

The child we think we remember may be constructed as much from more recent influences – films, books, stories relatives tell us about ourselves, family photographs – as from precise recollections from years ago. Memory is a slippery concept. My mother, for example, always claimed she remembered seeing Santa Claus fly across the night sky. The trickeries of memory, however, can also be manipulated by those who do not want children to remember abusive acts and behaviour: 'False Memory Syndrome' has become an important issue in the debate about child abuse. Who ultimately can decide the truth of a memory? Arguably we use images to express true feelings and experiences which the images *represent* even if what we think we remember seeing was not possible. My mother's vision of Santa, for instance, is quite a good and true expression of her belief in his existence at the time.

Moreover, there is a body of assumptions both within us as individuals and also part of our wider culture that defines what 'the child' and 'childhood' *should* be, and these forces may be as influential in forming our idea of who we think we were as a child as are more hidden memories.

We usually think of children as innocent, hopeful, angelic. Innocence is a defining characteristic of 'the child'. Childhood is seen, and represented as, idyllic, carefree, happy, but also something we have irretrievably lost. While loss is then an important way in which adults define childhood, at the same time children are seen as both symbolising and embodying the future. We see children both as the future generation of our culture and as those we hope, or assume, will in turn have children and carry on our family traditions, name and narratives. Such feelings of hope, futurity and joy are represented millions of times in posters, films, advertisements and family snapshots of smiling, apparently carefree children. Such images, however, are set up and constructed by adults for specific purposes. In the pornographic photos my father took, I was told to smile, and smile I did. My smile was not a reflection of happiness I was feeling, on the contrary, it was manipulated by him as part of the process by which he constructed an image to convey a meaning he wanted to dictate.

When used by the media, especially in advertising, representations of happy children often relate only very obliquely to the products being sold or the stories being told. As Patricia Holland points out concerning the prevalence of imagery of children:

> The imagery always draws on and nourishes the fantasy world of our longings. It mediates between our memory and our dreams . . . the nostalgia of imagery is part of the nostalgia each of us feels for a lost moment of satisfaction and a longing for a future of reconciliation and peace. (Holland, 1992, p. 12)

How children are represented by adults thus seems a crucial aspect of understanding what children mean. It seems clear that much of what children mean to adults relates to a sense of longing, yearning, and desire. This is often expressed in films, many of which focus on children and nostalgic yearning for a lost childhood: *Au Revoir les Enfants* is a good example of this.

Representations of children as joyful, innocent and carefree are not, however, universal; they are often contradicted by conflicting discourses of 'evil' or 'corrupt' children as in, for instance, representations of children who are violent and children who kill. Golding's *Lord of the Flies*, written in 1954, is a classic representation of this discourse. The recent film *The Good Son* also represents children in this way. The media drew on this discourse of children as evil when they reported on the two ten-year-olds who murdered James Bulger. Interestingly, however, perhaps because in our culture the equation of children with innocence is so deeply entrenched, Venables and Thompson were eventually defined not as 'bad children', but as 'non-children'. The enormity of their act defied our notions of what children can do and what children should be. The boundaries of childhood were thus shifted to accommodate adult definitions of children.

Arguably the idea of 'bad children' transgresses our idea of childhood because it accords children agency, independence. In our culture if children are not perceived as good, innocent and happy – and, most important, *dependent* – then they are represented instead as passive victims to whom bad is *done*. The media are full of images of damaged children: dying children, abused children, starving and war-damaged children. Almost all of them are represented as dependent and *dark* children, and they are overwhelmingly used as pleas for charity donations.

> Starving, ragged children stare out of news stories and advertisements for development charities. Even if the projects . . . are not directly related to children, children are frequently used to make the appeal; thus an association is constantly made between children who have a correct childhood and black children who have none. (Holland, 1992, p. 22)

Their darkness arguably distances them from how we like to think of *our* children while at the same time reminding us that childhood has a dark side. Instead of relating this to our own experiences, however, we can distant the apprehension such images evoke by locating it as Other, and 'out there'.

A National Children's Home charity advertisement in the early 1990s showed a picture of an abject little boy sitting on a bed; the message proclaimed was 'Kevin's Eight, but for him childhood's over'. Childhood was over, it seems, because he had been sexually abused. Contact with, or corruption by, adult sexuality is defined now as disqualifying a child from childhood. But who says? Children do not define who or what they are or who or what they should be. Adults do. If we want to understand 'the child' it seems, we need to understand first and foremost *what children mean to adults*. Meanings, of course, not only vary but also change. Is the child in some way universal or does it depend entirely on how adults have defined it? More than that, how were such meanings expressed through adult representations of 'the child' and 'childhood'? *Who* exactly was declaring through posters of abused children that sexual abuse disqualifies the abused from childhood? *Why* were such messages being conveyed, and to *whom*?

These questions lead to the central importance of understanding and disentangling *power relationships* affecting, and affected by, children. As Foucault makes clear (see, for instance, Foucault, 1972, 1977), power relations are complex, often contradictory, and arguably the most important ones are those that are least recognised and least visible. Power can operate on many levels: in material terms, for instance, through control of, and distribution of, material resources. This is most obvious at a macro level where certain groups and classes have less access to, or are denied, essential goods. Power is also implicit in definitions of dependency. Power relations are never, however, fixed, but shift and change over time. Education has only been compulsory for just over a century in Britain. Restrictions on child labour are historically recent. In 1900 working-class children smoked, drank and gambled and young children went into pubs. One woman who was born in 1903, for example, remembers that when she was six,

> Pubs weren't strict at all about children going in. I went with me mum and aunty and I used to have this gin spoon, which was a spoon layered with sugar then topped with gin. I'd have maybe three or four of them in the evening. I thought it was great! I had a real taste for it and I'd go rolling home with mum and aunty half drunk. (Humphries et al., 1988, p. 23)

Power relations also operate, of course, at a micro level within smaller groups and institutions such as schools, clubs, gangs and neighbourhoods. In family-households, for instance, girls and women often have less access to material resources such as food than do men and boys. At a discursive level, power relations imbue discourses which define and delineate who and what groups are entitled to what resources, who has control over others, who is represented in certain ways. These definitions are frequently contested, resisted and sometimes fought over.

Integral to power relations is resistance, and children's ability to resist in certain ways is rarely documented or deemed appropriate, so great is, presumably, both the material reality and the discursive reality of adult power over children. Yet children do resist, as any parent would testify. They refuse to eat certain foods (I remember insisting that I would eat peas only on Saturdays), refuse to wear certain clothes, say certain things, behave in adult-defined ways. Compliance by children is rarely gained without some struggle. The boys who murdered James Bulger, for instance, might be seen as resisting dominant adult representations of child and childhood that portray it as innocent, carefree and full of delight. How could such representations tally with their own experiences of poverty, cruelty and neglect? Part of the adult outrage at Venables' and Thompson's behaviour may have related to the boys' defiance of adult definitions of what childhood experience and behaviour *should* be. It could be argued, for example, that the stories adults tell of childhood and the images they create of it, may bear almost no relation to the actual experiences of many children. Perhaps this is why some resistant behaviour by children – violence, murder, 'hooliganism' – causes often extreme adult disquiet and protest.

At the trial of Venables and Thompson it was never asked *why* they did it. Such issues do not concern the legal system, which seeks only to establish whether or not a deed was done by certain individuals. To have asked such questions would have revealed the horrendous conditions in which the two boys had grown up, and might have led to awkward political questions about growing inequalities between children in Britain. Material embodied children live out their lives in an unequal society in which their standards of living, their health, their education, their life expectancy – in short, their life chances – vary enormously. Such issues are now rarely discussed and are increasingly denied, itself a prime example of 'invisible' power relations where inequality has been labelled as 'difference', thus effectively depoliticising the idea of inequality and its long association with ideas of social justice.

Crucial to this development has been the emergence of an apparently universal category of 'the child' and 'childhood'. The idea of '*the* child' and '*a* childhood' disguises difference and inequality at many different levels. Third World children do not have anything like the life chances that western children have; poor western children have far lower life chances than middle-class children; boys have better life chances than girls; black children have worse life chances than white children.

The child has arguably not only become simplified, but has also become universalised. Hendrick (1990) postulates four major ways in which this has occurred. First, there was a gradual shift from an idea of childhood as fragmented by group (especially urban/rural) and by class life experiences, to one much more coherent and uniform. Second, the rise of a 'domestic ideology' among the nascent middle classes from the late eighteenth century created new ideas about what childhood should be. Third, the evolution of an increasingly compulsory relationship between the state, the family, and welfare services enacted many of these new ideas. Finally, there was a political and cultural struggle to extend the developing concept of childhood through all social classes.[5]

The child has, in a real sense, become a myth, and become mythologised. Myth, Barthes ([1972] 1987, p. 143) argues 'is *depoliticised speech* . . . myth does not deny things, on the contrary, its function is to talk about them; simply, it purifies them, it makes them innocent, it gives them a natural and eternal justification.' Myth denies the complexities of history and historical construction; it 'gives them the simplicity of essences . . . it organises a world which is without contradictions because it is without depth' (Barthes, [1972] 1987, p. 143). To really understand what 'the child' means, therefore, it becomes essential to consider how and why contradictions, complexities and paradox have been denied and disguised. It becomes important to examine historically how and why children in the process of growing came to be set apart as special, different, Other, and how, in that process, differences and inequalities between them came to be erased and denied. How and where have these processes and problems been theorised? Where is the theory of 'the child'?

## Theory? What Theory?

It is my aim in this book to explore and attempt to disentangle some of the very real contradictions and complexities that are inherent in the apparently simple terms of 'the child' and 'childhood'. Broadly, I argue that to begin to understand these terms we must think of them as existing on at least three levels. First, there are embodied girls and boys whose life chances vary markedly according to the material circumstances into which they are born. Gender, class, ethnicity and nation are key factors here. Second, 'the child' exists in various representations in both imagery and texts; representations simplify what they represent, but are also presented as 'real'. Often, in fact, they are symbolic, but because they are taken out of their material, historical circumstances and thus de-contextualised, they can never be 'real' in any material sense. We may, however, believe them to be so, and such representations can arguably affect our ideas about 'the child' quite markedly. Third, we have all been children ourselves and thus harbour memories, associations and ideas relating to our own experiences of childhood which will affect, arguably determine, our ideas about 'the child' and 'childhood' generally. The symbolic, material and psychological levels undoubtedly overlap and intertwine, but it is crucial to recognise them, at least theoretically, as different spheres which can often contradict one another.

To tackle this has thus meant exploring a number of different subject areas and disciplines: history, literature, art, psychoanalysis and sociology. Because I, too, was a child and my views and attitudes undoubtedly influenced the material I chose to analyse and how I interpreted it, I have also drawn on some of my own memories and experiences. Not to do so, I think, would be dishonest. The result is a series of interrelated, and to a certain extent overlapping, essays from different perspectives. Because the map is so broad, of course, much detail is lost. My aim, however, has been to problematise and stimulate thought in general ways.

Theories, or more precisely, fragments of theories, relevant to studying 'the child' exist in many disciplines. In recent years, for instance, there has been a burgeoning interest in the history of child*hood* and child*rearing* (Ariès, 1960; Demos, 1970; de Mause, 1976; Greven, 1970, 1977; Pollock, 1983). Much of this work has grown from the wider field of the history of the family, into which 'the child' was subsumed. Much the same has been the case in sociology, where children have, until very recently, been generally studied as part of 'the family'.[6] Earlier, anthropologists such as Boas (1966) and Mead (1955a) made important explorations into cultural diversity in childrearing and attitudes to children, thus drawing attention to important issues around the question as to whether there can be any such thing as 'the' child. Psychologists have focused on physical and psychological development within the individual child, where the child is assumed to be universal and devoid of sexual, ethnic or class difference. Literature and art have explored the ways in which children generally are represented in texts and have related these to wider cultural meanings of 'the child'.

The theories are diverse, and will be referred to and discussed in subsequent chapters; it is impossible here to do all of them full justice and this is not my intention. Rather, I want to discuss briefly some of the key points arising from this diverse body of theories in conjunction with broader theoretical perspectives which help to elucidate the three levels on which it is necessary to consider 'the child': the material, the personal, and the cultural.

On a material level, Marxist theory highlights both the historical changeability of societies, and the material determinants of inequality, life chances, and living conditions. It elucidates ways in which poverty can be seen as not only a direct consequence of, but also a necessity for, a capitalist economy in which cheap labour is at the core of an overall drive to maximise profits. Children, like women and immigrants at different historical periods in different societies, have been, and in many countries remain, a key source of cheap labour. They have also been, and for many in Third World countries remain, a vital source of support to family-households, where survival often depends on several members being able to earn money. In such theories, however, children are studied only as part of the wider whole, both within the economic system overall and within the microeconomy of the family-household. Such theories are important in offering expla-

nations for the persistent inequalities between children in different countries and cultures. There has been a tendency in recent
years to downplay the centrality of material circumstances,
inequality and poverty generally. Yet, as Chapter 1 will show,
these are vital forces in determining the different life chances of
children worldwide.

Marxist theory, however, takes little note of differences between children based on gender. Historical and anthropological
data have made it abundantly clear that such differences have
been important in the past and remain so today. Feminist theory,
therefore, is important in the various ways in which it has qualified Marxism by focusing on ways in which ideas, beliefs and
ideology, but above all power relations based on gender, can
'determine' material conditions and life chances as much as
economic factors. The concept of patriarchy has been used by
some feminist theorists to try and explain this; Hartman's and
Eisenstein's arguments that capitalism and patriarchy should be
seen as co-existing systems were, for instance, very influential.[7]
Family-households, the education system and the legal system
ultimately seemed to work in the interests of capital, while at the
same time informed by, and informing, patriarchal ideology. The
concept of patriarchy, however, has always been controversial,
largely because it neither allows scope for historical specificity,
nor does it permit differentiation between black and white experiences of power relations based on gender. It is at least a way,
albeit a crude way, of expressing differences based on gender and
age rooted in inequalities often played out in, and expressed
through, both the metaphoric and material reality of family-
households.

The theories of Michel Foucault have become increasingly influential over the past decades by highlighting the ways in which
power relations are connected to, and determined by, knowledge
and communication (and their opposites, ignorance and secrecy).
Foucault's theories offer ways of understanding in more detail
patriarchal relationships based on gender and age, even though
this was not his intention. Indeed, Foucault has been criticised for
neglecting gender relations generally. His ideas, however, gave
insight into the ways in which information, representations and
discourse affect, and interact with, behaviour and practice. There
is much in these theories, in conjunction with historical practice

and research, to provide important insights into understanding the material circumstances of children and childhoods. At a personal, subjective and psychological level, however, they offer relatively little.

'The child' has been a traditional focus of psychology for at least a century. Theories of child development articulate ages and stages at which it is believed certain behaviours are appropriate/normal/necessary for psychological and physical well-being and maturation. Such theories, however, tend to assume a universal child who is without gender, class or ethnicity. They do not deal with difference, except in so much as any child who does not follow the prescribed patterns tends to be viewed and treated as pathological/abnormal/deviant. Nevertheless, Freud in particular developed many important ideas about psychological development that have been enormously influential and cannot be ignored.

Freud has been much criticised in recent years for various reasons. First, his theory of 'biological drives' not only lacked any substantiation (which is a particularly strong criticism to make since it purported to be 'scientific'), but can also be seen as essentialist in that it denied any possibility of change. Second, feminists condemned his theory of 'penis envy', though it could be argued that it has its merits, at least if we think of the penis symbolically as a cipher of male power; Lacan's more sophisticated notion of the *phallus* as the symbol of male power conveys this sense more clearly.[8] Third, and perhaps most of all, many (including myself) felt outraged by Freud's betrayal of women patients' confidence. Originally believing their accounts of sexual abuse by male relatives, Freud changed his course and claimed these could only be fantasies, thereby preserving his own precarious professional status in turn-of-the-century Vienna as well as condemning a century of abused women to disbelief.[9]

Nevertheless, there are aspects of Freud's theories that remain important, and which arguably stand the test of time. Most of all, perhaps, the unconscious is a crucial concept in understanding both self and culture, although Freud did not, in fact, create the concept. Similarly, the stress he laid on the importance of dreams and the centrality of sexuality makes a great deal of sense, even if they need qualifying. In contrast with Freud, Jung put far more emphasis on imagery and 'archetypes' – or symbols – both at an individual and a cultural level. Jung also argued that while sexuality was important, not everything could be reduced to it in the way Freud alleged. The attention paid by post-Freudians such as Klein and Irigaray to very early infancy has also been an important development from, and refinement to, Freudian theory.

If materialist theories such as Marxism paid scant attention to the psychological realm, psychological theories have offered little insight to the realm of culture and the ways in which cultural representations and ideas can affect both the material and the psychological realms. In recent years postmodernist theory has become increasingly influential and dominant, largely eclipsing materialist theories. A central tenet of postmodernist theory is the idea that all knowledge is uncertain and that there can be no universal truth. Lyotard (1979), one of the main proponents of postmodernism, argues that such 'meta-narratives' (that is, narratives about narratives, or all-embracing theories such as Marxism, which claim to be able to explain everything) are redundant and indicative of a repressive system of authority. As Skeggs (1991) points out, however, such a theory itself creates another meta-narrative. She also points out that Lyotard's argument that knowledge is particularised in a specific context denies all institutional and systemic phenomena such as racism or ageism.

Yet postmodernist theory is important in various ways, in particular its scepticism towards rationalism and scientific rationalism. The central importance of language and the ways in which meaning is created through language and discourse is another important tenet of postmodernist theory. Such insights provide a way to unite subjective experience with wider influences and experiences, a way to acknowledge the pre-eminence of language and narrative, imagery and representation. Some of these arguments are not unlike some of the points that Jung makes.[10]

Postmodernist theory, however, can be criticised for being overly abstract, deliberately inaccessible and, therefore, implicitly elitist. Of course, philosophy and philosophical debate has never been the most accessible of subjects, but so much of the work written seems unnecessarily obscure and abstract. Arguably it lacks a grounding in the 'real', material, world; how could it help in explaining the increase of homelessness, poverty, drug addiction or the slave conditions under which many Third World children are made to work? Nor could I truly believe that the chair I sat on, the pain in my lower back, the plaintive cries from the baby next door, were all discursively created. By arguing reality is discursively constructed, such a criticism is invalid; yet there are, I would contend, material realities which we ignore at our peril. Surely the human body can be seen as an example of a physical, material reality? But writers such as Susan Bordo (1992, 1993) show how the body, too, can be seen as 'discursively constructed'. Birke (1992), however, in arguing that biology and society interact makes an important point: we are *embodied* beings. Some of us undoubtedly have greater access to certain resources than others. Whether discursively constructed or not, poverty, hunger and material deprivation do have a reality that we would be foolish to dismiss.

None of these theoretical approaches alone seems to offer one clear-cut path to follow for a better understanding of 'the child'. All have their strengths and weaknesses. Because it is central to my project to consider 'the child' at three quite distinct levels, it is not surprising that there will be a consequent pot-pourri of theories from which to choose. I do not, however, intend choosing one alone, for that is not the purpose of this book.

In Chapter 1 I focus on the question of whether childhood is socially constructed. If we accept the argument that it is, how can we account for the embodied and material circumstances of children? I examine the central debates about the 'nature' of children, and in particular the doctrine of Original Sin in comparison with other discourses of 'original innocence' and how these debates have influenced ideas about child development and childrearing. I consider historical research on childhood, notably that of Ariès and some of his critics; this has been a crucial development in understanding how ideas and discourses about 'the child' and 'childhood' have varied and changed over time. The implication of this is that there can be no such thing as 'the' child. Similarly, evidence of marked differences and inequalities between children highlight the impossibility of there being a universal child. Nevertheless, I take issue with postmodernist theories that argue *everything* is 'discursively constructed', nothing is ultimately real. The political implications of this, if carried to its logical conclusion, suggest that children only really exist in our accounts of them and therefore issues such as abuse of power are simply narrative texts rather than material experience.

Dependency, responsibility for, and protection of children are the main themes in Chapter 2. I consider the historical importance of the idea of 'ownership' in relation to children, and its enshrinement in Roman law, as well as the changing and varying economic importance of children to parents, families, slave owners and the state. I look at eighteenth and nineteenth-century developments in middle-class domestic ideology and the growth of the central state in relation to the swelling body of nineteenth-century legislation that defined, determined and enacted definitions of 'the child' and 'childhood'. The notion of 'protection' is problematised in relation to the power it accords protectors over those they are supposed to protect.

In Chapter 3 I explore the psychological meanings of 'the child' and 'childhood'. The notion of interiority is examined in relation to various nineteenth-century developments, especially the idea of the unconscious. Key aspects of the theories of Freud, Jung and Lacan are discussed briefly in relation to this, in particular the idea of projection. Projection arguably links the realm of the individual psyche with the wider world of society and culture, and I am particularly interested in the ways in which unconscious memories and emotions may be projected on to other individuals and groups who then become stereotyped and ostracised. For this reason I also consider the studies by Alice Miller, whose work, though arguably naïve and oversimplified in certain aspects, has none the less suggested important ways in which psychological experiences in childhood determine ideas about, and parental patterns of, childrearing generally and violence towards children specifically.

In Chapter 4 I examine the idea of representation, especially in relation to visual art and family photography. A brief discussion of how representation works and what it means is followed by specific examples of representations of children in art and family photography. Themes that come out of this include nature, futurity and dependency. I then turn to further discussions about how the ways in which children were represented generally in the nineteenth century resulted in their becoming a myth – a myth which Cunningham (1991) has argued represents above all a story, a symbol, of the nation itself.

Innocence is the subject of Chapter 5. I consider it in terms of adult morality, sexual knowledge, and knowledge/ignorance generally. I then examine conflicting discourses of innocence and evil with reference to St Augustine, Locke, and Rousseau. I discuss representations of children and innocence in literature in relation to Blake, Wordsworth, Dickens, George Eliot, Twain, and Henry James. Knowledge and understanding are the key concepts in these sections and, in particular, the issue as to whether children think and understand differently from adults and, if they do, when and why this changes. I suggest that the idea, and indeed the ideal, of innocence as related by adults to children, also implies deliberate witholding of knowledge and thus ultimately disempowerment.

The final chapter is concerned with ideas about children's sexuality, but in particular with what this means to adults. Returning to some other aspects of the theories of Freud and Lacan, I suggest that desire is the crucial concept here. Desire is arguably constructed in all of us during early infancy; this is subsequently manipulated and played upon by wider cultural forces such as the advertising industry. I also consider the importance of the symbolism of the body and how this developed historically. Particular examples focus on the Cleveland crisis of 1987 and the moral panic over masturbation in the eighteenth and nineteenth centuries.

Much of this book is therefore about what children mean, and have meant, to adults. This, I believe, is vital given the enormous amount of power that adults have, and have had, over children. While not denying the importance of, for example, understanding the problems of children who have been abused, ultimately if we want to get to the roots of such abuse we need to understand more about why adults abuse children in the first place and, indeed, what 'abuse' means in a wider sense. I cannot pretend to offer any wide-ranging or all-encompassing solutions, the very subject-matter and construction of this book is far too diverse and general for that. What I do hope, however, is that it will provoke discussion, controversy and further thought and research in all kinds of ways.

# 1

## IS CHILDHOOD SOCIALLY CONSTRUCTED?

What could be more universal than a child? Each and every one of us is born of a mother, born utterly helpless, powerless, unable to speak or control our bodies. The human infant, the infant's body, must surely be a biological given, an essential fact that cannot be regarded as 'constructed' in any other sense except a physiological one? Yet a baby is born into a social world, a linguistic world, a gendered world, an adult world. Arguably the infant in its utter helplessness, without control or language, is given meaning by adults in the context of a wider culture:

> Childhood, the invention of adults, reflects adult needs and adult fears quite as much as it signifies the absence of adulthood. In the course of history children have been glorified, patronised, ignored, or held in contempt, depending upon the cultural assumptions of adults. (Walther, 1979, p. 64)

This highlights the importance of differentiating from the start between the concepts 'child' and 'childhood'. The notion of a child denotes an individual embodied being that is, in one way or another, not adult. Definitions of maturity, the boundary between the child and the adult, however, vary enormously, from the chronological to physical sexual maturity to legal status or cognitive ability. The child is first and foremost a transitory being that is constantly changing, growing, developing; this in itself both defines it and leads to confusion about it. What do a newborn infant and a 17 year old, for example, have in common? Perhaps only that they are both defined as children by adults living in a certain culture at a certain historical point in time.

Some social groups, however, in fact remain forever character-ised as childlike: women, slaves, the colonised and the insane have at various times been defined as not fully mature and thus akin to children. As soon as we try to delimit the boundaries of 'child', therefore, we come across a range of social and cultural categories.

The word 'child' carries a number of meanings that could be seen to be contradictory; it defines both the biological embodied being *and* connotes dependency, powerlessness and whatever other criteria are used by a given culture to define the non-adult. In contrast, 'childhood' is by definition a social and cultural con-cept, an idea as well as a category, but it never refers to an individual, embodied child. Focused on the general state of being a child, 'childhood' indicates an ill-defined period of time as it is (variously) defined by adults. 'Child' and 'childhood', of course, overlap and to a great extent define one another, but by differentiating them it is possible to see that, for example, a cul-ture might well have a concept and word for 'child' without *necessarily* having a concept of child*hood*. Childhood suggests a separate, different, other group. Children as adults-in-the-making need not, however, be treated as separate, different or other, and indeed have not always been so. Postman (1985), for instance, argues that childhood is 'disappearing'; this he at-tributes primarily to the development and influence of the media, especially television.

The debate as to whether a child is 'biologically given' rather than 'socially constructed' (or 'Nature versus Nurture' as it is often called) has been ongoing for centuries in one form or another, and can be seen to relate to wider debates on the 'nature' of humanity itself. Bradley, for instance, in discussing child psy-chology, points out that:

> The main issue . . . is whether findings about babies primarily serve science as a means to construct a coherent picture of what goes on in the mental lives of babies themselves, or whether babies are mainly discussed in science to represent how scien-tists (not babies) see the world. (Bradley, 1989, p. 3)

Conservatives, including Functionalists, drawing on St Augus-tine's idea of Original Sin,[1] have defined the child as born weak and innately prone to sin and corruption. First and foremost, this can be seen as a statement about 'human nature'. The implications of this for child*rearing* are that children need strict discipline and control by adults.

In contrast with the idea of Original Sin, however, Marxists and liberals, following the ideas of Rousseau, saw the child as born innocent and corrupted by society. This perspective also needs to be seen primarily as a view of 'human nature' that is *symbolised* by the child. In terms of ideas about childhood and the practice of childrearing, this discourse implies the need to give children a maximum amount of freedom in the context of an area/time protected from corrupt influences. It also leads to the conclusion that humanity generally is innately good; then society itself, as corrupting, must be changed. These ideas have had a great influence on progressive education as well as on political revolutions.

The core issue, however, is whether a baby is born with innate characteristics or whether the process of growing and developing in a social and cultural context determines the baby's life chances and personality. If a baby has innate characteristics, then it would seem these are biologically determined and in some way fixed and immutable. As Riley points out, however:

> The peculiarity of developmental psychology, that it must deal both with the appearance of 'progressive entry' into social institutions and the ageing of the subject in that process – a double history – does intensify the possibility of biology getting used here as a myth of origins. It is often stated that the infant is born in an animal-like state and over time acquires a social or a human nature. Being 'helpless' is equated with being 'animal-like', so that having to lose your animal nature is the precondition for achieving your humanity. (Riley, 1983, p. 34)

If the infant is originally natural, at what point, how, and why, does it become 'social'? Essentialist arguments, or 'biological determinism', have been criticised as both conservative and reactionary, because whatever is biological is seen as unchangeable. Clearly, however, with regard to the human infant, change is itself a defining characteristic. Recently it has been pointed out by Lynda Birke (in Crowley and Himmelweit, 1992, p. 71), among others, that biology itself is misunderstood and misrepresented in such debates; biology is not necessarily fixed and static, but is also changed by social and environmental factors, the two more often than not interacting.

Technology is a prime example of how the social and biological can interact to effect change quite dramatically – witness the development of reproductive technology. Insisting that the biological, the body and embodiment, are entirely socially constructed can result in the idea of social construction itself becoming essentialist (Fuss, 1990). We experience society and culture as embodied individuals, and while it would be controversial to claim that human behaviour is *caused* by biological factors alone, just as it would be controversial to claim all behaviour is caused by environmental or cultural factors, it is important to accept that children are born into society as embodied creatures. Bodily needs are then mediated, adapted and controlled by human society.

Having said that, however, it is important to note that much of the work of child development over the past century or so has tended to be premised on the idea of children developing along a linear, clear-cut, essentially pre-ordained and biological process of becoming adult. With a few important exceptions – Héroard's study of the early years of the future Louis XIII in the seventeenth century[2], and Tiedemann's account of his son's first three years in the late eighteenth century (see Archard, 1993) – accounts of child development did not attract adult interest until the late nineteenth century. Preyer's *Die Seele des Kindes*, published in 1882, and G. S. Hall's 'Contents of Two Children's Minds', published in 1883, are generally seen as the first texts in child psychology (see Archard, 1993).

Different theories of child development presuppose different norms of adulthood, where adulthood is taken as an ideal, an end-state, without any specific chronological age. Just as one could speculate that a neonate shares little with a 17 year old, so it could also be argued that a 21 year old is rather different from an 80 year old, despite both being characterised as adults. Be that as it may, one of the most influential theories to nascent child development studies in the late nineteenth century was that of Ernst Haeckel, who argued in his 'biogenetic law' of recapitulation that 'ontogeny is the short and rapid recapitulation of phylogeny' (Archard, 1993, p. 32). In other words, the development of the individual human being from conception to adult (ontogeny) reiterates and repeats the complete development of the whole species (phylogeny).

It is easy to see the influence of Darwin in such an idea. Darwin sought to demonstrate that even those aspects of our humanity that we see as most 'human' originated naturally rather than being created by any supreme being. In his *The Expression of Emotions in Man and Animals* (1872), Darwin set out to show that 'human minds, like human bodies, were products of an evolutionary history linking us to animals, not to God' (see Bradley, 1989, p. 17). It is also clear that Haeckel's theory was full of imperialist assumptions about the childlike 'nature' of 'primitive' people, and the conversely 'adult' nature of the 'civilised'. The whole theory has a fixed and predetermined inevitability about it that is inherently biological. Nevertheless, it was taken seriously at the time and influenced psychological theory generally.

Freud was also influenced by Darwin's ideas in his theory of child development, premised as it was on the idea of sexual development. For Freud the 'normal' adult is one whose sexual desire has been negotiated through certain key stages in childhood and adolescence to become 'genital in aim and heterosexual in object' (Bradley, 1989, p. 33). Freud's theory was biologically determinist in that it presupposed everyone's development was ultimately determined by innate 'drives'; he never offers any cogent proof of the existence of these. Yet it can also be seen as a social constructionist theory because he recognised that the individual's development was also affected by environmental and social factors interacting with the 'drives'.

If Haeckel's idea of 'normal' adulthood was a recapitulation, a mini-version of 'civilisation' incarnate, and Freud's theory presupposed (hetero)sexual maturity as the crucial qualification for adulthood, Jean Piaget proposed yet another criterion for marking adulthood: the capacity for abstract and hypothetical thinking:

For Piaget, intelligence was the product of a process of biological adaptation. The structure of intelligence at any age consisted of schemes or 'schemas' representing in knowledge the basis of a baby's response to, let us say, the movements of a mobile. (Bradley, 1989, p. 93)

Cognitive development then becomes the crucial way in which children develop. Piaget insists that each and every child reaches a certain stage of cognitive development at a certain chronological age, a supposition that has been much criticised. As Bradley (1989, p. 15) wryly comments: 'Two decades of demonstrating how Piaget underestimated the intelligence of infants means that the baby is now deemed to be able to conceptualize in the womb, if not the gene.'

Theories of child development are concerned first and foremost with the individual child in its embodied state. None of them, for instance, pays attention to the different social, economic, political and cultural contexts of childhood. Is it really the case that an undernourished, uneducated child living on the streets of Bogotá develops in exactly the same way as a well-fed, well-protected child living in a middle-class home in Paris? Does a girl growing up in !Kung society go through identical stages of psychosexual development as did a girl in early twentieth-century Vienna? They are all, moreover, conceived on a linear model where 'adulthood as a state is seen as accomplished absolutely, once and for all, when childhood, its contrary, is left behind' (Bradley, 1989, p. 36). Where theorists of child development focused on what they saw as linear patterns of change shared by virtually all children regardless of class, gender, ethnicity or historical era, historians in recent years have turned their attention to children as a social group, that is, to child*hood*.

## History and Childhood

It was the historian Philippe Ariès who first drew attention to the idea that childhood is socially and historically constructed rather than innate or 'natural'. Attitudes to children, he argued, changed over time, and with these changing attitudes there developed a new concept: *childhood*. In the Middle Ages, he maintained, children mixed freely with adults, and although adults were not exactly indifferent to children, they were less concerned with their development and well-being than he sees as being the case in modern European society. Children were seen as adults-in-the-making rather than as separate individuals with a distinct world-view:

In mediaeval society the idea of childhood did not exist; this is not to suggest that children were neglected, forsaken or despised. The idea of childhood is not to be confused with affection for children: it corresponds to an awareness of the particular nature of childhood, that particular nature which distinguishes the child from the adult . . . In mediaeval society, this awareness was lacking . . . as soon as the child could live without the constant solicitude of his mother, his nanny or his cradle-rocker, he belonged to adult society. (Ariès, [1960] 1986, p. 125)

Ariès based much of his theory on, first, the absence of childrearing handbooks in medieval society and, second, on the paucity of representations of children in medieval art, none of which portrayed childhood as in any way distinct from adulthood. Children, he pointed out, when and if they were represented, were painted as small adults. From the late Middle Ages onwards, however, children began to be increasingly differentiated from adults, as evident in the development of specialised clothing for them, the rise of new ideas on work, the growth of education, and the increasing amount of literature written specifically for children. At about the same time, children in western art became an important subject for representation, both alone and as part of family portraiture. To say 'children', however, is misleading because it was above all *boys* who were first targeted as a different and special social category: 'Boys were the first specialised children. They began going to school in large numbers as far back as the late sixteenth century' (Ariès, [1960] 1986, p. 56). Not just *boys*, but *middle-class* boys were singled out as a distinct social group. Childhood was a gendered concept.

His theory, however, has been in some ways controversial. It raises important questions, for instance, as to the relationship between representation and reality and to what extent representation not only is influenced by, but also influences viewers' behaviour. It is a debate that continues in contemporary culture, for example, about possible connections between children who watch 'video nasties' and subsequently commit violent acts. In 1988, for example, Comstock concluded that 'a large majority of studies show that viewing television and film violence does not help children to get rid of antisocial, violent inclinations. Quite the contrary, it leads to increases in aggressive and antisocial behaviour' (Miedzian, 1992, p. 209).

Paintings are usually commissioned by a particular person for a particular purpose, and the painter, if the patron is to be pleased with the product, needs to portray the subject as the patron would like it to be remembered. In the Middle Ages paintings were overwhelmingly painted for churches and religious purposes; they illustrated religious themes and usually employed symbolism, rather than being concerned with realism. It was never their aim to represent ordinary medieval life or mundane concerns.

Medievalists have been critical of Ariès. Nelson, for example, argues that Ariès was wrong about the Middle Ages:

> He mistook the absence of handbooks on child-rearing for lack of concern with children, instead of looking in medical treatises for relevant material: focusing on artistic representations of children as miniature adults, he ignored a mass of textual evidence . . . for the recognition of childhood as a human stage with specific characteristics and needs. (Nelson, 1994, p. 82)

Nelson also maintains that Ariès neglected the variety that existed in the Middle Ages in terms of *class* and *place*, and that he ignored altogether shifts that occurred during the different centuries labelled 'the Middle Ages'. By so doing, she argues, Ariès underestimated the love of medieval parents for their children.

Martindale (1994) criticises Ariès for ignoring 'immutable and universal elements' in the care and socialisation of children by adults which, he maintains 'were indeed present in the Middle Ages if one bothers to read the evidence'. There did exist, for example, an intellectual schema in the Middle Ages that was concerned with the processes of infancy, childhood and adolescence: 'the evidence for this is so overwhelming that it must require some sort of modification of Ariès' thesis' (Martindale, 1994, p. 206).

Martindale also maintains that Ariès was wrong to suggest that the high rate of infant and child mortality in the Middle Ages led parents to feel relatively indifferent to them emotionally, because they defended themselves against the almost inevitable probability of losing some of their children. This is not, in fact, a central tenet of Ariès' thesis, but one that has been put forward by other modernisation theorists, such as Lawrence Stone (1977), Edward Shorter (1975) and Peter Stearns (1975). It is not really a valid argument, because although mortality crises declined from the eighteenth century, infant mortality remained particularly high until the end of the nineteenth century, while modernisation theorists see this shift in sentiment as occurring from a much earlier period.

Notwithstanding the various critiques, Ariès' work has had an enormous influence on the study of children and childhood. By drawing attention to childhood as something that is socially and historically constructed, he gave the impetus to a body of historical research on childhood which has burgeoned since the early 1960s. Such research has become increasingly diversified:

> One approach to the history of childhood examines changes in private dispositions toward the young. Another approach concentrates on the proliferation of public institutions for managing child life. The history of sentiments has led to a futile debate over the relative extent of dispositional change or continuity in feeling for children without considering the ways in which notionally primordial or elemental dispositions were constructed or contaminated by the normative, politicized meanings of childhood, arising from inter-group moral conflict, returns to haunt current interpretations in the guise of timeless psychological or bio-social truths. Studying the official processing of children errs in the opposite direction, losing sight of the personal thought and action of children and their parents, as if their historical experiences were fundamentally comprised of policy and administration. Actual children vanish and an implausibly intrusive account is offered of policy itself. (Bellingham, 1988, p. 347)

Childrearing has been central to much of the debate in historical studies on children and childhood. Historians of the 'modernisation' school have argued that a revolution in childcare and attitudes to children arose in Early Modern Europe, particularly in the sixteenth century with the rise of Puritanism (which was influenced by the idea of Original Sin). At this time preachers exhorted parents to be severe with tiny children in an effort to eradicate the sin that was innate in them. Much of the debate among modernisation theorists has revolved around the question as to whether or not childrearing was more or less cruel in the past and to what extent Puritanism, and later, Evangelicalism, determined the severity of childrearing techniques.

Pollock (1983, 1987) argues that parents have always been loving and caring towards their children. Both perspectives, however, seem intent on proving that one or other type of child-rearing existed at a certain point in time; they form an integral part of more grandiose theories of social change which charac-terise periods of history with one specific emotion or trait.[3] It is important, however, to distinguish, first, what preachers, politi-cians and writers *say* about children and childhood – that is, the discourse and rhetoric of childhood and childrearing – from how embodied girls and boys were in fact being treated. Furthermore, it can plausibly be argued that parents are *never* wholly consistent throughout the period of their children's upbringing; at times indulgent, at times distant, at other times erupting into violence, is any parent always, without exception, consistent over time? As Jordanova (1989) argues, 'It was not that people suddenly changed their child-rearing habits, but that a group of middle-class professionals and intellectuals strove to rethink the nature of childhood as a part of their approach to "nature".'

One of the most influential groups of historians has been known as 'psychohistorians', most prominent of whom is Lloyd de Mause. De Mause put forth what he called a 'psychogenic theory of history' which maintained, first, that the evolution of parent–child relations constitutes an independent source of his-torical change; second, that the history of childhood is a series of closer approaches between adult and child; third, that childrearing practices are the very condition for the transmission and development of all other cultural elements (de Mause, 1976, p. 4). Psychohistorians have similarities with modernisation theo-rists, in that they tend to see parent–child relations as gradually improving in a linear and progressive way from a time when children were valued hardly at all and often sacrificed, to modern co-operative and loving relationships. Modernisation theorists, however, do not give centrality to the unconscious in the way psychohistorians do.

Influenced by Freudian theory, psychohistorians tend to focus on key stages of childhood, such as breastfeeding/weaning, toilet training, sexual relations, and so forth. It is, however, contestable that Freudian theory can be applied in this way to earlier historical periods. It assumes Freudian theory to be universal in a way that many would argue it is not. It allows for little cultural variation; who is to say that what we think of as abusive to children now, for instance, was seen in such a way 500 years ago? It does not allow for variations between different social classes and groups. It has been important, however, as a vanguard for a whole body of research that has focused on the history of 'sentiments' and the emotional value of children to parents.

Linda Pollock, for instance, has claimed that 'parents have always valued their children: we should not seize too eagerly upon theories of fundamental change in parental attitudes over time . . . There are some basic features of human experience which are not subject to change' (Pollock, 1983, p. 17). Emotional relations between children and adults, according to Pollock, are biologically given rather than socially constructed: 'Pollock has a socio-biological theory and believes parental solicitude is invariant across cultures' (Pollock, 1983, p. 349). To claim that parents have always valued or loved or cherished their children is probably a reasonable generalisation to make. What it does not tell us, however, is what 'love' or 'value' or 'cherishing' actually meant to, for example, fourteenth-century parents living in a one-room hovel with six children. How might their meanings differ from the meanings we ascribe to children in late twentieth-century Europe?

Words change meaning between groups and over time. The meaning of words is constantly subject to subtle shifts and variations in the course of social interaction and cultural change. Zelitzer (1985), for instance, argues that the 'value' parents put on children up until the nineteenth century was largely an economic one; as children ceased to be economically valuable, they became 'emotionally priceless'. Because this occurred first among the middle classes, Zelitzer argues, there was a cultural conflict that affected different family systems in the nineteenth century. Such a conflict model suggests it is wrong to think of 'evolving psychic dispositions toward children as somehow cumulating into new norms by a Durkheimian mystery of cultural acclamation' (Zelitzer, 1985, p. 352). The meaning of children to parents and thus the meanings ascribed to childrearing and childhood shift and vary, of that there can be little doubt. This is not to deny that children have always tended to have emotional importance, but what exactly that emotional importance has been, and whether it can be argued it is in some way universal in terms of content, is less certain.

The history of childhood has tended to concentrate on studying children in terms of childrearing, adult sentiments about children, and the role and value of children in families. Less attention has been paid to children in terms of *difference*, whether in relation to social class, gender, ethnicity, region or religion. The word 'child' disguises as much as it informs. We have touched on the confusions about boundaries between children and adults and also between children at different stages within childhood itself. The idea of 'the child' suggests a uniform, universal being that is, to a great extent, biologically given rather than socially constructed or differentiated. Yet the differences that exist between children warrant reflection and lead to consideration as to whether the term 'child' is that useful a tool for analysis.

## Different Children, Different Lives

Consider life expectancy: a child born in Cameroon has a life expectancy of 50 years, less than two-thirds that of an American child. In the Middle Ages, the life expectancy of a peasant child at birth would have been about half that of a child born in Cameroon today. The average life expectancy in the least developed regions of the world in 1990–95 was 51 years, compared with an expectancy of 74 years in the most developed regions during the same time period (*Guardian*, 4 March 1995). Low birth weight is often taken as a sound indicator both of poverty and of poor life expectancy; every year 23 million low-birth weight babies are born – 90 per cent of these are in the Third World. About one-quarter of all the world's deaths are those of children, and 97 per cent of those are of Third World children (Vittachi, 1989, pp. 43–5). In terms of sheer chances of survival, then, there is a vast difference between children in the West and in Third World countries.

There are also, however, huge differences in life expectancy and health between children *within* western countries. Nearly 40 per cent of the American poor, for instance, are children. In 1984 14.4 per cent of all Americans – 33.7 million people – lived below the poverty line. From 1980 to 1984 the number of poor people increased by four and a half million. The poverty rate for children under six was 24 per cent in 1984 (Sidel, 1987, p. xvi). The gap in life expectancy between children living in poverty and the more affluent classes in the UK is wider now than it has been for 50 years. Despite the 'consumer revolution' and the flood of surplus food and inessential goods to the West – often produced by children living in conditions amounting to slavery in the Third World – poverty within western countries has escalated in the past few years. An estimated 15 million people in the UK and 30 million in the USA are currently living on or beneath the poverty line (Lee-Wright, 1990, p. 8).

In February 1995 the Joseph Rowntree Foundation Inquiry into Income and Wealth (reported on in the *Guardian*, 10 February 1995) found that the gap between rich and poor in the UK is 'now so wide that it is damaging the cohesiveness of society without bringing any attendant economic benefits'. It found that income inequality in Britain had grown faster in recent years than any other comparable industrial country; since 1977 the proportion of the population with less than half the average income has more than trebled. The poorest 20–30 per cent of the population had failed to benefit or share in economic growth since 1979. Children, they pointed out, were particularly vulnerable, and were often locked into neighbourhoods characterised by severe poverty with little community support.

The Conservative government, however, has effectively out-lawed poverty by refusing to admit it exists. Even the 'new' Labour Party under Tony Blair seems relatively uninterested in the concept or prevalence of poverty. Poverty in the UK, although it is increasing, has become increasingly rendered both silent and invisible. Children born poor in the West, although their condi-tions relative to children in the Third World are better, still suffer from poor health, lower life expectancy and have a far greater chance of being unemployed than do the children from the more affluent classes.

Children's life chances depend to a large extent on the colour of their skin. Black and Hispanic children in the USA suffer a far

higher rate of poverty than do white children. In 1984, for example, 39 per cent of Hispanic children were poor (Sidel, 1987, p. 3).
In the Rowntree Report mentioned above, poverty in Britain was
experienced differentially according to race. While only 18 per
cent of the white population was in the poorest fifth of the population, for example, *more than one-third* of the non-white population was in this group. Most of the people in this group were of
West Indian and Pakistani/Bangladeshi origin (*Guardian*, 10 February 1995). In South Africa in 1980, 12 out of every 1000 white
babies died, but 300 out of every 1000 black babies died. In the
same year in the USA, there were 11 deaths per 1000 infants for
whites, but 21 deaths per 1000 for blacks (Vittachi, 1989, p. 45). In
terms of less quantifiable but equally powerful factors such as
prejudice, racism, and low self-esteem children from ethnic minorities almost certainly suffer immeasurably more than children
from dominant white groups. Moreover:

> If a baby is not only poor and black but a girl, her chances
> of survival dwindle still further. Girl babies are biologically
> stronger at birth ... Nature favours girls: human society fa-
> vours boys ... In Barbados ... for every 100 deaths in boy ba-
> bies, only 93 girl babies die, but ... by the age of 4, for every
> 100 boy deaths, there are 200 deaths in girls. (Vittachi, 1989,
> p. 45)

Gender is a prime determinant of life chances. Girls are rarely
welcomed in the same way as boy babies. In India today, finding
dowries for daughters remains a serious problem for many families. Indeed, 7 per cent more boys are born in India through
the deliberate use of selective post-amniocentesis abortions or
subsequent female infanticide (Miles, 1994, p. 81). Men and boys
command higher wages than girls and women. Most family-
households depend for survival on multiple incomes from the
earnings of all members who can work; in Muslim countries girls
are not supposed to work at all and thus their perceived economic value is diminished further. Moreover, of 251 couples
treated in sex selection clinics in America, Asia and Europe, 236
chose boys (Miles, 1994, p. 81).
  Girls were rarely welcomed in European peasant households

because by tradition they were not supposed to work on the land, even if the work they did within the household was in fact just as essential to its survival. Even where there are no worries about inheritance, labour or dowries, however, girls continue to be not only less welcome than boys in many western households, but are also treated differently from birth. This still applies in cultures where there is little apparent material rationale for such attitudes. Witness the following account: 'Furious that her fifth grandchild was yet another girl, Romanian grandmother Niculina Ureche, aged 60, threw the week-old baby out of a second-floor window. The girl survived' (*Guardian*, 10 February 1995).

In contemporary Italy a study of a sample of babies of both sexes showed that 34 per cent of mothers refused to breast-feed their daughters, yet with only one exception *all* the boys' mothers wanted to breast-feed (Odette Brunet and Irene Lezine, *I primi anni del bambino*, 1966, quoted in Belotti, 1975, p. 32). The same study found that girls who were breast-fed were given less time at the breast than boys: boys were given on average 45 minutes at the breast, but girls only 25 minutes. Bottle-fed girls got eight minutes, bottle-fed boys, 15. Girls were weaned much sooner than boys (Belotti, 1975, p. 33). Greed, they found, was seen by mothers as a positive trait in boys, but a negative one in girls:

> Thus, while no one ever interrupts a boy during his feed to moderate his greed, the girl who sucks in too greedy a way is interrupted by having the teat taken from her mouth, by being made to wait until she will approach the breast with more 'feminine grace'. (Belotti, 1975, p. 37)

Girls were taught to feed themselves before boys were, usually at around two, while boys had help from their mother until they were four or five.

In family-households where food is scarce, it is the girls and women who almost invariably go short or go without altogether, though even in affluent family-households there seems to be an unspoken norm that women and girls need less food than men and boys, regardless of age or size. I remember when we used to visit my Welsh ex-in-laws, my mother-in-law rarely sat to table with the rest of us, but spent most of her time serving and clear-

ing. If she did sit down, she would scarcely eat at all, but would
'pick' on scraps before and after the meal, in the privacy of 'her'
kitchen. One of the complaints my husband made of me when
our marriage was breaking up was that I served myself as much
food as I did him, although we were similar in weight and size
and were both working.[4]

Major differences thus exist between children according to
where they live, their social class, gender and ethnicity. Differences also exist according to religion and religious practice. Religious and ethnic groups, for example, often receive very different
educations, sometimes imposed by the state, such as in Nazi
Germany or South Africa under the apartheid system, and sometimes chosen by parents: schools of different denominations are
common in the West. Religion itself can divide children. Wole
Soyinka (1991), for instance, wrote in his autobiography, *Aké*,
how as the son of Christian parents in colonial Nigeria in the
1930s, he was both fascinated by, and felt increasingly different
from, local children who retained their belief in such phenomena
as spirits and reincarnation:

> My mother gave a sigh, shook her head and left us to listen to
> Osiki's tales of the different kinds of *egùngùn*, the dangerous
> ones with bad charms who could strike a man with epilepsy
> and worse, the violent ones who had to be restrained with
> powerful ropes, the *opidan* with their magical tricks. They
> would transform themselves into alligators, snakes, tigers and
> rams and turn back again into *egùngùn* . . . Apart from Giro, the
> cripple contortionist to whose performance we had once been
> taken in the palace compound, only those *egùngùn* appeared to
> be able to tie up their limbs in any manner they pleased.
> 'Can I come back as an *egùngùn* if I die?' I asked Osiki.
> 'I don't think so,' he said. 'I've never heard of any Christian
> becoming an *egùngùn*.' (Soyinka, 1991, p. 34)

Similarly, orphanhood, illegitimacy, as well as variations within
family-households themselves contribute to patterns of difference between children and childhoods. One aspect of such relationships that is rarely examined historically or sociologically is
that of sibling relationships.[5] It is, however, often central in auto/
biographies and novels. M. V. Hughes, for instance, in her auto-

biography *A London Child of the 1870s*, was aware from an early age of her difference from her four older brothers; her experience of the difference, however, was positive:

> A girl with four brothers older than herself is born under a lucky star. To be brought up in London, in the eighteen-seventies, by parents who knew how to laugh at both jokes and disasters, was to be under the influence of Jupiter himself . . . I suppose there was a fear on my mother's part that I should be spoilt, for I was two years younger than the youngest boy. To prevent this danger she proclaimed the rule 'Boys first'. I came last in all distribution of food at table, treats of sweets, and so on. I was expected to wait on the boys, run messages, fetch things left upstairs, and never grumble, let alone refuse. All this I thoroughly enjoyed, because I loved running about, and would often dash up and down stairs just to let off my spirits. Of course mother came in for some severe criticism from relations in this matter, but I have never ceased to thank her for this bit of early training. (Hughes, [1934] 1989, pp. 1 and 7)

Had her brothers perhaps been less loving, or she of a less generous spirit, such experiences of enforced difference and inequality might have proved very painful and humiliating. De Salvo (1989) has suggested, for instance, that Virginia Wolf's experience of her elder brothers included sexual abuse, which may have been a major determinant in her suffering from depression. For my sister and I, though our family-household was comfortable in material terms, the almost total lack of positive emotional resources combined with clever manipulation on our father's part, left us like two starving dogs fighting over one small, rather fetid, bone.

A study by Marjorie Shostack (1990) in which she carried out extensive interviews with a !Kung woman, Nisa, who had lived all her life in the Kalahari Desert, revealed interesting insights into sibling rivalry in that context. The !Kung are nomadic and rely on a combination of meat killed by the men and berries, roots and honey gathered by the women for survival. The diet is not a good one for infants, and thus breast-feeding is crucially important to a baby's health. Weaning does not usually occur until the birth of a younger sibling, or otherwise around the age of three or four. Nisa, however, was quite a frail infant and the birth of a young brother not long after her own incurred huge jealousy in her, and this incited angry encounters between Nisa and her mother:

> I wanted the milk she had in her breasts, and when she nursed him, my eyes watched as the milk spilled out. I'd cry all night, cry and cry until dawn broke. Some mornings I just stayed around and my tears fell and I cried and refused all food. That was because I saw him nursing. I saw with my eyes the milk spilling out, the milk *I* wanted. I thought it was mine . . . Another day, my mother was lying down asleep with Kumsa [Nisa's younger brother], and I quietly sneaked up on them. I took Kumsa away from her, put him down on the other side of the hut, and came back and lay down beside her. While she slept, I took her nipple, put it in my mouth and began to nurse. I nursed and nursed and nursed . . . I had already begun to feel wonderfully full when she woke up . . . She grabbed me and pushed me, hard, away from her. I lay there and cried. She went to Kumsa, picked him up and laid him down beside her. She insulted me, cursing my genitals, 'Have you gone crazy? Nisa-Big-Genitals, what's the matter with you?' (Shostack, 1990, pp. 57–8)

When relationships are particularly difficult between children and adults, the proximity of other sympathetic kin is often a godsend. Nisa, for instance, went to live with her grandmother for a while soon after the above incident. At other times she turned to her aunt for comfort. Children's lives vary quite markedly according to the composition and structure of their family-household and kinship networks. One important way in which western children's lives have changed over the past century is that few now live in large family-households, many have no or only one sibling, and particularly with increased geographic mobility, accessibility to wider kin networks is often rare.

## Children and Nature

In the summer of 1968 two little boys were murdered in the Scotswood area of Newcastle: Martin Brown, aged four, in May, and Brian Howe, aged three, in July. Eventually Norma Bell, aged 13, and Mary Bell, aged 11 (they were not related) were accused of the murders. The trial, in an adult court, resulted in Mary Bell being found guilty on two accounts of manslaughter. Norma was found not guilty on both accounts (Sereny, [1972] 1995). As with the Bulger case 25 years later, there were two distinct reactions from the public and the media. On the one hand, there was an overwhelming sense of horror and grief for the brutal deaths of two little children. On the other hand, there was what amounted to an even more vehement response of fury and outrage at the murderer, who was also a child. The rage vented at children who kill far surpasses any rage witnessed against *adult* murderers of little children. There was a case in the 1980s, for instance, where a man murdered his three children – and got a three-year sentence (*Guardian*, 28 January 1994).

No attempts were made to enquire into the reasons for Mary Bell's actions or her background; no interest was expressed in the poverty and severe distress that characterised her childhood. Nobody took notice at the time of her mother's abandonment of her, her mother's repeated nervous breakdowns, or the fact that Mary had to have her stomach pumped from drug overdoses four times, the first time when she was only a year old, possibly as a result of her mother's actions. Mary was singled out by both the media and the court as 'evil', a 'fiend' and a 'Svengali'. Both the court and the public tried to explain Mary Bell's transgression of childhood innocence by insisting she was a result of 'evil birth'. Her victims, of course, were innocent: as children they were in any event innocent *by definition*. Mary, however, because she was not innocent, could not be a child. Hence her denouncement as monstrous, evil, a 'non-child'.

The rare instances of children who kill[6] challenge the meanings adults ascribe to 'child' to the core, and can result, if only momentarily, in an unsettling awareness that there is no universal child, that childhood is socially constructed by adults. But this recognition, if it really occurs, is soon obliterated by a more acceptable and all-pervasive conclusion that such children are simply *non-children* who are some kind of freaks, monsters and thus able to be treated as adult criminals, incarcerated at the discretion of the Home Secretary. For children to manifest such behaviour has been seen not only as pathological, but also as 'unnatural', where to be a child is premised on a notion of nature more akin to the tenderness of plants than to the brutality of tigers or lions. Nature is not a straightforward concept.

The notion of 'nature' is sometimes used to describe groups or phenomena seen as other than, separate from, and in opposition to 'culture'. But what exactly is meant by 'nature' and 'natural'? The very definitions are themselves cultural products. When I go into the local park and sigh at the beauties of nature, I conveniently forget that the whole park was landscaped by humans, planted by humans and is carefully tended and managed to conform to a cultural concept we call 'nature'. As Jordanova argues with regard to the long-standing analogy between nature and children:

> The relationship between children, childhood and nature has existed at a number of different levels. It is as complex as our ideas about nature itself: the state of childhood may be seen as pure, innocent, or original in the sense of primary; children may be analogised with animals or plants, thereby indicating that they are natural objects available for scientific and medical investigation; children could be valued as aesthetic objects . . . but they could equally well be feared for their instinctual, animal-like natures. Two fundamental points . . . arise out of the association between children and nature: First, the polyvalency of nature led to a variety of concepts of childhood, and second, these diverse meanings of childhood were deeply imbued with moral values. (Jordanova, 1989, p. 6)

The concept of nature has changed and varied over time and arguably still has different connotations, like any idea or work, according to the context in which it is used.

In the seventeenth century the idea of the dichotomisation between body and mind came to a peak with Descartes and the rise of scientific rationalism. Descartes' rigid separation of body and mind, with clear preferences ascribed to mind/rationality/ masculine over body/irrational/feminine, resulted in a number of new attitudes developing. Animals, for instance, were further downgraded, while children, who were increasingly compared to angels, came to be seen as more in need of careful protection and nurturing.

There was at this time an increasing concern to clarify and demarcate boundaries between humans and animals: 'Men stood to animals as did heaven to earth, soul to body, culture to nature' (Thomas, 1983, p. 35). Bestiality was regarded as the worst of all sexual crimes and became a capital offence in 1534. It remained so until 1861 (Thomas, 1983, p. 39). It was during this period, too, that farmers began to move animals out of their homes and into separate accommodation. Theologians preached strict separation between people and nature:

> In the sixteenth and seventeenth centuries the so-called 'long-house' . . . in which men and cattle slept under the same roof . . . was evolving into an exclusively human residence, with the erection of a party wall or a separate entrance for the cattle or . . . the moving out of the animals to separate buildings. (Thomas, 1983, p. 95)

In a culture that was anxious about widespread socioeconomic changes and the shifting of boundaries generally, animals became increasingly equated with 'below': with dirt, with the body, with instinct. People, however, were equated with 'above': the head, rationality, cleanliness, adulthood and masculinity. Children and women, however, were arguably in a rather ambiguous position, on the threshold between the animal/lower and the human/ upper. This contradiction and the paradox of trying to force into a pair of binary opposites categories that were too diverse and complex to fit such overly simplified schemes arguably contributed to crises over, for example, the discipline of children, where preachers were exhorted to beat 'the sin out of' children as young as 18 months for their 'animal behaviour', while older unmarried women were persecuted as witches, accused of having 'unnatural' and magical relations with, and over, animals.

By the eighteenth century, ideas about nature had changed markedly. In particular there was a shift from *mechanical* views of nature that made a sharp differentiation between body and mind, and where the body was seen as akin to a machine, to *organicist* views:

> In the late eighteenth century, life was commonly associated with activity and plasticity, with the adaptive powers of organ-

isms to respond to the environment, and with organization, that is, the structural complexity of a living being, a concept used to explain the special properties of animals and plants. Life was a notion of synthesis, system and fusion... A rigid demarcation between mind and body thus made no sense ... the moral and the social emerged out of the natural organization of living matter. (Jordanova, 1986a, pp. 106–7)

Ideas about children and childhood were also changing noticeably at this time, and women and children were marked out in the organicist view as special because they were closer to nature, 'women because they gave life, children because they had recently received it. In them the full mystery of life was manifest' (Jordanova, 1986a, p. 112). Life was in this way placed in opposition to 'commodity' in a similar way to other pairs of binary opposites such as woman/man, private/public and, of enormous relevance to changing ideas of 'the child', dependent/independent and asexual/sexually active.

Debates on child labour, masturbation, and child prostitution, all reflect, according to Jordanova, these broader changes in definitions of nature and the natural and the issues they in turn raised:

The awkwardness of growing up, both in reality and in imagination, could not be solved easily. One approach was to select an age at which the passage from one status to another could be deemed to have taken place ... At a deeper level, these debates were about when children might pass from the private to the public, when they might enter the world of commodities, and when they might become sexually active. Once working, they lost their special status close to the source of life. (Jordanova, 1986a, p. 115)

It is interesting to consider how current debates about nature and the environment also often relate, sometimes implicitly and sometimes explicitly, to concerns about children, childhood and, indeed, animals. Not only has it now become possible for women to bear other women's babies, but the organs of other people, and indeed of animals, are being transplanted into human beings. As the last areas of the world's wilderness vanish under bulldozers, so we increasingly revere the 'natural' and the 'wild'. The intense concern over childhood 'innocence' and its opposite, corruption, can be seen to reflect a wider cultural shift in notions of nature itself, a notion that has, in fact, always been cultural.

## If it's all Constructed, is it all Just a Story?

It all comes back once again, so it would seem, to how adults define, and have defined, children and childhood. Children do not define themselves as a social group, but are born into a cluster of meanings, meanings that may often vary and shift both at a micro and a macro level. Such meanings are part of adult discourse, adult representations, adult culture and politics. Representations and discourses are expressed through language and imagery. As a result, according to the Stainton Rogers (1992), who draw on postmodernist theory of language and narrative, *all* our ideas and concepts of 'the child' are created by language and by narrative. Thus all apparently factual information such as statistics on child mortality, birth weight or household size, are just as much 'stories' as are more obvious narratives of fictive children such as Alice or Tom Sawyer or Peter Pan. The result of this, so the Stainton Rogers argue, is a tapestry of texts of childhood in which:

> that whole cloth contains not only fictive children but what we may think of as real ones: Victorian 'kids int' Mill'; child prostitutes in Bangkok; the child subjects of developmental psychology; the 'children within' uncovered by psychoanalysts; ourselves when young – even our own children! (Stainton Rogers and Stainton Rogers, 1992, p. 6)

Thus the whole world, it is argued, is created through narrative and language, and children are drawn into this network of narratives that both affect and define their material lives from the very beginning.

Certainly this postmodernist model is persuasive, for it is hard to argue that stories and narratives do *not* envelop our lives and consciousness in myriad ways from the beginning. Even the body, which we tend to think of as supremely physical and material, is arguably defined through social meanings created through discourse and narrative. Susan Bordo, for instance, says:

> The body – what we eat, how we dress, the daily rituals through which we attend to the body – is a medium of culture. The body, as anthropologist Mary Douglas has argued, is a powerful symbolic form, a surface on which the central rules, hierarchies, and even metaphysical commitments of a culture are inscribed and thus reinforced through the concrete language of the body. The body may also operate as a metaphor for culture. (Bordo, 1993, p. 13)

The problem with the Stainton Rogers model, however – and arguably this applies to much postmodernist theory generally – is that it can end up by trivialising and even denying inequalities based on difference. In a rather more frightening way, it is possible to see that it could be used to dismiss real problems, real pain, real suffering of real embodied people at a number of levels.

To argue that child prostitution in Bangkok is just another story, which could then easily also be applied to the whole 'story' of Third World poverty and underdevelopment, may be interesting and clever academically. To deny that there are real embodied children suffering physical pain, degradation and illness and to classify such phenomena as 'stories' begs the question, as it were, and lets us off the hook. Poverty, sexual abuse, physical cruelty and starvation then become interesting texts to analyse from a position of security and affluence in the western world, rather than subjects which might be seen as relevant for political concern or action.

Similarly, it needs to be pointed out that one of the main ways in which children have suffered, particularly if they have been abused physically and/or sexually by adults, is not only through experiencing physical pain and feelings of degradation, humiliation and shame, but also through the pain of *not being heard or believed* when they give accounts of their suffering. If we take on board the Stainton Rogers' thesis, children's accounts can be regarded simply as stories, narratives, which may be interesting, may even be moving, but nothing to be concerned about ultimately, except perhaps as interesting texts.

The physical pain of being raped by your own father or stepfather as a small child does not last so much as physical pain *per se*, but it does become engraved on your body, embodied in your memory. Because you have always been told, and believed, that parents can do no evil, that parents only wish you well, the only interpretation a small child can put on such devastating behaviour is that her own body is in some way evil, transgressive, overwhelmingly bad, a place of horror. I do not mean to dismiss the importance of either language or narrative in the construction of meaning, but what I do find unacceptable about this approach is that too rarely does anybody ask: *Who* is telling the story? *Why* is it being told? Why are some stories believed while others are not? And by whom exactly? How are certain stories used to affect, indeed to determine, the life chances of others and *their* ability to tell their own stories and have them believed? In other words, it seems there is a real danger of forgetting the centrality of power and power relations in such models.

Power relations envelop our lives at a multitude of levels; children are born into webs of power relations as well as of discourse and narratives. They are not unrelated. They affect a child's life chances from the start and inscribe themselves on a child's body in myriad ways. The body is neither outside culture, nor is it just biological. Rather it interacts constantly with culture so that its very chances of survival are largely determined by the tangle of relationships and narratives with which it is constantly negotiating, being affected by, resisting. The life chances of 'the child', in all aspects, depend on definitions of 'childhood' which are arguably entirely made up of discourses and narratives. But discourses and narratives in turn affect policies and behaviour and become implemented in ways that directly affect the bodies of children. The very fact that it is possible to see how different children's life chances are and have been attests to the social and historical construction of childhood. But neither should it be forgotten that children are embodied beings and as such their experiences of childhood, different and variable though these undoubtedly are and have been, are still lived out in a physical body.

# 2

## WHO OWNS CHILDREN?

'"Look Emma", the man said, as he rose and came over in a threatening manner. "You belong to us now, so shut yer row and be quiet"' (Smith, 1954, p. 27). Emma Smith was born in England at the turn of this century and was illegitimate. When she was six she was sold to a hurdy-gurdy man, who overworked and abused her in a number of ways. From the 1860s in the USA the *padrone* system sent children from poor regions in Italy to the USA in return for payments to their parents. In exchange, the *padrone* kept the children's earnings. The children usually were made to work as street musicians, often with organ grinders, and were not uncommonly sold to other owners. Later, a similar system operated which dealt in Irish and Chinese children (Gordon, 1989, p. 40).

Those held responsible for the care of infants and children literally hold the power of life and death. Children, because they are born totally helpless, are by definition wholly dependent on others for care and protection, at least for the first few years. At various times and in different cultures this dependency has been dealt with in different ways. In some cultures, children are seen as a collective responsibility. In western culture, responsibility for children has generally been defined as lying with the biological parents or, more specifically, and until very recently, the father; this notion has been closely associated with private property. Increasingly, however, the state has intervened in areas relating to what is defined as child welfare and this has become an area often characterised by conflict between parents and state agencies.

Aristotle argued that a child is in some fundamental sense a part of the parent's body, and that being the case the parent should have ultimate control over the child. Plato, on the other hand, argued that the state should have direct control of children's education and upbringing. Childrearing, he argued, need not be the sole preserve of women, whom he saw as capable of fulfilling important offices in the state (although this was qualified by social position). The state for Plato, therefore, took primacy over biological parenthood and family ties. Similar arguments about the connections between private property and the family were made by Engels and, in more recent years, feminists such as Shulamith Firestone.[1] Locke, on the other hand, associated ownership with labour. It could be argued from such a premise that childbirth, as labour, should therefore entitle women to own their children. Locke, however, denies that children should be 'owned' at all, given their status as citizens-in-the-making and thus *potentially* free. It is a complex and often contradictory debate.

Parentage and kinship are not universally defined. Though we assume biological kinship to be the ultimate definition of 'family' and the crucial tie between children and parents, in some non-western cultures the primacy of blood ties is not necessarily even acknowledged and is often seen as far less important than the fact of an individual's belonging to a wider group. In Banaro society, for example:

> After the first few days of infancy, the raising of children is in many respects a public activity. There is always an alternate caretaker available and the mother is never isolated with her child or left without help . . . even small children are free to change residences, at least temporarily, if they become angry or feel mistreated . . . a parent is never put into the situation of being the sole satisfier of a child's needs. (Langness, 1981, p. 27)

Wet-nursing has been used for centuries as an alternative to breast-feeding by the biological mother. Wet-nursing, for instance, was prevalent in Ancient Egypt, Greece and Rome: 'In Greek and Roman Egypt unwanted children were often exposed on rubbish heaps. People requiring an inexpensive slave could visit such places, choose an abandoned baby, and then select a wet nurse to feed it for periods of up to three years' (Fildes, 1988, p. 5).

Wet-nursing continued to be widespread in medieval Europe and apparently became even more common among households of the wealthy after the eleventh century (Fildes, 1988, p. 34). In England it reached a peak in the late seventeenth and early eighteenth centuries. From that time on, it was increasingly condemned by medical and religious writers. In France, however, it remained common until the end of the eighteenth century. Babies from more affluent households were often dispatched within days of their birth to wet-nurses in the country, who would feed and raise them until around the age of three or four. Sometimes wet-nurses were brought into the parents' household, as was, for example, the nurse for Paul Dombey in Charles Dickens' *Dombey and Son*. Early forms of bottle-feeding – 'nursing horns' – date back until at least the ninth century (McLaughlin, 1976, p. 151). Thus a baby's dependency is total and constant, but the person on whom it is dependent can vary and shift. It is by no means always the birth mother or indeed an adult; young children have often been entrusted with care of younger siblings while their parent/carer goes out to work. Similarly, older relatives often take responsibility for their children's babies.

Under Roman law, which has shaped and influenced western law, *patria potestas* allowed the father to sell, or indeed to murder, his child, at least until the age of seven. In feudal society, where the legal system was deeply influenced by Roman law, children below the age of majority (10 in the sixth century, 12 in the seventh century, but 21 in the eleventh century) had no legal rights whatsoever. A father was by law entitled to sell a child below the age of seven. Children were defined as the father's property. Mothers held no rights over them at all.[2]

As land ownership and tenancy became increasingly hereditary in western Europe, so control of land inherited by a minor became more and more problematic. This was clarified in England after the Norman Conquest, when it was decided that an heir who was a minor was to be made a ward of the feudal lord to whom the tenant owed service: 'The Lord was also entitled to the body of the heir. Should the latter escape or be seduced away from the Lord's custody, the Lord could compel his or her return. The Lord could sell the heir in marriage' (Thane, 1981, p. 13). The only rights stipulated for a child in such cases were those of 'adequate maintenance'. These laws, of course, were formulated for the wealthy and landed; the issue of inheritance was at the centre of debates and legislation affecting children, so that from at least Roman times they were closely associated with, and defined in relation to, property and ownership.

As wage labour became more prevalent and feudal ties weakened, however, guardianship of minors passed from feudal lords to close male kin, and fathers in particular: 'From very early times, the role of the law was chiefly to protect the rights of the parent or guardian against the loss of the property or service which the minor represented . . . Only from the 1870s did the law acknowledge that the first consideration in deciding who should have custody of a minor was the interests of the child' (Thane, 1981, p. 15). Much of the power and control once allocated to the feudal lord, therefore, was used to define the position of the father over his children, and the notion of ownership remained largely central to this until the latter half of the nineteenth century.

## Slavery

Historically and globally, it is possible to see how the idea that children can be owned contributed to a rationalisation for millions of children being sold into slavery:

> In the ninth and tenth centuries, young boys were among the principal categories of slaves exported from France to Spain and other parts of the Moslem world . . . they seem to have been mainly pagan (Slavic) children captured and then castrated chiefly at Verdun . . . according to the thirteenth century German *Schwabernspiegel*, the sale of children in cases of dire necessity was permissible, but they were not to be delivered to death or to the heathens or to prostitution. (McLaughlin, 1976, 161, footnote 124)

The slave trade and slave labour were essential components in the development of western capitalism and were fundamental to imperialism between the fifteenth and nineteenth centuries. For over 400 years Africans were viewed by Europeans as non-human commodities to be bought and sold for profit. Edward Said (1994) has shown how important slavery and imperialism have been to western culture. Despite the increasing importance attributed to the family and 'family values' among the nascent bourgeoisie in late eighteenth and early nineteenth century Europe, slaves were sold separately, regardless of their kinship ties or connections, which were, indeed, often seen as a hindrance to effective control by masters.

Many children were sold into slavery at only a few years old, never to see their family again. The following extracts were written by Mary Prince, the first black British woman to escape from slavery. She was born about 1788 on a farm in Bermuda. Bermuda had been a crown colony since 1684 and its major industries were shipbuilding and salting. In 1788 less than 200 acres of land were cultivated and the population numbered between 10 000 and 11 000 people, of whom 5000 were slaves (Ferguson, 1987, pp. 2–3). Mary Prince published an account of her experiences in 1831, *The History of Mary Prince, a West Indian Slave, Related by Herself:*

> I was born on a farm belonging to Mr. Charles Myners. My mother was a household slave; and my father . . . was a sawyer belonging to Mr. Trimmingham . . . When I was an infant, old Mr. Myners died, and there was a division of the slaves . . . I was bought along with my mother by old Captain Darrel, and given to his grandchild, Miss Betsey Williams . . . who was about my own age. I was made quite a pet of by Miss Betsey and loved her very much. She used to lead me by the hand, and call me her little nigger . . . I had scarcely reached my twelfth year when my mistress became too poor to keep so many of us at home; and she hired me out to Mrs. Pruden. (Ferguson, 1987, pp. 47–51, passim)

She stayed with Mrs Pruden for some three months, but Mrs Williams then died and she was sent back to Mr Williams to be sold. Her mother had to dress and take her own children to market to be sold:

> She placed us in a row against a large house, with our backs to the wall and our arms folded against our breasts. I, as the

eldest, stood first . . . and our mother stood beside, crying over
us. My heart throbbed with grief and terror so violently . . . But
who cared for that? . . . At length the vendue master . . . arrived. He took me by the hand, and led me out into the middle
of the street, and, turning me slowly round, exposed me to the
view of those who attended the vendue. I was soon surrounded by strange men, who examined and handled me in
the same manner that a butcher would a calf or a lamb . . . It
was a sad parting; one went one way, one another, and our
poor mammy went home with nothing. (Ferguson, 1987, pp.
52–3, passim)

Her subsequent owner inflicted myriad cruelties and punish-
ments on her.

Abolition of the slave trade was, of course, a key issue in late
eighteenth and early nineteenth-century Britain. Interestingly,
though, even after the slave trade had been abolished it was not
until the middle of the nineteenth century that some of the duties
and responsibilities towards children accorded in law to fathers
began to be conceded to mothers. It is almost certainly not coin-
cidental that such changes in state law came at a time when
children were ceasing to be of great importance either as inheri-
tors of land/capital or as wage earners in propertyless families.[3]

Yet children who could not be supported by their families,
whether because they were orphans or illegitimate or suffering
severe poverty, remained (and remain) a problem for the state.
Prior to the nineteenth century in Europe, such children were
apprenticed to other family-households until they reached the
age of majority. With the demise of the apprenticeship system,
the rapid growth of population, and especially of a younger
population, such measures were no longer feasible. Orphanages
were one response to what was perceived as a crisis, although, in
fact, it was often the case that the children who went into orphanages were not actually orphans at all, but children of parent(s)
suffering unbearable poverty and unemployment. Another solution was to send children to the colonies. Parr relates how in the
'dark days' following the 1848 revolutions 'The Poor Law Act
was amended . . . so that [Poor Law] Guardians could send orphaned and deserted children abroad . . . Over 4000 Irish girls
were sent to New South Wales and South Australia' (Parr, 1994,

p. 28). In Britain between 1868 and 1925 80000 boys and girls were sent from institutions to work under indentures as agricultural labourers and domestic servants. Most of them were under 14 and none gave consent to their enforced emigration. Between 1854 and 1891 American city youngsters were sent to the midwestern states in a similar programme (Parr, 1994, p. 46).

Crucial to the definition and position of children in society, as we have seen, is their initial total helplessness and thus dependency on others for care and protection. Of equal importance, however, is their transitory nature. Helpless they may be, but they are adults, or at least older children, in the making, and as such, if they survive, can have enormous value as both heirs and workers to their parent(s). They can, of course, have great potential for giving emotional pleasure and satisfaction to parent(s). They are also, however, future citizens and members of a wider collective. As such they both represent and literally *embody* the future of a society and the future of a polity. States want future citizens who will not challenge their authority or laws, whatever these may be. The state also acts as arbiter in cases where custody is contested. There are an increasing number of custody disputes between foster parents and biological parents, as well as occasionally between surrogate mother and biological mother. Surrogacy in particular raises important issues about 'ownership' and whether ultimately a child can be truly said to *belong* to anyone at all. Such debates raise further questions as to what should be the criteria for deciding a child's best interests: blood ties and kinship, or material comfort and security?

Children are thus crucial to society and the state as well as to parents in a number of ways. The western state, however, has rarely been interested in, or willing, to take on the *economic* burden of providing care for its future citizens while they are young and helpless. Historically it is possible to see how the state has at times taken responsibility for children in certain situations, while refusing to take responsibility in others. This tension between state responsibility and intervention, and the responsibilities and rights of parents (and only very recently, of course, the rights of children themselves), continues to be a contested area in many ways in contemporary society. Consider, for example, the recent acrid conflicts over the Child Support Agency,[4] the Cleveland crisis,[5] or old and ongoing debates about illegitimacy and single mothers.

## Illegitimacy

In recent years illegitimacy has largely ceased to bear the stigma it did for centuries, although single mothers continue to be a controversial political issue. Judaeo-Christian codes of sexuality, marriage and reproduction which have dominated western culture for over two millennia, have stipulated specific rules on the boundaries of legitimate sexuality and reproduction which are firmly premised on the notion of heterosexual monogamous marriage. One of the first ways in which the nascent state intervened to define responsibilities surrounding children was in regard to illegitimacy. Because the fatherhood of illegitimate children can be uncertain or unknown, the body of laws pertaining to his responsibility and rights concerning the child do not apply. In the Middle Ages the church usually accepted unwanted babies and children, and took on all responsibilities for them, raising them as oblates in monasteries. Children and Christianity were in many ways closely connected, and as God's creatures children were also accepted as to a large extent the responsibility of the Church (Boswell, 1989). After the Reformation and the dissolution of the monasteries, however, this service was no longer available in Britain and the sixteenth century was a time when various attempts at prescribing responsibilities for illegitimate and orphaned children were made by the state.

First it was decreed that illegitimate children should be the responsibility of the local parish where they were born; this, however, proved to be a drain on local resources and was much resented by local taxpayers, with the result that pregnant women were often driven from parish to parish. Second, they resolved that illegitimate children and orphaned children should be bound as apprentices: boys until they were 24, girls until they were 21 (McLure, 1981, p. 125). For girls this meant almost invariably working as household servants. Until illegitimate children were old enough to be apprenticed, however, they were either raised by their mothers with the aid of parish funds, or else found shelter in parish poorhouses, which were usually characterised by mortality rates running as high as 100 per cent (McLure, 1981, p. 13).

In seventeenth-century France 'foundlings' proved a useful source both of souls for the church and as soldiers for the French standing army. By the eighteenth century in England, however, the apprenticeship system was very much in decline, largely as a result of the spread of wage labour and a 'free' market concomitant with the rapid development of urbanisation and industrialisation. Parallel with these was a surge in population growth, brought about partly by changes in mortality,[6] partly by an increase in birth rates, and illegitimate births in particular. Infanticide was increasing.

In 1722 Thomas Coram began his plan to try and help alleviate the problems of increasing illegitimacy by setting up his Foundling Hospital in London. Here illegitimate children, strictly separated by gender, were given a regimented and carefully supervised life, well fed compared to those without such help, yet always reminded of their pernicious and lowly status. The governors, for instance, stipulated clearly that the children should:

> learn to undergo with Contentment the most servile and laborious Offices; for notwithstanding the innocence of the Children, yet as they are exposed and abandoned by their Parents, they ought to submit to the lowest Stations, and should not be educated in such a manner as may put them upon a level with the Children of Parents who have the Humanity and Virtue to preserve them, and the Industry to support them. (McLure, 1981, p. 48)

It is interesting to note that the parents are blamed for lacking humanity, virtue and industry – not money, health or physical ability. Such 'lapses' were at this time, and for a long time afterwards (and, indeed once again now), seen as primarily *moral* problems and failings on the part of the *mothers*, not as problems relating either to poverty or to the vulnerability of women in many situations to male harassment and violence.

Implicit in rules and codes governing legitimacy and inheritance is also the issue of the control of women's sexuality by men:

'Fathers, brothers and husbands have a right and a duty to protect and regulate the sexual activities of daughters, sisters and wives' (Ennew, 1986, p. 37). A child born to an unmarried woman is thus 'evidence of an unsanctioned sexual act or, to put it another way, a woman out of control' (Ennew, 1986, p. 37) *as well as* being an immature person without material support from a man, and thus liable to be or to become dependent on the local community and/or state.

That the sins of the fathers should be laid on the children was clearly articulated and reinforced in the children at Coram's, who were made to sing this version of the 51st Psalm:

Wash off my foul offence,
   And cleanse me from my sin;
For I confesse my crime, and see
   How great my Guilt has been.

In Guilt each part was form'd
   Of all this sinful frame;
In Guilt I was conceiv'd and born
   The heir of Sin and Shame.
   (Quoted in McLure, 1981, p. 232)

Throughout the nineteenth century, Coram's was the only institution to care for illegitimate children and, indeed, for every child taken in, five were turned away (McLure, 1981, p. 251).

The stigma of illegitimacy remained. It branded children from an early age: branded *poor* children, that is, for the aristocracy had for centuries produced large numbers of illegitimate children. Their wealth ensured the stigma on their illegitimate children was relatively slight, for their economic dependency was not a problem to the state. For illegitimate children born in poverty, however, it was a different matter. Emma Smith, quoted at the beginning of the chapter, was raised initially by her grandparents and then sent to the workhouse before she was finally sold to the hurdy-gurdy man. She became increasingly aware of her difference from other children, who teased her because of her cropped hair and called her 'old Union maid' (the workhouse was often called the 'Union'). She grappled with the status of illegitimacy, which she found difficult to understand:

At that early age I did not know the meaning of the word 'bastard'. I only knew that the angry tone in which the word was always used conveyed to my sensitive mind the realisation that Harry (her younger brother) and I were in some dreadful mysterious way different from other children; that indeed we had no right to be in the world at all. (Smith, 1954, p. 20)

Harry, however, stayed with their mother, while Emma was sold into a life of sexual abuse, squalor and hard work. She spent some time in a Salvation Army home, then ran away back to her mother, who was by this time living with another man and had more children. Her mother turned her away, saying: 'Look Emma . . . my man comes first' (Smith, 1954, p. 73). When she was 12 she contracted acute chicken pox and was put in a penitentiary for prostitutes, where she was made to feel intense shame, but still could not understand why.

It was not until the 1871 Bastardy Laws Amendment Act that a mother's claim for maintenance from a putative father was strengthened. The earlier Bastardy Law Amendment Act of 1834 had laid all blame and responsibility for illegitimate births on to the mother. Stigmatisation, however, remained fierce until at least the 1960s. At that point the 'sexual revolution', the growing importance of multinationals and monopoly capitalism all meant that inheritance and knowledge of paternity had declined in importance both economically and politically. Where the illegitimacy rate in Britain had stood stable at around 5 per cent of all births until the 1950s, this had risen to 8 per cent by the end of the 1960s, rose again to 11 per cent by the end of the 1970s, and in 1990 stood at an all-time high of 28 per cent (Social Trends, 1992, quoted in Fox Harding, 1996, p. 35).[7]

The rise in divorce rates, decline in marriage rates and second wave feminism also arguably helped to reduce the stigma of illegitimacy. The recent increase of unemployment, however, and concomitant spread of dependency have meant that the government, sporadically trying to resurrect 'family values' and 'Victorian values', has focused on single mothers as the target of cuts specifically and opprobrium generally, so that single mothers have become in Conservative rhetoric scapegoats for much wider economic and political problems. Since dependency is now dealt with at the level of the central state rather than at a local parish level, it is arguably less easy to target specific individuals for discrimination and shaming, as was the case for children such as Emma Smith. Poverty, however, continues to be a problem for most single mothers and their children.

State concern with children thus focuses largely on the problem of children's dependency and who should be responsible for them until they can be responsible for themselves. Wherever and whenever possible, the state has tended to define responsibility for children as lying firmly in the lap of the parents/father, extolling in rhetoric 'the family', while handing over the expensive tasks of upbringing to parents whenever possible. Changes in the economy and in society, however, have meant that this is often challenged, resisted and renegotiated. Key areas in which, for various reasons, the state has intervened in relation to children's dependency, have been those of child labour and education.

## Work

Children in contemporary western culture are to a great extent defined in terms of economic dependency. To be a child means not to work for a living. If and when children do work we tend to feel pity, outrage, horror; at one level we question their entitlement even to be considered children. Yet work for Third World children is as normal as it was for many poor western children up until the nineteenth century. One-third of all domestic workers in Brazil, for instance, are children, some of whom have been handed over to middle-class households as servants from the age of three or four, often as settlement for their parents' debts (Vittachi, 1989, p. 96). The ILO estimates that 100–150 million children work every day. The numbers are increasing.

Child labour, of course, is cheap labour, and hence its immense value to the West. Our ability to buy cheap tea, coffee, chocolate, shoes, clothes and 'ethnic' home furnishings depends on Third World cheap labour, which is to a great extent child labour. A bonded slave boy in India making carpets may be paid around $7 for his work when his master is paid $225 for the carpet the boy makes . . . The carpet may then be sold in London for up to $9000

(Vittachi, 1989, p. 97). Children in the Third World are sold into slave labour. Many are sold into prostitution. We feel horrified; how, we might wonder, could their parents do such a thing?

It is done because not just children, but also adults – parents – live in poverty and destitution. The western media tend to focus on images of poor children working and starving because the notion of *children* working and starving is immoral to us. *Poverty,* however, is now less emotive to us, having been virtually denied by recent Conservative governments. As a result poverty tends now to be seen increasingly as an individual shortcoming rather than as a social problem. Charities arguably use images of starving or damaged children in advertisements because we still 'care' about children in a way we no longer seem to care about poverty. Little is said to convey the fact that for most children who work, their earnings are essential to the survival of their family-household.

A principal difference between children globally is thus that of work. Of course western children do 'work' in the sense that they expend effort attending school. Girls in particular are often involved in carrying out unpaid domestic work at home. Child labour is not unique to the Third World. Just as middle class children in the Third World do not work, so an increasing number of poor children in the West, and especially in the UK, live in poverty and often have to work illegally. A survey carried out in Birmingham in 1991 found about three-quarters of school children were working in some capacity. The Low Pay Unit estimated that approximately two million children in the UK do part-time work, and this is the worst record in all Europe (*Guardian*, 10 February 1995).

As increased cuts in health services have bitten deeper, many disabled adults have become more dependent on the care and services of their – often young – children. Such work, however, is largely invisible and is rarely paid. For family-households living in poverty both in the Third World and in the West the contributions made by children to the family economy thus often make the difference between survival and starvation. Of course the scale and amount of child labour in the Third World is huge compared to the UK, but in the UK a persistent unwillingness to endorse EU legislation restricting child labour has meant that it continues to grow steadily. Cheap labour, after all, is cheap labour, and profit levels continue to depend on it. Cheap labour and child labour, if not quite synonymous, are nevertheless intimately linked.

Children are, and have been, economically important to adults/parents in several ways. For those with wealth and land, children, and boys in particular, are and have been crucial, as discussed earlier, as *heirs*. Inheritance, of course, has also been of central *political* importance; many of the wars that raged through medieval Europe focused on contested inheritance of lands and kingdoms. Henry VIII's successive wives were all about his desperate quest for a male heir. While such issues were most pressing for the aristocracy and ruling families, heirs to any landed group are always a crucial problem.

Children have also been regarded as a form of insurance for old age. In eras and cultures where there was no form of welfare, people who became ill, disabled or unable to work were dependent on kin generally and children specifically for support. As the Conservative government in Britain has cut welfare services, so it has tried to emphasise the importance of 'family values'. Many middle-aged 'children', for instance, care for their ill and infirm elderly parents; such 'children' are overwhelmingly women. Children, however, have not been and are not always the most reliable form of support for aged parents, except where care has been contingent on inheritance of land/wealth. Children with nothing to inherit have been more likely to move away, marry and make their own lives and family-households.

For the landless, children have been of great importance economically in terms of labour both in the labour market and within the household. Girls particularly, but sometimes also boys, have provided enormous amounts of labour within the home, labour which, though invariably unpaid, is often vital in releasing the mother or other female kin for productive labour – whether on family lands or in the wage labour market. Who did what in terms of gender, however, depended to a great extent on the gender composition and the age composition of the particular household, as the following extract by George Muckford, who was born in Sussex in 1826, shows:

My parents were poor, the occupation of my father being a shepherd. I was the eldest surviving member of a large family of twelve children, the first born having died in infancy; and this being the case, I had, as soon as I was old enough, to be mother's help, to nurse the baby, clean the house, and do sewing like a girl, so that I was not only prevented from playing with other boys, but also from going to school. (Burnett, 1982, p. 72)

Equally, in households where there were daughters but no sons, daughters might well work on the land or in the labour market. More probably, a girl might work on the land for a short time until a younger brother was able to take her place, thus releasing her for other duties, which might or might not be in the household. George Muckford, when he was eight, stopped taking care of younger siblings because a younger sister could now take over that task. Instead he began to work by scaring birds from the fields for a wage of one shilling a week. By the age of ten he had become a shepherd boy and earned two shillings a week:

> ... though I never had the money, as of course my father took it ... I was always rather delicate in health ... Having commenced my new occupation in the winter, I felt it much; my feet and hands became covered with chilblains, which soon broke out into open sores ... [His father] had no sympathy with his white-faced son; he said I must be hardened to it, or I should never be any use. I began to have a great dread of him, and all I did for him was done under fear of the lash. (Burnett, 1982, pp. 72–4)

It was assumed that most children, certainly the children of the poor, should work. The jobs they did would vary by their age, gender, position in relation to siblings, class, and geographical location, but work – often with and among adults – was part of a child's life from an early age. The work they did and, most important of all, the money they earned, was always assumed to *belong* to the parent(s).

In 1724 Daniel Defoe reckoned a child 'could fend for himself from the age of four or five' (quoted in Vittachi, 1989, p. 12), though evidence suggests this was regarded as very early except among the most impoverished. Yet the majority of children, to a great extent regardless of social and economic background, were sent away as apprentices or servants in other family-households, often from the age of seven or eight. An estimated 75 per cent of children in early modern Europe lived and worked in other households (Gillis, 1981). An Italian observer visiting England around 1500 remarked:

> The want of affection in the English is strongly manifested towards their children; for after having kept them at home till they arrive at the age of seven or nine years at the utmost, they put them out, both males and females, to hard service in the houses of other people, binding them generally for another seven or nine years. And these are called apprentices, and during that time they perform all the most menial offices; and few are born who are exempted from this fate, for every one, however rich he may be, sends away his children into the houses of others, whilst he, in return, receives those of strangers into his own. (Quoted in Rosen, 1994, p. 24)

Among poor families some children might stay at home to help on the farm or in a trade, while others would be sent away. The main benefit to parents was that if the children were not needed as labour at home, they ceased to be a burden on family expenditure while living and working elsewhere. Apprenticeship often entailed a fee, and this was one way in which children were differentiated in the past, but once paid, the master was responsible for the child's board, lodging and training. The potential for cruelty and abuse in such a situation was presumably great, but the overall issue was a collective one concerning the best option for the family-household.

As the economy became increasingly characterised by wage labour and labour-intensive industry, especially from the eighteenth century (although this varied enormously between different regions and, of course, countries), a premium was put on children remaining at home where they could contribute actively, through wage labour, to the household economy. In such a situation, which was typical of working-class families in the late eighteenth and early nineteenth centuries in many areas of Britain, children who were economically active usually handed over all their earnings to their parent(s). Implicit in such transactions was the notion of ownership and indebtedness. Yet there was also potential in such relationships for increased independence for children, should they find their home situation unbearable.

James Dawson Burn, for example, who was born about 1806, lived initially with his mother and stepfather. His stepfather was an alcoholic and abusive ex-soldier, and made James work with him peddling and begging from an early age. When he was around 12, his mother and stepfather hired him out as an agricultural labourer. Soon after, they sent him to his real father in Ireland, who was a cord weaver and whom James had never known:

> My mother had an interview with my father, after which I was duly consigned to his care . . . I went to him with my mind surcharged with a living hatred of his very name. He had a family of three children and a step-mother . . . My new-found brother and sisters were strangers to me. I was there as a living memento of [my father's] perfidy. I was neither inconvenienced with shoes nor stockings . . . my clothes were reduced to rags. During the winter my feet were hacked into innumerable fissures from which the blood was continually starting . . . During the whole time I was with him, he never once called me by name. (Burn, 1978, pp. 72–5, passim)

James ran away and never returned.

It was at least partly this potential for working-class children to be independent that frightened the middle classes, who were deeply committed to their own domestic ideology that defined children and women as 'natural' dependants on men within the family. There was also a discourse of rescue, which was particularly promulgated by the Evangelicals, and focused on *morality* rather than issues of cruelty or hardship for children working. It is perhaps not surprising, therefore, that the initial target of state intervention and middle-class outrage was on the most visible and dirty of children's occupations: chimney sweeping and coal mining. Exploitation was less at issue in the debate on these than what was seen as a great moral danger to children who were 'exposed' to work alongside adults, both women and men, in the case of mining, and where workers often had to wear scanty clothing to cope with the extreme heat.

From the 1770s onwards debates about child labour, and about chimney sweeps in particular, grew and became increasingly acrimonious. Jordanova argues that the controversy focused on sweeps because that particular occupation

> was visible, it affected young children (roughly five upwards), and it had tremendous symbolic potential (black, dirt, sin, slavery, and so on). On what grounds was it deplored? Children were tender, impressionable, vulnerable, pure, deserving of parental protection, and hence all too easily corrupted by the market-place. Two main justifications existed for this characterisation of children: a Christian one, which portrayed children as in a 'sacred state of life'; and an ideological one, according to which they were somehow 'naturally' incompatible with the world of commodities. (Jordanova, 1989, p. 20)

The urge to 'rescue' and 'protect' working-class children by the middle classes can also be seen, however, as a result of fear. Children who lived and worked in the streets, in public, were regarded as 'out of control', 'wild' because they had no apparent adult supervision or control and were not dependent directly on adult protection and surveillance. The idea that children could, and can, survive in the world without adult protection, without conventional (middle-class) families, defied (and defies) middle-class notions of masculinity as defined in terms of independent men who must support 'naturally dependent' women and children, and who alone are capable of instructing, guiding and controlling such weak/needy/Other beings.

The character of Fagin in Dickens' *Oliver Twist*, for instance, can be seen as the epitome of all traits that a Victorian middle-class father was supposed not to be: exploitative, living off the (illicit) earnings of others who by definition should be protected and innocent (that is, little boys), self-interested, greedy, and living in filth and darkness. Of course the fact that he is represented as Jewish reinforces old stereotypes of evil, greed and otherness (echoes, for instance, of Shakespeare's Shylock in *The Merchant of Venice*). Oliver Twist's redemption depends on middle-class money, philanthropy and (Christian) family values. Only through these can he be reinstated into 'true childhood' by being removed from the public world of work, street, money and corruption, spheres only negotiable by strong and independent

men, who in turn serve to protect him within the private world of
the family as a total dependant.

Jordanova argues that it was the often complex and contradictory concept of 'nature' as it was applied to children in the eighteenth century that was used to justify children being defined as
'naturally' ill-suited to hard labour. Interestingly, however, the
whole range of work done by children was by no means under
attack. The middle classes were quite happy to employ girls as
young as seven as their domestic servants, who often carried out
hard physical tasks such as lugging full coal hods and large jugs
of water up several flights of stairs. Children's work in agriculture was not condemned, nor was industrial work except, increasingly, the most visible forms of industrial work in large
factories (where moral danger was seen as greatest because of
close proximity to adult men and women). Children who worked
in mines, however, in black, shadowy, hot and 'underground'
work, became the focus of renewed controversy over child labour
in the early nineteenth century. It was primarily *public* labour (or
labour that was seen as such) that concerned the middle classes
in relation to children, while the 'private' realm of family-
household was left uncriticised, uninvestigated, because that
realm was defined as sacrosanct by the middle classes themselves. Such views largely let the middle classes 'off the hook' as
regards their own widespread employment and exploitation of
young girls as servants: 'To patrol industry on behalf of the
young was England's Christian duty. To patrol the home was a
sacrilege' (Behlmer, 1982, p. 9).

Such well-entrenched beliefs die hard. Part of the shock to the
public surrounding the Cleveland crisis in 1987 was not just that
many of the abusers were respectable, married, middle-class men
– this aspect was silenced very rapidly – but that the state should
deign to intervene in *middle-class* families at all. Perpetrators
(largely fathers and stepfathers) and victims (girls and boys)
became invisible and silent as figures in the drama, as the focus
of the spotlight quickly shifted to the battle between families –
usually, though not exclusively, middle class – and state agencies; the agenda was only very briefly about the pain and suffering of children caused by adults allegedly responsible for
protecting them, and it soon shifted to the audacity and horror of

state agencies (and in particular 'feminist' state agents such as paediatrician Marietta Higgs) intervening in the sacrosanct homes of the middle classes. State intervention is always described – some might say 'disguised' – as in the interests of the child and its protection. But the state itself is not neutral; it is composed of a number of different agencies such as the civil service, the National Health Service, Social Services, local government, and so forth. These are generally staffed by middle-class people, who tend to be carefully scrutinised for their (middle-class) values and orientation.

Issues surrounding state intervention in child labour were not, of course, confined to Britain alone. In France, where there was a substantial peasant population throughout the nineteenth century (and, indeed, well into the twentieth century), children were expected to start some form of work on or around the farm from the age of six or seven. Heywood points out that children in nineteenth-century rural France were still highly visible in all spheres of life: the street, the workshop and the farm 'were still very much part of their territory, where they mingled freely with the world of adults' (Heywood, 1988, p. 1). Children and adults ate, worked and relaxed together. As in Britain, children were also frequently sent away to work as servants, apprentices and sweeps, often developing an itinerant life style early on, moving regularly from farm to farm. Many children in France, both girls and boys, began work as shepherds, where they lived separately from their family-households, sometimes with other shepherds and sometimes alone. Where several of them worked nearby, they often yodelled to each other, played games, and shared meals in an adult-free world, although for most it was a lonely, fearful existence (Heywood, 1988, p. 50).

In France, too, the middle classes were juggling attitudes towards their own children, defined as dependent, innocent and in need of protection from the outside world, with the situations of poor children who continued to work long hours from an early age. Where a village school was available, some poor children were able to attend during the winter months when work was scarce, but 'the impression remains that right up until the First World War, the primary school perched uneasily in the villages as it struggled to insert itself into the mainstream of rural life'

(Heywood, 1988, p. 61). Apprenticeship, both formal and informal, remained the chief means of education for poor children in rural nineteenth-century France.

Thus undoubtedly one of the most dramatic, even revolutionary changes with regard to children was a changing attitude, a different discourse, that saw work and child*hood* as incompatible, regardless of social class. It is possible to see the nineteenth century as the period during which a notion of a universal childhood was fought over, negotiated, renegotiated. Dependency was coming to define a universal child and childhood. As Walvin (1982, p. 61) notes, however, it was a 'view that was often furthered by the declining viability of child labour.' The shift from a labour-intensive industrial infrastructure in early nineteenth-century Britain to an increasingly capital-intensive one from mid-century onwards can be seen as linked in many ways to changing discourses of childhood. The relative continuity and size of the rural peasantry in France and a comparatively weak industrial infrastructure can similarly be seen as related to different ways and timescales in the development of such discourses, and relevant legislation, there.

In Lancashire in 1836 there were 30000 children working in the mills, where six year olds often worked from 5 a.m. to 9 p.m. In some areas boys started work in the mines from the age of four (their smallness, like chimney sweeps, made them extremely useful in cramped conditions). The 1842 Act, however, restricted children's and women's work in mines; from then on they were forbidden to work underground. Many, however, continued to do surface work. From chimney sweeping and mining, legislation developed to encompass other occupations and spheres:

> By 1850 factory legislation had reached its high water mark and had, from its original base in textiles and mining, come to afford increasing protection to children (and other workers) in a host of industries . . . there remained worries of children working beyond the pale of such legal safeguards. (Walvin, 1982, p. 68)

Children continued to work long and arduous hours in London's clothing and furniture trade which were based in small workshops and often involved outwork at home. In 1851 over one million girls and women worked as domestic servants. Girls and boys continued to work in coastal areas gathering cockles and mussels, preparing nets and cleaning fish. Farm work of all sorts still employed children extensively, often in organised gangs. The Gangs Act of 1867 brought under control some of the worst abuses of gang labour and the 1873 Agricultural Children's Act forbade the employment of children under eight. None the less, particularly in areas dominated by smallholdings, children's labour in agriculture continued to be important well into the twentieth century (Walvin, 1982, p. 75).

Middle-class efforts to ban all children working needs to be seen as part of their domestic ideology that regarded children and women as dependants:

> It was assumed by adults of the middle and upper classes that children were dependent on adults and subservient to them. They did not work; they played and learned. Responsibility for their care and education lay with adults: mother, father, aunt; nursemaid or other servant; governess, tutor or schoolteacher. They belonged in the home, preferably in separate quarters . . . Boys were sent to school after about eight . . . girls too might spend some time in school . . . whether at home or at school, children were to be segregated from the adult world. They were to accept whatever they were told by adults and ask no questions; girls especially were to know nothing of such adult matters as money or sex, and to be innocent and unworldly. (Davin, 1990, pp. 37–8)

Davin shows how once these ideas became consolidated into a code of ethics that claimed to offer a 'natural' definition of what children were, they came into conflict with the conditions of working-class children. Working-class children lived much more as part of the adult world; they worked, they earned money, they spent much of their time in the street. Middle-class reactions to this crystallised into two contrasting stereotypes of the 'child-as-adult': the 'little woman' (domestic and female, but often very young and having to take responsibility prematurely for younger siblings, domestic work, and so forth), and the 'Street Arab' (male, street-based and dangerous) (Davin, 1990, p. 39). The images of

these two types of working-class child were used widely to portray them as transgressive, dangerous, problematic.[8]

In 1848 Lord Shaftesbury estimated there were some 30000
children living in London's streets (Davin, 1990, p. 43). From the
middle of the century onwards there was a growing attempt to
deal with this perceived problem of children living in a way that
negated middle-class ideals of childhood. The number and powers of charities dealing with poor children grew and developed.
Some people, such as Mary Carpenter[9] and the writer Charles
Dickens, argued for a kind and loving approach that stressed
reform for a group that needed to be seen as different and thus in
need of special treatment. Others favoured a far more punitive set
of policies, arguing for the continuation, for example, of imprisonment of children for minor offences. In 1856, 1990 girls and
boys under the age of 12 were imprisoned in England (Behlmer,
1982).

When Mayhew carried out his research into London's poor in
the 1880s, he discovered boys of six years old incarcerated for
throwing stones, knocking on doors, and obstructing the high-
ways. In York a small child was jailed for a week for playing
cricket in the street (Walvin, 1982, p. 57). Scores of young children
were transported during the first half of the nineteenth century,
often for minor offences. Increasingly, however, reformatory
schools took the place of prison; legislation in 1854 and 1857
empowered courts to send children between the ages of 7 and 16
to reformatory schools. 'Vagrant' children under 14 were sent
to industrial schools. Both were established as alternatives to
prison. Yet imprisonment of children under 14 continued until
1908, despite a growing awareness that children had different
needs to those of adults and were, in some fundamental sense,
both different and special.

Legislation forbidding children to work protects them from
physical stress and strain and often dangerous conditions. It also,
however, excludes them from adult society, from a sense of personal worth and status that undoubtedly come from work, and,
most important, it prevents them earning money. As discussed,
children's earnings were often essential to the survival of their
family-households; forbidding children to work can thus affect
their standard of living adversely. Enforced economic and social
dependency both protects and excludes. Moreover, by taking

greater responsibility for children's welfare, the powers of the state over parents are thereby increased, as are the powers of parents over children.

## Education

Increasingly powerful state legislation was enacted in the western world during the second half of the nineteenth century that gave both the state and new voluntary agencies such as Dr Barnardo's in England the power to intervene in working-class children's lives. The acts, of course, specified 'children', yet in practice they referred only to working-class children. Many such acts endeavoured to 'regulate' working-class children's lives in ways more congruent with middle-class ideals of childhood. Working-class family-households and streets were coming under a closer surveillance than ever before. At the same time, however, the working classes themselves began to organise and pressurise for changes, many of which related to working-class children: the struggle for a 'family wage' was a classic example of this.

Education had for a long time seemed to the middle classes an obvious solution to the problem that working-class children, by working and spending much of their time on the streets unsupervised by adults, posed to middle-class discourse of dependent childhood. Yet a coherent primary education system was a long time coming, largely because of a prolonged tension between the radicals, who wanted a secular education system, and the Evangelicals, most prominent of whom was Hannah Moore 'who was determined to convert the nation's children to a proper outlook, partly through her cheap publications . . . but more significantly . . . through the Sunday School' (Walvin, 1982, p. 110).

Moreover, there were still many among the middle classes who regarded the idea of universal education as deeply threatening to the social order. They feared literacy would result not just in a radicalisation of politics, but also in revolution, as had occurred in France. While on the one hand many groups within the middle classes wanted to put into effect aspects of their overall discourse of dependent childhood that defined children as innocent and in need of adult supervision and guidance, on the other hand there were others who were afraid of working-class children becoming less different from middle-class children in relation to knowledge, information and, presumably, political skills. As inherited wealth became less important in the late nineteenth century, so education became more important, for it was through elitist and exclusive educations and professional training that the middle classes were able to develop and maintain a position of dominance in relation to other groups. This increasing importance of what Bourdieu calls 'cultural capital' arguably remains crucial in contemporary society where different educational opportunities remain a focus of debate and controversy.

In the nineteenth century, however, the issue was never one relating to a universal and identical education for all children, but the idea was carefully defined in terms of tailoring an education system to what were seen by the middle classes as the 'needs' of working-class children, such as obedience, deference, punctuality and cleanliness. 'Education was seen as being for work rather than for life' (Burnett, 1982, p. 168). Paradoxically, however, the middle classes were simultaneously emphasising that *all* children had similar needs and traits, while at the same time stressing the differences *between* children – mostly in terms of social class, but also in relation to gender and, implicitly, imperialist discourses of race and racial superiority.

Debates over, and provision of, education, however, were not new to the nineteenth century. From the seventeenth century onwards education had been a growing concern. Ariès attributes this to a new notion of childhood, which is effectively a modernisation argument, while Marxists have pointed to the correlation between a developing education system for middle-class boys and the rise of a capitalist economy (Hoyles, 1979). Schools for the aristocracy such as Eton and Harrow, of course, dated back to the late Middle Ages. The first grammar schools were established in the sixteenth century and were used mostly by the sons of local merchants. Literacy in seventeenth century England was about 40 per cent. Where there were 34 schools in all of England in 1480, by 1660 there were 444, a school for every 4400 people (Postman, 1985, p. 40). Small private schools and academies were set up in abundance during the eighteenth and nineteenth centuries, with competition often fierce between them. Mostly they were single-sex schools, and what schools were established for girls during this time tended to teach social deportment and perhaps a bit of French and music, while for boys the emphasis was largely on commercial subjects (Plumb, 1975, p. 72). The cost, and quality, of such schools varied enormously, but Plumb argues that the fees were low enough in many of them for the children of shop-keepers, small farmers, tenant farmers and some artisans to be able to attend.

Expansion of schools in the early nineteenth century was not, however, confined to the middle classes. Many villages, for example, had dame schools where poorer children attended for paltry sums and where they received some rudimentary instruction in reading. No doubt then, as for many now, such schools were also useful to mothers as childminding facilities. Dame schools continued to operate during the nineteenth century and tended to be run on a shoestring. Witness this account by Frederick Hobley, who was born in 1833 in Oxfordshire and was sent to school just before he turned three:

> I was sent to a Dame's School, kept for very young children . . . I have a distinct remembrance of the teacher giving me a needle and thread and a piece of rag to pass away my time during one of the afternoons . . . If a boy was naughty he was shut in her dark pantry as a punishment, and on one such occasion the little culprit ate up some old plum pudding that was in the pantry . . . Ma'am Lund eked out her living by selling Bulls-eyes and Brandy-balls. (Burnett, 1982, p. 178)

As the strength and influence of the working-class movement developed, particularly in the latter part of the nineteenth century, so working-class pressure for improved education also influenced the ongoing controversy and the eventual form that state education took.

Education, one way or another, was a key issue in the late eighteenth and early nineteenth centuries, and continued to be so throughout the nineteenth century and, indeed, up to the present day. It is of prime importance because it is a focus for debates on who should make decisions on children's behalf, how long children's dependency is seen as lasting, whether children from different class and religious/ethnic backgrounds could, or should, be taught different agendas and subjects, and so forth.

Debates over working-class education and state education continued during the nineteenth century and onwards, but there
were also fundamental debates and developments regarding
middle-class education. Corruption in boys' public schools was
overhauled by the efforts of Arnold[10] and others; public schools
increasingly became a melting pot between the aristocracy and
the middle classes. Increasing professionalisation and the need
for younger aristocratic sons[11] as well as those from the middle
classes to work in the professions led to increased competition
through the exam system, and this in turn led to generally higher
academic standards in the public schools. It also, of course, el-
evated standards and thus boundaries between classes at a point
when the working classes as a group were finally gaining access
to basic educational provision. Public schools and day schools for
middle-class girls were founded. Though in the vast majority of
these emphasis was on the acquisition of domestic skills and
social graces, none the less a more rigorous academic programme
was introduced in some.

Schools varied enormously, from the elitist public schools to
the kind of school represented by Charlotte Brontë in *Jane Eyre*,
where a regime of semi-starvation, beatings and evangelical discipline were the norm in the context of a charity school for orphaned lower middle-class girls. Certainly beating does seem to
have been common in *all* schools during the nineteenth century,
both for girls and boys, working class, aristocracy, and middle
class alike. Obedience and punctuality were cardinal virtues in all
schools, while deference was given particular emphasis among
working class pupils, though it was also deemed important
among elitist schools. Schools for the middle classes were run by
the middle classes. Schools for the working classes, with the
exception of dame schools, were run by the middle classes. Thus
in the latter there was, and to a certain extent still remains, conflicts between different codes of behaviour, language, habits
between middle class teachers and working class pupils.

By the early twentieth century, by which time free and compulsory universal primary education was established, working-class
children were further controlled and watched not just by the
growing army of 'child rescue' organisations, but also by officials
such as the school nurse and the 'nit-nurse'. Such officials of
course also provided overall benefits in terms of a new awareness

of health and hygiene, but they can be seen as part of a growing surveillance of children in state schools. Faith Osgerby, for instance, who was born in 1890 in East Yorkshire, gives the following account of her early memories of school:

> We sat in 'galleries', row above row, so that it was easy for the teacher to see us *all* at *all* times. I can hear Mrs Buttery even now shouting in her loud voice 'Faith Campey, come down here!' and I knew I was in for a swish of that cane. I suppose I had been whispering to my neighbour which was a grievous sin. (Burnett, 1982, p. 93)

Universal education gave more children access to literacy, and for a few, eventually, social mobility. Yet, again, it meant the demise of children's ability to help sustain their own family-households through work. The accepted narrative that such legislation inevitably improved children's conditions must thus be questioned seriously. It presumes, for instance, that children are not part of a family-household, and it fails to acknowledge how working-class households frequently pooled wages from all working members to survive. That poverty continued, possibly even accelerated, for the poorest in the latter nineteenth century is to a great extent confirmed by the fact that infant mortality, often taken as an index of poverty, reached its highest rate ever recorded in 1899.

Children's experiences of education thus differed markedly according to social class, gender and whether or not they were educated in boarding school, orphanage, private day school, public day school, dame school, tutored at home by parent or tutor, or worked at home or elsewhere, legally or illegally. Frequently educational opportunities depend and depended on the composition and parity of family-households. Often older siblings had to go to work as soon as they were able to help support the whole family-household, while younger siblings were then able to attend school because the overall income was being boosted by their older siblings working. Often all resources were poured into the education of a son or sons at the expense of a daughter or daughters, regardless of academic or intellectual ability. Such, for instance, was the case of Tom and Maggie Tulliver in George Eliot's ([1860] 1979) *The Mill on the Floss*, where Tom, utterly uninterested in academic work, was sent to a boarding school to learn the classics 'like a gentleman', while Maggie, much brighter than Tom and keen to learn languages, was denied an education. Such decisions were made by parents in the first instance, though by the end of the nineteenth century the state had resolved that all children must attend primary school. Such a change can be seen as indicative of the growing intervention of state agencies in delineating the needs and indeed definitions of children and childhood. It can be seen as at once showing an increased concern with children as the future of the nation, the race, as well as a concern that working-class children represented potential danger to political stability if not taught deference, obedience and respect.

## In Whose Best Interests?

What is good for children? Who should decide? Who is responsible for their well-being in all its senses: physical, mental, emotional, spiritual? These are arguably the core questions relating to the problem of children's dependencies. They are now articulated overwhelmingly in terms of one universal child, one universal childhood. What is inherent in this issue, however, is the concept of *protection*. An individual or group is, for one reason or another, deemed to be responsible for the protection of a dependent child. The duration and character of such dependency, which can be seen more logically as a cluster of different dependencies (physical, emotional, economic, legal), vary according to historical period, state legislation, parent-household, and individual circumstances. The notion of protection is premised by definition on a clear power differential between protector and protected. Paternalism is implicit in such a relationship. Paternalism can be benevolent, like a benevolent dictatorship, but it also has the potential for malevolence and harm, as do dictatorships. When apparent benevolence is the order of the day in relation to the protection of children by parents, nobody intervenes. It is when the relationship becomes malevolent, violent, destructive that crisis occurs in terms of responsibility and ownership of children. It is important to remember, however, that there is no universal definition of cruelty. What was seen as 'good discipline' 50 years ago would now be condemned as abuse. Rituals such as infant circumcision or infibulation, both of which involve extreme pain, are none the less important aspects of different cultures. The crucial issue is ultimately who decides what the standards of cruelty and abuse should be.

Much of the legislation affecting children that has burgeoned since the second half of the nineteenth century can be seen as concerned with delimiting the boundaries between parents and state. The boundaries are blurred and are frequently being challenged and redrawn. It is possible, however, to discern patterns in which 'protection' of children has developed over the past 200 years. Late eighteenth and early nineteenth concern tended to focus primarily on the *moral* and *spiritual* welfare of the child; hard physical labour was not seen as posing anything like the problem that susceptibility to adult immorality and corruption was. Discipline was seen as essential to such goals, and physical punishment was applauded by some and tolerated by many.

With the growing importance of the medical profession and medical discourse during the nineteenth century, it is possible to detect a shift towards concern with the *physical* well-being of children and their bodies. In the USA, for example, Gordon relates how child abuse was 'discovered' in the 1870s. Although undoubtedly ill treatment of children long preceded this, it was at this point that it became defined as a social problem. There was a rapid development of societies for the prevention of cruelty to children and by the end of the decade 34 such societies existed in the USA, and 15 elsewhere (Gordon, 1989, p. 27). This can also be seen as resulting from Darwin's theories and, in particular, an increased obsession with the overall condition of the 'race' and the nation's well-being as symbolised by its children. Early acts dealing with such issues in Britain were the Infant Life Protection Acts of 1872 and 1897, as well as the Prevention of Cruelty to Children Act of 1889. These preceded the Boer War (1899–1902), which is usually regarded as a watershed because it led to a critical assessment of the nation's health. What amounted to a moral panic occurred when it was discovered widespread ill health, disability and disease were endemic among the working classes. As a result there was a growing awareness of how the future of the British Empire, its 'racial stock' and overall prosperity related directly to the health of its future generations. Hence the Liberal reforms of 1906–14 focused to a large extent on children's well-being: school meals were initiated; medical inspection (although not treatment) was brought in to schools; the juvenile justice system was set up and the death penalty for children abolished; smoking was forbidden, as was children's presence in pubs.

Parallel with this increasing concern for the health of the nation generally and its children in particular ran a discourse about children's social behaviour and the issue of *control*. This had been at the heart of many debates about work and education during the course of the nineteenth century; the First Industrial Schools Act and various subsequent acts provided for the removal of children from parental custody if it could be proved that parents were unable to 'control' their children adequately. Standards and norms of 'control', of course, vary and varied widely, by gender, class, neighbourhood and culture.

Overwhelmingly, concern articulated about 'control' of children has been synonymous with control of *working-class* children. Violent incidents at public schools such as Eton, for example, are almost inevitably passed off as instances of 'boyish pranks' or 'high spirits', while similar incidents carried out by working-class children are labelled as vandalism and hooliganism and are generally punished fiercely. The current policy to set up 'boot camps'[12] for male juvenile offenders bears witness to the continuing power of this discourse. Once again, as in Victorian times, children's anti-social behaviour is seen as the result of bad parenting rather than as the result of wider social and economic problems such as homelessness, unemployment and poverty. Because childhood is now defined as if it were universal, evidence of *difference* is treated as pathological and/or deviant, rather than as evidence of diversity and different life chances between children and childhoods according to class, ethnicity and culture. The little boys who murdered James Bulger, for example, came from appalling social and economic backgrounds, yet this was never an issue.

While tolerance of children's aberrant behaviour would seem to be diminishing in some ways in recent years, at the same time there has been an increasing concern with the idea of children's rights. The recognition that children can be, and sometimes are, exploited and abused by their 'protectors' has led to increased state involvement in trying to protect children from their protectors. Under the Children Act of 1989, for instance, parents are defined as having 'parental responsibility' in relation to their children, rather than having rights over them as such (Fox Harding, 1996, p. 166). Responsibility (primarily and implicitly *financial* responsibility, but also power and control) continues for parents regardless of whether or not they live separately or divorce. Only if neither parent is able to provide financially or keep their children 'controlled' and/or 'protected' will the state intervene.

When, how and under just what circumstances the state is entitled to intervene in family-households to protect children from their protectors, however, remains a highly controversial issue. As discussed earlier, governments forced emigration on thousands of children, many of whom still had living kin, from the mid-nineteenth century until the third decade of the twentieth century (Parr, 1994). Governments have endorsed and supported putting children in reformatories, orphanages, industrial schools, prisons, and, of course, schools. Sometimes they have encouraged children without viable family-households to be institutionalised, sometimes to be fostered, sometimes sent away altogether. After the Second World War fostering and adoption were favoured over institutionalisation in Britain, as family bonds were given much emphasis. The acknowledgement of baby battering[13] as a social problem from the 1960s led to renewed debates, and the death of Maria Colwell at the hands of her stepfather in the 1970s resulted in a demand for more state intervention to protect children from their protectors. In the 1980s the deaths of Tyra Henry (aged 22 months), Kimberley Carlile and Jasmine Beckford triggered off widespread criticism of social services for non-intervention. In 1987, however, social services were pilloried for their interventions in Cleveland. In Cleveland, of course, they were intervening in *middle-class* family-households, where in all previous cases intervention had been into working-class family-households. It is perhaps, then, not surprising that the outcry over Cleveland was far more powerful and vociferous than it had been in any of the other cases.

The 1989 Children Act has attempted to balance some of these ongoing debates and conflicts about where responsibility ultimately lies for children, and whether they themselves can be given more say in their own lives. Children's initial physiological dependency is soon outgrown, and what remains in relation to their dependency and disempowerment – the right to vote, work, smoke, drink, drive, live where they choose – is arguably all socially constructed. Beyond the first few years of life when children are overwhelmingly dependent physically, older children are dependent because dependency is forced on to them. This can be seen as a result of the development of the concept of a universal child and a universal childhood, both of which are gender-neutral, apparently classless, but in reality premised on a middle-class ideal of childhood, which is in turn deeply influenced by assumptions about an ideal family. The 'ideal family' is firmly based on middle-class ideology and rhetoric of 'the family'.

There are arguably, then, what amount to myths about 'the family', 'the child' and 'childhood'. None of these allows for differences in any substantial way. They might also be seen as part of a trend that has increasingly denied the concept of 'community' or 'collective' as in any way relevant to the well-being of children. James Bulger, for example, was *seen* by many people being dragged away by his captors; he was crying and obviously hurt. Only one woman bothered to stop the boys and try to find out what was wrong. It is common to see children being quite viciously hit by parents for minor transgressions, such as crying or whining when they are tired or hungry, yet nobody says anything, nobody protests, everybody looks the other way. On a television programme in the mid 1990s a man admitted that he knew his neighbour's children were being seriously abused, but he still believed he was right not to intervene. Regardless of legislation it is still the case that the vast majority of the population believes children *belong* to parents, and that parents can do pretty much what they want with them. Children are still seen, I believe, as property; to speak out when a child is hurt by its parent remains as transgressive as to tell a stranger you do not like their jacket or the colour of their eye shadow.

We idealise children. We claim to adore them. We weep when they are hurt or destroyed, as so many people did for the slaughter of the schoolchildren at Dunblane in 1996. Yet we rarely intervene when children are being hurt or even tortured. In some cultures, past and present, children are defined as belonging to the collective and as such everyone carries almost equal respon-sibility for their well-being and protection. Why is it in our own culture, in which we purport to idolise and idealise children, we persistently turn a blind eye to abuse and cruelty when we are in a position to intervene? Is it a result of living in a culture where self-interest, individualism and the worship of wealth and greed are not only tolerated, but endorsed and encouraged? Is it as a result of such values that individual children are seen as some-body else's problem, somebody else's property? Is there then a gap between cultural, symbolic meanings of children and child-hood, and how we deal with individual children specifically? If so, is this something that is internal to us as individuals, or is it a wider cultural phenomenon?

# 3

## Is there a Child Within?

In my early twenties, I thought of my childhood as having been essentially idyllic, although in some way that I did not fully understand, marred by my own 'badness'. I was a peculiar, odd child, I told others. I made my parents' lives hell by refusing to go to school, by teasing my sister, by generally not co-operating and conforming in myriad ways. In my late thirties (mid-life crisis!), I had to reconsider this child and her childhood when I went into therapy. I found an abused girl who felt horribly betrayed, abandoned, and was full of rage, pain and fear. I saw myself, at least for a while, as a total victim of sadistic and disturbed parents.

After a while, however, I worked with another therapist, a woman this time, a Jungian, and discovered through my dreams a number of images of children, some that seemed to be of myself as young, and others I did not recognise. Sometimes I dreamed of babies, of myself as a four-year-old with no head, or myself at eight or nine with long hair but no face. Yet one image in particular recurred from time to time: a small child of perhaps six or seven dressed in blue, a deep sea blue, with curly golden hair. This child seemed in some way extraordinary and special, seemed almost to glow, and when I woke I always felt incredibly joyous, at peace with my body and mind.

Working with these dream images of children – painting them, writing poetry about them, talking about them – had a profound healing effect on me. I would be reluctant to categorise the children in my dreams, because to categorise them would confine them to rationality, reduce them to some theoretical construct, like putting a bird of paradise in a cage. They *could* be seen as symbolic of all manner of aspects of my self: a Freudian, for instance, would soon reduce them to an entirely sexual content. For me, however, the child in blue was of a different 'type' of dream image and seemed to bear no relation to my own personal past or present, yet it felt vital to my sense of self. Though in rational terms the idea of a 'child within' may sound maudlin, corny, clichéd, at a subjective level there was a numinosity about that child image that convinced me, if nothing else, of the supreme importance of 'the child' and, indeed, of the 'irrational', both in relation to personal subjectivity and at a wider cultural level.

In retrospect, I think all the insights I gained from working with different perspectives about my personal past and my childhood(s) had a certain amount of truth. I would be reluctant, however, to say one or the other was *the* 'true' interpretation, just as arguably there can be no ultimate truth, no one 'meta-theory' that offers a universal knowledge to explain all aspects of either the self or the world. What I did discover, however, was that one way or another there was something about images of children in my dreams, and fragments of memories of myself as a child, that seemed absolutely central to my whole sense of who I thought I was or who I might become. The more I looked within, the more important 'the child' seemed to be.

## The Child and Interiority

The early Romantics – Blake, Wordsworth, Goethe – first drew attention to the idea of the child and childhood as an area of self-knowledge lying within each individual. The notion that we all retain an aspect of our individual pasts within our psyches was discussed and debated throughout the late eighteenth and nineteenth centuries, and it remains an important issue today. From the late eighteenth century it is thus possible to trace a growing interest in the idea of interiority. As Gullestad comments in relation to the metaphor of 'the child within':

The starting point of its development lies in the eighteenth-century notion that human beings are endowed with a moral sense, an intuitive inner feeling for what is right and wrong.

Instead of being in touch with God or the Idea of the Good, human beings had to be in touch with their own deeper selves. This subjective inward turn, implying a conception of humans as beings with inner depth, has now been transformed into the idea that the nature deep inside human beings is a vulnerable child. (Gullestad, 1996, pp. 8–9)

Recently Carolyn Steedman (1995) has analysed the notion of interiority in relation to 'the child' in the nineteenth century. She considers it through the various representations of Mignon, the homeless orphan who was dislocated by adults training her to be an acrobat, originally portrayed by Goethe in *Wilhelm Meister*. Throughout the nineteenth century this image, this mythical figure, was a source of extensive – and intensive – adult longing and desire. Mignon's dislocation, Steedman argues, is crucial for it represents 'the loss that provides the aetiology of the self; the imagined child embodies the loss and dislocation' (Steedman, 1995, p. viii). In this way the remembered child combines with the imagined child to create a quest for the lost child. This process can be seen, she argues, as occurring both within the individual (as in my own case outlined above) and outside, in wider culture, in terms of the desire of many to 'rescue' real children. Mignon, of course, is fictional, but what she represents is of great importance: 'All she represents is really not to be found at all. The search is an impossible one, for the past is lost and gone' (Steedman, 1995, p. viii).

The past may be lost and gone, yet surely it continues within us as memory; and without memory, would we have a self at all? As Luis Buñuel, the Spanish film director, once commented: 'You have to begin to lose your memory, if only in bits and pieces, to realise that memory is what makes our lives. Life without memory is no life at all. Our memory is our coherence, our reason, our feeling, even our action. Without it, we are nothing.' Memory, however, is elusive and cannot always be read as direct evidence. We think we know who we were as a child, yet memory itself can be structured and re-structured from scraps of stories and images, whether from photographs or stories we have been told by significant others or stories we have read of other children we identified with and imagined, or still imagine, to have been as we think we were or, more probably, as we would like to have been. Memory is constantly being revised through the accounts we take in and the accounts we give out, and we cannot take memories as necessarily always 'objective' or true, although it is arguable that the very act of remembering signifies an event of great importance. Memories are often symbolically significant if not 'factually' true. Of course the whole notion of truth and objectivity is itself neither fixed nor finite. As Samuel and Thompson point out:

> Like myth, memory requires a radical simplification of its subject matter. All recollections are told from a standpoint in the present. In telling, they need to make sense of the past. That demands a selecting, ordering, and simplifying a construction of coherent narrative whose logic works to draw the life story towards the fable. (Samuel and Thompson, 1990, p. 8)

The past may be irretrievable in terms of material reality, but fragments of it survive and continue to shape our sense of who we (think we) have become.

Various factors can be seen historically as contributing to a developing interest in interiority. Foucault, for instance, saw the period 1775–95 as a time

> in which the idea of life (as a force, an entity, a category of thought) became absolutely necessary to scientists attempting to categorise natural beings ... From this period onwards ... classifying things in the natural world would involve relating the visible to the invisible, to that which lies deep within. (Quoted in Steedman, 1995, p. 53)

Scientific developments at this time, and cell theory in particular (founded in the period 1840–70), contributed to this growing fascination with the invisible, the interior, although, as Steedman points out, cell theory was only one manifestation of a much wider scientific attempt to describe what lies within. The cell, as the smallest unit of life, was seen at the time as the 'ultimate fact' needed by physiology as well as being 'a Romantic quest, for unity in diversity, for the common source of life' (Steedman, 1995, p. 58). The cell, however, also implied death 'with its ceaseless making and unmaking' (Steedman, 1995, p. 59).

## The Unconscious

Arguably the culmination of developments and debates about interiority was Freud's formulation, during the early years of the twentieth century, of the theory of the unconscious. Freud, however, did not *discover* the unconscious. Goethe and Schiller, for instance, saw the origins of poetic creation as lying in the unconscious. In *Faust* (started in 1775 and published in two parts in 1808 and 1832), Goethe explores the duality of life and the problems inherent in divisions within one's own personality. Coleridge refers to 'the twilight realms of consciousness'. The German philosophers Schopenhauer (1788–1860), Schelling (1775–1854) and Nietzche (1844–1900) were all fascinated with the 'shadowy', irrational aspects of the human mind and human behaviour:

> Though his theory of the unconscious was one of Freud's most original contributions to general psychology, his view of the mind had a long and prestigious prehistory. Plato had envisioned the soul as two spirited winged horses, one noble and beautiful, the other coarse and insolent, pulling in divergent directions and virtually beyond their charioteer's control... Christian theologians taught that once Adam and Eve had fallen, humanity was torn between its duties to its divine creator and its carnal urges. Certainly, Freud's ideas about the unconscious were in the air in the nineteenth century and had already assumed some sophisticated guises. (Gay, 1988, p. 366)

What Freud did that was innovative was to develop these more subjective ideas into a precise theory, which he used as the foundation of what he saw as a rational and scientific system of human psychology.

Crucial to Freud's theory of the unconscious was the idea of repression. The young child, he argues, cannot cope with the enormity of feelings, images and thoughts which it encounters relating to sexual desire and sexuality during the Oedipal crisis.[1] It then represses them, that is, stores them away into an area of the psyche beyond conscious thought or memory:

> Most of the unconscious consists of repressed materials. This unconscious, as Freud conceptualized it, is not the segment of

mind harboring thoughts temporarily out of sight and easily recalled; that is what he called the preconscious. Rather, the unconscious proper resembles a maximum-security prison holding antisocial inmates languishing for years or recently arrived, inmates harshly treated and heavily guarded, but barely kept under control and forever attempting to escape. Their breakouts succeed only intermittently and at great cost to themselves and to others. (Gay, 1988, p. 128)

Repression is itself an unconscious process and continues to operate beyond early childhood. The fears, desires and feelings that are repressed in the 'maximum-security prison' of the unconscious are inherently irrational:

The unconscious is not a submerged consciousness, a rational system that is somehow invisible; it is an entirely *other* form of reason, logic, and pleasure, one not reducible to those available to consciousness. It undermines the subject's conscious aspirations by its symptomatic intrusions in behaviour which are uncontrolled by, and maybe even unknown to, consciousness.' (Grosz, 1990, p. 10)

Repressed material only finds expression by devious means: certain character traits, slips of the tongue, jokes.

Yet the unconscious for Freud was not a *static* 'maximum-security prison', rather, he saw it as a dynamic force. In fact, he argued, the unconscious plays a central part in the mental life of the individual, taking energy from what he called the 'drives'. Drives in Freud's theory differed from earlier notions of 'instinct' in that he argued they were a relatively undifferentiated energy capable of enormous variation through experience. For many, however, the theory of drives comes very close to biological determinism; the effects of these 'drives' may be socially constructed, but it is questionable as to whether the existence of the drives themselves can ever be substantiated. By arguing they are a root and causal force of human behaviour, but a force that cannot be proved, Freud lays himself open to the criticism that the whole body of theory is invalid. Nevertheless, the idea of the unconscious arguably still remains central to late-twentieth century ideas about the human psyche, its developments, traits and contradictions.

Freud's one-time colleague C. G. Jung also used the idea of the unconscious in his theoretical works, while according less primacy to sexuality in its creation. Jung did not agree with the causal/mechanical model of the unconscious, but saw it instead as relating more to the realm of meanings and images that are crucial to the development of the adult psyche. In this, his concept of the unconscious was in many ways closer to that of earlier thinkers such as Goethe, Schiller and Schelling. Jung believed there were several layers to the unconscious; the upper ones relate to the individual's life experiences, repressions, trauma, and so forth, while the lower, more profound, ones come from culture itself, inherited rather in the way physical traits are inherited genetically. This area he called the 'collective unconscious'. The collective unconscious stores inherited patterns of thought and imaging, or what he called 'archetypes'. These are not experienced as such by the individual, but 'manifest themselves as symbolic images in myths, art, dreams and fantasies – an interlocking system – like maps projected by the psyche onto the world' (Clarke, 1992, p. 117). Examples of archetypes are the shadow, the wise old man, the divine child.

Jung's theory of the collective unconscious and archetypes has been viewed with much scepticism:

> Since John Locke supposedly demolished the concept of innate ideas in the seventeenth century, it has become virtually a dogma of Western thought that the mind is furnished only with ideas which come through the senses during the lifetime of the individual ... Any idea that the mind already has at birth a stock of knowledge, or that we inherit from our parents anything other than our physical constitution, smacks of metaphysics or, worse, of mysticism. This is linked with the widespread assumption amongst modern psychologists that all distinctively human behaviour is acquired through learning. (Clarke, 1992, p. 116)

Jung's writings are undoubtedly less logical and coherent than those of Freud, partly at least because Jung was above all interested in the contradictions and complexities of the psyche, and in writing about these it is not always easy to get a sense of logical development or rational theory. Personally, however, I found that this approach and his ideas, at least in therapy, were incredibly fruitful. The archetype of the divine child for me was of enormous importance, particularly as it seemed to relate both to images in my dreams and to wider issues about the symbolic importance of 'the child'.

Jung and Kerenyi studied various myths about the 'divine child', and found that they usually related to mythological concepts of origin, not in a biographical sense, but in a much wider sense altogether: 'the mythologies speak in the image of a divine child, the first-born of primeval times, in whom the "origin" first was; they do not speak of the coming-to-be of some human being but of the divine cosmos or a universal God' (Jung and Kerenyi, [1949] 1985, p. 9). Divine children – Hermes, Apollo, Moses – are often abandoned foundlings and are usually under great threat from outside forces. They express a kind of primal solitude while at the same time showing how 'from the miserable plight of the orphan there emerges a god' (Jung and Kerenyi, [1949] 1985, p. 32). They do not offer any neat explanation, except to suggest that myths of divine children give an approximate description of an *'unconscious core of meaning'* (Jung and Kerenyi, [1949] 1985, p. 75) that relates generally to futurity, potential and the synthesis of conscious and unconscious elements, that is, it unites opposites and has the potential to heal and make whole. Psychologically the archetype can both illuminate individual process and convey a sense of a more universal meaning:

> It is a striking paradox in all child myths that the 'child' is on the one hand delivered helpless into the power of terrible enemies and in continual danger of extinction, while on the other he possesses powers far exceeding those of ordinary humanity. This is closely related to the psychological fact that though the child may be 'insignificant', 'unknown', 'a mere child', he is also divine. (Jung and Kerenyi, [1949] 1985, p. 89)

The importance of Jung in relation to the question of whether or not there is a 'child within' is, it seems to me, that he attempts to unite the different planes on which 'the child', particularly as image and symbol, exists: in the individual psyche, in wider culture, and in a material sense. Jung remains in academic circles, it seems, an object of criticism and scepticism. Yet while he may lack the apparent logical coherence of writers such as Freud or Lacan, it is arguable that his attention to contradiction, complexity, the uncertainty of knowledge and the centrality of subjectivity and the role of imagery within that, brings him close to many contemporary postmodernist thinkers.[2]

The theories of the Neo-Freudian Jacques Lacan, however, have been of far greater influence, at least in academic circles, in recent years with regard to debates about the unconscious and interiority. There was a joke making the rounds of the Open University a few years ago:

> *Question*: What do you get when you cross the Godfather with Jacques Lacan?
> *Answer*: An offer you can't understand.

Be that as it may – and certainly Lacan is not easy to make sense of – there are key aspects to his work which have been, and arguably remain, of great significance.[3]

First and foremost, Lacan maintains that the unconscious is *symbolic*, that it is organised like language, that is, it is characterised by metonymy and metaphor. This refinement of Freudian theory was crucial because it got away from the contradiction of Freud's pseudo-scientific notions of biological 'drives' which reduced all individuals to identical development patterns and thereby conflicted with the rest of his theory that human psychological development is socially constructed. Lacan brings together linguistic theory and Freudian theory to give centrality to language, both as symbol-system, and as the watershed in the child's development process. Language, and the meanings created by it and through it, are mutable. Thus Lacan's insistence on the primacy of language introduces the possibility of change, of social construction, in terms of personal development, gender construction, subjectivity and identity.

Crucial to Lacan's overall theoretical system is his theory of the 'mirror phase'. At around the age of six months, he argues, the infant, who had until this time thought of itself as part of its mother and not as a separate being, begins to become aware of being separate. Lacan uses the metaphor of a mirror to illustrate this process; looking into a mirror for the first time the infant suddenly finds a coherent image reflected back, which contrasts dramatically with its earlier feelings of being unco-ordinated and without control. Suddenly the baby feels transformed into a coherent and unified whole, both subject and object. Yet in fact the object it sees reflected back is its mother/other: 'The baby narcissistically arrives at some kind of sense of "I" only by finding an "I" reflected back by something outside itself and external – its (m)other' (Minsky, 1992, p. 189). This process splits the human baby, the human psyche, into two, because we identify with something/someone which looks like what or who we want to be, and yet which is also at the same time separate and alien.

As the baby develops, it falls deeply in love with its mother (or female carer) and sees the father as threatening to its desire to have the mother all to itself. It is this longing for the mother, and its denial by the father who symbolises culture, law and the outside world, which, when it is by necessity repressed *'creates* the unconscious. It also splits the newly created subject, now encapsulated within the social domain beyond the mother and child couple, into consciousness and the unconscious' (Minsky, 1992, p. 190). Integral to this process is the child's acquisition of language and simultaneous acquisition of gendered subjectivity.

Language always represents something else; the word 'tree' can never be a real tree, and if it could it would cease to be a word. Language is premised on difference and is above all else a symbol-system. The child, desiring its mother and feeling unified with her, sees the father as representing difference and the threatening outside world of language and culture. The child misinterprets the symbolic representation of the father as lying in the physical penis rather than in the symbolic phallus.[4] Little girls think that what they think they lack – a penis – is a sign that they are not entitled to be in, to have power in, the outside world, while little boys see their mother's apparent lack of a penis as a sign that they are susceptible to castration by the father, and thus also liable to exclusion from the outside world. These painful and difficult lessons are part of their developing sense of difference, which occurs both in relation to children's own bodies and simultaneously in relation to their ability to use language, which itself is only useable when the notion of difference at an embodied level and symbolisation generally is understood.

Language emerges as the child represses the horror of these (mistaken) realisations about embodiment and sexuality. The process of repression itself creates the unconscious and conscious and divides the child's psyche; an integral part of this process is the ability to understand how one thing can stand for something else. Language, then, acts as a compensation to the experience of loss and pain that both girls and boys repress into the deep recesses of the unconscious: 'Language serves to cover the nakedness of painful experience with its rational, linguistic clothes' (Minsky, 1992, p. 193). What is repressed and the sense of lack this creates in the individual become a key aspect of the formation of *desire*, and this is considered later with regard to children's sexuality. A crucial aspect of all theories of the unconscious, however, which can be seen as a bridge between ideas about 'the child' and how these affect adult behaviour, is the notion of projection.

## Projection

Projection was introduced as an important aspect of the psychological process, and the unconscious in particular, by Freud in 1895. Essentially, it is the idea that the individual, or more specifically the individual's ego, wants to take in – or *introject* – to itself everything it feels and sees as good, while at the same time ejecting from itself everything it feels or sees as bad or threatening. In this way the ego gets rid of all aspects of itself perceived as in some way dangerous. Integral to this process, however, is that these unwanted aspects of the self are then attributed to someone else; they are *projected* on to another. In this way certain unwanted aspects of the individual's self become located elsewhere, seen as faults or unattractive characteristics of somebody else. The result of this process is that on the one hand the individual feels a weakened sense of self and identity because part of the self has been denied, while on the other hand 'others' tend to become stereotyped as bad and unattractive.

The idea of projection is crucial to Steedman's thesis about interiority and dislocation. She argues that Freudian theory was seminal in the first two decades of the twentieth century in 'summarising and reformulating a great many nineteenth-century articulations of the idea that the core of an individual's psychic identity was his or her own lost past, or childhood' (Steedman, 1995, p. 4). The theorisation of the unconscious, and an increased awareness of interiorised subjectivity became most clearly expressed and represented through the figure of the child and the notion that childhood, now seen as something sacred and special, was also increasingly being seen as dark, sexual and fearful. Thus it could be argued that the pairs of cultural binary opposites of middle-class child and working-class child, dependency and independence, good and bad, light and dark that prevailed and so troubled the nineteenth century, shifted in our century to a universal image of *the* child and a universal ideal of *a* childhood – myths that eradicated difference, denied history and can be seen to have forced the dichotomies inwards in such a way as to colonise our psyches with an even deeper split.

The notion of a split psyche, while not new, was taken up and investigated in depth by the second-generation Freudian, Melanie Klein. Klein saw the roots of this split as lying in the very early stages of infancy, when the baby seems to experience alternating feelings of love and hate for the mother. When it feels full and warm and satisfied, the baby experiences both itself and the mother (not being able to distinguish between self and (m)other at this stage) as all-bountiful and good and idealises her/self. When, however, it feels empty, hungry, or frustrated it experiences both itself and her as bad and in danger of total psychic disintegration. To survive this experienced danger, the infant then splits off its bad feelings and projects them on to the mother, who it then sees and experiences as not loving, but attacking. Thus the baby, like the adult

who 'projects' in later life, is actually suffering from a paranoid fantasy: it feels itself under attack from its own externalised 'split-off' feelings of hatred and envy now embodied by the mother – its psychic 'other half'. As an adult, suddenly being angry with someone who is close to us when we are feeling very vulnerable harks back to this very early period of infancy. Being 'in love', and the sense of euphoria it produces, also refer back to the baby's earliest feelings of 'fullness' and love when it experienced the mother's breast as satisfying and fulfilling. (Minsky, 1992, p. 188)

Generally this can be seen as integral to the stage in early infancy when a baby switches from seeing everything as an extension of self to an increased awareness of difference. Wardell points out that Klein's theories, although located within the Freudian tradition,

> resulted in what amounted to a fundamental reframing of psychoanalytic thought. Drawing on her pioneering play technique with children, she stressed the pervasive force of infantile impulses in adult life and suggested that human development was less a matter of an evolutionary progress from one psychosexual stage to the next (Freud) than of different states of mind, each typified by particular anxieties and qualities of relationship. (Margot Wardell in the *Guardian*, 17 April 1996)

Thus Kleinianists see the child from the beginning as shaped more by relationships than by any biological drives. British Kleinianists such as Isaacs, Bowlby and Winnicott, have all stressed 'the "innate" – and grim – nature of the infant, and the isolated mother–child couple as the terrain on which the child's psychic development is fought out' (Riley, 1983, p. 21).

Gilman has argued that the early psychological process of projection in infancy is at the root of the *social* process of stereotyping:

> The child begins to combat anxieties associated with the failure to control the world by adjusting his mental picture of people and objects so that they can appear 'good' even when their behavior is perceived as 'bad' . . . the child's sense of self itself splits into a 'good' self, which, as the self mirroring the earlier stage of the complete control of the world, is free from anxiety, and the 'bad' self, which is unable to control the environment and is thus exposed to anxieties . . . with the split of both the self and the world into 'good' and 'bad' objects, the 'bad' self is distanced and identified with the mental representation of the 'bad' object. This act of projection saves the self from any confrontation with the contradictions present in the necessary integration of 'bad' and 'good' aspects of the self. The deep

structure of our own sense of self and the world is built upon the illusionary image of the world divided into two camps, 'us' and 'them' . . . this is a very primitive distinction which, in most individuals, is replaced early in development by the illusion of integration. (Gilman, 1985, p. 17)

In other words, the 'other' is originally created within the infant's psyche and at the same time collective representations of the 'other' are fed into it, and are fed by it. The Other – that which the self denies and defines as different – can be both an object of fear and an object of glorification. In the case of 'the child' it becomes possible to see how children have *both* been venerated *and* feared/abused. The process of projection is particularly powerful in the notion of 'the child' because it is in this state that projection first begins; dividing the world between 'good' and 'bad', self and Other, is not only a defining characteristic of being a child, being a 'self', but it can also be easily translated into the pair of opposites 'good child/bad child'.

Culturally the 'bad child', like the 'bad', the 'shadow' generally, has tended to be played down and/or denied *at the same time* as it is projected outside, located elsewhere, in others and in the Other. A good example of this has been in the moral panic over children who kill, and the little boys who killed James Bulger in particular. The extreme reactions of adults to the three boys – one for whom everybody felt intense sympathy and two others who were literally hated and attacked in myriad ways – encapsulates well the good child/bad child dichotomy both in culture and within the individual psyche. Arguably all of us contain unconscious rage and negative feelings towards children, much of which could, for instance, be repressed animosity towards siblings. What older sister or brother has not, however fleetingly, wished with all their might to destroy the younger child that has suddenly usurped its place, stolen all the attention and love that once belonged to them? Yet how quickly such deep and overwhelmingly powerful feelings tend to be punished, denied and repressed as utterly bad and unacceptable. Could it have been a re-surfacing of such feelings, long incarcerated in the maximum-security prison of the unconscious, that were triggered so violently by Thompson's and Venables' actions?

## Poisonous Pedagogy?

Recently the Swiss psychoanalyst Alice Miller has tried to apply psychoanalytical theory, and projection in particular, to social and political factors in an attempt to explain violence generally and violent individuals, such as Hitler, in particular. She argues that the roots of violence lie in child-rearing, and points to a correlation between the belief in, and implementation of, strict discipline – what she calls 'poisonous pedagogy' – and a general receptiveness to totalitarianism. She has been greatly criticised for ignoring crucial intermediary elements such as a historically specific economic and political context. Moreover, she fails to distinguish between different kinds of abuse and different degrees of abuse. Furthermore, and perhaps most important, she accords children themselves no agency.

Despite such criticisms, however, I think Miller deserves to be taken seriously because she posits none the less cogent arguments about how dependency evokes in adults *both* a desire to protect *and* a desire to control and hurt their children. She illustrates various ways in which children become instrumentalised on behalf of adult needs, and shows how most of these adult needs are legitimised and rationalised as 'normal', and indeed seen as 'highly necessary' for the child's 'own good'.

Because an infant is wholly dependent on its carer(s), not only for physical sustenance, but also for emotional nourishment – love, trust and consistency – and because babies, who seem to have an innate ability to love, love their carer(s) regardless of their behaviour, indeed accept whatever behaviour is meted out to them because they know no other, adult carers are automatically given an enormous amount of power. When adult carers are themselves insecure, Miller argues, the child's total helplessness and neediness awakens in them a strong awareness of their own power and their own ability, possibly for the first time in their lives, to control someone even more helpless and vulnerable than they themselves feel.

*All* adults, Miller insists, have themselves been hurt as children. Even with the most mature and caring of parenting, a child can still be hurt by feeling powerless or unjustly disciplined. The hurt parents experienced as children, however, has almost always been repressed and lies deep and unacknowledged in the unconscious. Bearing and rearing one's own children tends to evoke these old feelings that have been incarcerated, denied, in the unconscious. These feelings, according to Miller, tend to become translated into both intense love for, and an intense desire to control, one's children. Part of this uneasy conjunction of strong but contradictory feelings is the desire to make one's own children experience what parents themselves suffered as children ('it didn't do me any harm' as proclaimed, for instance, by the Labour leader Tony Blair in the early 1990s with regard to corporal punishment).

This process occurs almost entirely in the unconscious. We learn to disguise as rationalisations and legitimations those feelings deemed to be socially unacceptable, and the often extreme behaviour that sometimes results from them in our 'disciplining' of children. Our rationalisations virtually always project our own guilt on to the children themselves. As a result we, as parents, glibly pass off a child's pain and grief at being hurt by us as 'she asked for that' or 'it's about time he learned a good lesson' instead of asking, why did I do that? Whatever made me inflict so much pain on the child I think I love so much?

Because small children adore their carer(s), they cannot believe or accept that the one(s) they love so much, the one(s) they worship as if they were gods, could possibly hurt them:

> The love a child has for his or her parents ensures that their conscious or unconscious acts of mental cruelty will go undetected . . . The child's dependence on his or her parents' love also makes it impossible in later years to recognize these traumatizations, which often remain hidden behind the early idealization of the parents for the rest of the child's life. (Miller, 1987)

When they *are* hurt by them, therefore, they find the feelings so overwhelming that they repress the feelings, the memories and the pain into their unconscious. It is arguable, however, that many of these overwhelming feelings are not just a result of parental inability to confront or understand their own unconscious pain, but are an almost inevitable result of the Oedipal crisis when the young child has to deal with the pain of realisation s/he cannot have the mother exclusively. This is not to deny the validity of much of what Miller argues, but rather to suggest that the process may be rather more complex, and that some of the deepest wounds occur virtually inevitably as a result of separation from the mother.

Miller sees aphorisms of childrearing such as 'spare the rod and spoil the child' or 'you have to be cruel to be kind' are part of a wider discourse on childrearing, which includes textbooks and various theories of childrearing, that she entitles 'poisonous pedagogy'. Poisonous pedagogy is the process by which adults rationalise their own needs and unconscious conflicts and re-enact their own humiliation and disempowerment experienced – and repressed – in childhood. The end-product of such rationalisation on the part of parents is a body of discourse on 'childcare' and 'education' that disguises, often in the rubric of scientific objectivity, adults' own negative and unacceptable feelings and experiences. Such treatises then legitimise at a wider cultural level adult cruelty to children:

> In beating their children, they are struggling to regain the power they once lost to their own parents . . . for the first time they see the vulnerability of their own earliest years, which they are unable to recall, reflected in their children. Only now, when someone weaker than they is involved, do they finally fight back. (Miller, 1987, p. 16)

Parental and adult abuse of children, whether physical, sexual or verbal, is therefore always, according to Miller, for adults' own psychological reasons as a result of their own psychological needs. These needs have been rationalised and reconstructed as a set of principles of 'what's good for children' and enshrined in both popular beliefs and formal (poisonous) pedagogy. Humiliation of children, thus rationalised, always satisfies the *parents'* needs rather than those of the child.

It would seem, then, that the apparently contradictory response of most adults to smaller and more vulnerable beings is one of both a desire to protect and a desire to hurt (and there may well be other forms of desire that connect with both of these). The desire to hurt arises from the unconscious, and because it is unacceptable the conscious mind tries to repress it once more. Yet it is not always successfully repressed. Rather, it can motivate

irrational and cruel behaviour which, once carried out, is immediately justified and rationalised by the (shocked) conscious mind
as 'discipline' or 'experience'. In other words, Miller's theory
points quite definitely to the conclusion that all adults have the
potential to abuse children.

Policies and discourse that single out child abuse, in whatever
form, as the result of a handful of psychopaths or deviants or
'monsters' thus obviate the reality of each and every one of us
having the potential to behave as irrational, deviant monsters.
The extent to which our cruel and irrational behaviour towards
children can be hidden, disguised, rationalised and, of greatest
importance, controlled, depends arguably on the extent of our
own psychic damage as children, our material circumstances, our
present support networks.

Thomas Hamilton, the man who massacred 16 small schoolchildren and their teacher at Dunblane in 1996, came from a
background under which any individual would be severely
marred and damaged:

> Hamilton's childhood was not the normal background of a
> white-collar man. Shame, deception and, possible, hatred, were
> the dominant emotions in his family. His grandparents pre-
> tended to be his parents and his mother pretended to be his
> sister. No one has yet said when Hamilton discovered the truth
> about the peculiar arrangements his family made to avoid
> embarrassment in a more censorious age.
>
> His mother, Agnes, was born in 1931, the illegitimate daugh-
> ter of a widow . . . To prevent a scandal, the baby was given
> away to a childless couple who were relatives [who] looked
> after Agnes until she was 19 and fell in love with Thomas Watt,
> a bus driver. On 10 May 1952, their son Thomas was born.
> Eighteen months later, the father ran off with another woman
> and a second 'scandal' was hushed up. Agnes went back to her
> adoptive parents [who] adopted Thomas as their child. His
> mother became his 'older sister'. (*Guardian*, 17 March 1996)

It would seem that Hamilton struggled to control his anger and
his paedophiliac desires, and in a way cried out obliquely for help
by showing outsiders the pictures of semi-naked little boys on his
walls and by repeatedly writing to the school and the press about

his anger at not being allowed to rejoin the Scouts as a scout-master. Nobody can be blamed for not having been able to prevent the tragedy that occurred. Yet the lesson seems to be that we need to find ways of listening to, and hearing, cries of help that are often (thinly) disguised and which we are all too ready to dismiss as Other, loony, perverted.

I cannot help but wonder, naïve though it may be, that if somebody had been able to intervene and ask Hamilton to talk about his desires, his feelings, his own painful childhood experiences, could his actions then have been prevented? His father dismissed his own son as a 'monster', having himself abandoned the child before he was two years old. What better example of the way adults constantly excuse and rationalise their own cruelty to children? How often do we hear, in supermarkets, trains, bus queues, the refrain 'God, I could have *killed* Jason [or Shulamith or Lev or Tracy] yesterday!'? Is our outrage at such tragedies fuelled by its closeness to our own unconscious, shadowy and violent feelings of murderousness, jealousy, envy, rage – feelings we constantly struggle to deny and repress?

Two studies published in 1993[5] both found that disabled children are far more vulnerable to physical or sexual abuse than are other children:

> Communication barriers combined with frequent hospital stays and institutionalization leave many isolated, unprotected and powerless to speak out. Yet often signs of abuse go unnoticed by child care professionals who find it difficult to believe that disabled children are preyed upon. (*Guardian*, 23 February 1993)

Perhaps it was difficult to believe because to do so might mean confronting one's own repressed pain of humiliation when 'disabled' – in the sense of being physically wholly dependent on others – and the resultant rage and desire for revenge this might provoke in turn by wanting to 'disable' others.

The feelings of rage and humiliation experienced by a child at the hands of an adult are repressed, but they none the less remain, and continue to influence, albeit obliquely, subsequent development and behaviour. They reappear usually in a form split off from the self and then projected on to another – a child, perhaps, or a disabled person or some other helpless and vulnerable being that somehow reminds the psyche of its pains. It is this process of projection that contributes to, arguably determines, stereotyping, ostracism and persecution at a social and political level. It can be seen as a vital determinant of the 'monstrous' behaviour of those who have become so damaged they can no longer effectively repress their murderous feelings: Thompson, Venables, Hamilton, Hitler could all be arguably better understood in this way.

Denying the Other, the shadow, the unacceptable within ourselves, we project it outside ourselves through clever and intelligent use of rationalisation, legitimisation, intellectualisation. We project our dark and unattractive aspects of self on to those more vulnerable, whether children, ethnic minorities or foreigners – anyone we can rationalise away as 'different'. Collectively when such individual projections focus on a group – or individual – that group or individual then becomes defined in terms of the traits we so loathe in ourselves. Collectively we then seek to destroy, banish, punish those people who are in fact carrying those own aspects of ourselves we find so unbearable, so impossible to own.

## Memories, Violence, Mothers

Over the years I have struggled to understand two early memories of my mother. In the first, I am simply looking at the dark green window blind drawn down beside my parents' bed, yearning to pull the round silky handle that would release it and let the light in. This image always made me feel deeply disturbed and nauseous. In therapy I eventually accessed the rest of the image; it concerned my mother's sexual abuse of me and her subsequently telling me I was disgusting and calling me names I did not understand.

The other memory was of lying on the living room sofa and waking up from a nap with a jolt as my mother jabbed her lighted cigarette on to the back of my hand. She then walked out and returned with a wide grin on her face, asking me, what had I done to myself? She gently dabbed my wound with iodine while telling me I must never, ever play with lighted cigarettes again. I remember feeling utterly confused. I hadn't wanted to do those disgusting things, had I? It wasn't me who burned myself, was it? Or had I? Did I? Surely she had to be right – she was my mother – and yet . . .

Not only did I learn – slowly and painfully – not to trust her, but I also learned I could not trust myself. (Perhaps one of the most destructive results of her behaviour was that it led to a great confusion as to who I was and whether I really was separate from my mother at all.) It must have been my fault, because she said so. I learned to hate myself for what I had not done. I turned the rage that should by rights have been directed towards her against myself instead. The one time I really did let go of my anger I was severely punished by my father. The punishment was rape. It makes me wonder about different ways in which such behaviour operates according to gender. It seems to me, for instance, that because anger is undoubtedly less acceptable in girls and women, we may grow up more prone to express our rage and humiliation through self-damage as well as through more indirect (verbal, emotional) cruelty to our children, while boys and men are apt to express it more openly, physically, directly.

Eventually I had to admit that I too made terrible mistakes in bringing up my own children. It was the worst, the most miserable, the most painful aspect of therapy: 'For children who have grown up being assailed for qualities the parents hate in themselves can hardly wait to assign these qualities to someone else so they can once again regard themselves as good, "moral", noble and altruistic' (Miller, 1987, p. 9). I had somehow to accept that I had had responsibility for others more vulnerable than I, and that I had at times abused that position of trust and had acted with cruelty. Yet what I can now realise as cruelty all those years ago was not how I saw it, or rationalised it, then. I did genuinely believe I was doing the right thing. In my early twenties, of course, I had not ventured into therapy and had not explored my own unconscious, my contradictions, my pain. This, I think, is one area in which Miller's theory is seriously flawed; we rationalise cruelty to our own children as parents because we cannot face and do not yet acknowledge our own pain. This is what is known as *denial*, the process by which we detach the unwanted from ourselves until it eventually confronts us in all its horror. We deny, we forget, because we cannot bear to remember or to acknowledge. Having said that, however, I think there *were* times when I knew perfectly well I was being cruel. It wasn't *all* unconscious – and that is the hardest bit: it is never easy to accept the grim reality that we simply are not always very nice people.

If it has been difficult to accept the ways in which I was cruel to my own children, it has been even more difficult to accept the abuse inflicted on me by my own mother. It has been far more difficult to accept this than the abuse suffered at the hands of my father and stepfather. Feminism helped me to locate and express the rage I felt towards men who had abused me, but the rage I felt towards my mother was far less acceptable, more hidden, more contradictory and in the end more painful. Diagnosed as psychotic in her early forties, how could I feel anger towards a poor sick woman? Then again, it was clear she was pathological – a kind of 'freak', a mad woman, a nutcase, who was in no way representative of women or mothers *generally*. I so wanted to believe in, to have had, the kind of mother eulogised by mentors such as the poet Adrienne Rich, who represented mothers as infinitely gentle, kind, loving and connected to all that is good in life and on this earth. But I think my mother would have liked to have been like that, too, and I know she wished *her* mother had been.

Violence by women, like violence by children, has until very recently been seen as so transgressive as to be a 'one-off'. Indeed, it is very rare in comparison with violence by men: an estimated 85–90 per cent of sexual abusers are male. Yet it raises crucial questions about gender, parenting and children. It relates to a central issue in feminism and the women's movement: if women are truly equal, then surely their capacity to abuse, kill and inflict cruelty and violence generally must be the same as men's? Radical feminists, however, have argued that women and men are different in certain fundamental ways and that consequently women are more peace-loving, nurturing, intuitive, and closer to nature.

In 1989 Joel Steinberg, a rich lawyer from New York, was convicted of beating his illegally adopted six-year-old daughter, Lisa, to death:

She had been battered and sexually abused for most of her life. Originally Steinberg's lover, Hedda Nussbaum, who had herself been appallingly beaten by him, was also charged. But the charges were also dropped and she was never tried. She received psychiatric treatment, testified against Steinberg and walked out of the courtroom a free woman. (*Observer*, 7 April 1991)

In an article about the case (*Guardian*, 12 March 1991) Ann Lloyd raised the issue of how controversial it had been for a white, educated, middle-class woman, though abused herself, to take part in the abuse and murder of a child. The article points out that violent crimes by women form a tiny minority of crimes, some 10 per cent of those committed by men, and yet this is still a large number of crimes. Lloyd suggests society's reluctance to face women's violence may be to do with men's fears of women's anger, or a result of men separating out their own feelings in the construction of their masculine identity, thereby dividing off women as emotional, caring, experts on childrearing who *can't* by definition be aggressive. Women like Nussbaum (and my mother) become labelled as mad or as passive victims or so at the mercy of their 'feminine nature' and hormones as to not be capable or responsible for their own actions.

Yet if the theory of projection is correct, then *all* adults, women and men alike, will harbour a varying degree of rage and resentment at their humiliation, betrayal and disempowerment by adults when they themselves were girls and boys. What is at issue here is not so much the fact that both women and men have immense, almost total, power over their children, especially when very young, but that abuse of that power is easy, accessible and implicitly endorsed by adult culture. It may, however, be expressed in different ways, and these differences can be seen to relate to gender: verbal abuse and sarcasm (my favourite as a parent), humiliation of all sorts, controlled violence (i.e. corporal punishment), uncontrolled violence. Any of those can be sexualised.

What seems likely is that gender influences the *type* of abuse mothers and fathers inflict on their children (and, indeed, on and against themselves and one another). This may, however, be changing as an increasing number of women have sole responsibility for children in what amounts to a 24-hour job that is essentially unpaid and unrewarded, undertaken if not exactly for life, then for a substantial number of years. It has been argued, for instance, that we are witness to an increasing feminisation of poverty and, in tandem with this as a result of the burgeoning of single parenthood and divorce, a pauperisation of children. Poverty, isolation and little respite from sole responsibility for childcare may be contributing to an increase of abuse by women of children, although this is hypothetical.

It would seem that virtually all girls and boys experience some form of abuse in childhood, although the type and extent and severity varies considerably. Miller's thesis, however, is not so much about extreme abuse, such as the Steinberg case or the Dunblane massacre, but about *general* abuse that poses as 'normal' childrearing methods and discipline yet which is experienced by children as humiliating, unfair and disempowering. Above all, and contrary to adult rationalisations, it is not about what *children* need, but about what *adults* need and act out on to children. Miller, however, does not acknowledge that the *meaning* of abuse is not fixed or static, but is historically and culturally variable. What was regarded as good discipline once is now seen as physical abuse. Cultural rituals such as circumcision, which cause great physical pain, are none the less regarded as essential milestones in certain cultures.

What is important in Miller's thesis, however, is the way it makes us consider how parents are in fact dependent on children psychologically as a focus for the projection of their own unresolved conflicts and rage. By projecting much of their own shadow, unconscious, unwanted aspects of themselves on to the child, they arguably make themselves feel more 'adult' and more powerful, clear their own backyards as it were, while as a result their children feel increasingly disempowered, humiliated and hurt. This process, however, is not deliberate or conscious, but operates largely at an unconscious level, a fact that Miller does not adequately confront.

So far the discussion has focused largely on parents, but it is arguable that a similar process goes on for those adults who work in a professional way with other people's children. As Oldman (1994) has pointed out, many adults are now dependent on children for their living: this 'childwork' forms an important dependency relationship between children and adults. Under the guise of professionalism, part of which stipulates that, unlike parents, professionals should not love those in their custody, many undoubtedly help to nourish, protect and heal many damaged children. For those whose own conflicts and repressed feelings have never been dealt with, however, it is perhaps not so surprising that they can be projected on to the children in their care.

In 1991 scandal erupted when it was discovered that a regime of cruel abuse of children in children's homes in Stoke, in Britain, had been established and in operation since 1983. This regime – known as 'pin down' – relied on humiliation, isolation and confrontation. Log books examined from the homes recorded typical reactions of the children as:

> anger, depression, weeping, sobbing, anxiety, talking in sleep, talking to self, staring into space, lost confidence in people, frustrated, bored, banging on wall, loneliness, desperation . . . incidents of wrist-slashing and the taking of overdoses. (*Guardian*, 31 May 1991)

The regime was allegedly instigated 'against a background of serious shortages of money and staff, arising from relative underinvestment in social services' (*Guardian*, 31 May 1991). When we talk of 'the state' taking care of and responsibility for children, or making policies and decisions 'on behalf of children' it is important to remember that policies are not only designed and legislated on, but they are also *implemented*. What may begin as an apparently philanthropic and well-intentioned measure or policy may end up when it is actually implemented as an altogether different policy.

Policies, obviously, are implemented by people. Perhaps it is time to ask in greater depth why some people are attracted to 'care' for children in homes and institutions. Such a relationship carries an enormous amount of power on the part of the carer, and if the carers themselves have experienced abuse and disempowerment in their own childhoods, to work with children who have already been severely abused and victimised must surely put them in a position of vulnerability to their own – undoubtedly unconscious – desire to re-enact their own abuse and cruelty. Wages for such posts are notoriously low. Care assistants are recruited from the untrained. Social work training has been cut by the government, and social services funding cut as well. Pin down may represent only the tip of an iceberg.

Be that as it may, it has become increasingly clear that children in virtually *all* situations are vulnerable: in their own families, at school, in children's homes – all institutions ostensibly designed to protect children – we see children being abused in myriad ways by their protectors. Of course the majority of children in these situations *are* protected to a greater or lesser extent, yet the evidence does suggest that those who abuse children are not just occasional psychopaths, but that adults generally, and particularly those who have control, care and thus power over them, do abuse that power relationship, whether as fathers, mothers, priests, uncles, care workers or scout leaders. Abusers come from different class backgrounds and those who abuse are, in many cases, those who also protect.

Fred Fever, for example, who was placed in residential care as soon as he was born and spent his childhood in Barnardo's homes, gives graphic accounts of the abuse he suffered there from those supposed to protect him. When he was seven, for instance, new wardens came to his residential home and took an instant dislike to him:

> Staring at walls wasn't the only punishment Patrick dealt out to me. He also smacked me. The smacks came in various degrees of severity from hard, to very hard, to extremely hard. Most of these blows fell upon my legs, although occasionally he smacked me around the head. The severity of the smacks didn't really bear any relation to the seriousness of the supposed misdemeanour but depended on what sort of temper Patrick was in at the time. I was hit fairly often. I always felt most vulnerable when wearing shorts. Long trousers didn't cushion the blows, but psychologically I felt happier wearing long trousers. When you were wearing shorts the smack always left a horrible and very visible bright red mark, a perfect imprint of Patrick's hand upon your leg . . . The bright red brand on my pale white skin was a symbol of my helplessness, and of a life lived at the mercy of others. Whenever I wore long trousers it didn't feel quite as bad. The badge of my powerlessness was then not apparent to the naked eye. (Fever, 1994, p. 43)

Patrick moved Fred to share a bedroom with David, a boy who was then 14 or 15 and who 'stood over six feet tall and was enormously built for his age. He was capable of putting the fear of God into men much older than myself' (Fever, 1944, p. 45). David sexually abused Fred regularly, threatening him with castration if he told anyone. Wardens beat and humiliated him – and others – regularly. It transpired later that the wardens had known Fred was also being sexually abused by a local man; their only response was to tease him by calling him 'queer'.

If we accept the theory of projection, then all adults carry unconscious desires and needs to act out their own early pain and feelings of powerlessness. These will vary according to the type and severity of abuse, no doubt, but it needs to be truly taken on board that *all* adults have the capacity to abuse children. Abuse of course is ultimately a vague concept, one which can be re-defined and re-negotiated over time and between groups and cultures. Nevertheless, it seems important to accept that the potential for abuse lies within us all and is not a characteristic of a few 'nut-cases' who are utterly different to ourselves. It might be most useful to consider abuse in terms of a continuum where all adults abuse to some extent, and where all children are abused to some extent. Only to focus on the extremes in both instances ignores the more endemic nature of the phenomenon and leads to different questions being asked than if we accept it as a predisposition in *everyone*.

Because western society has defined – indeed, constructed – childhood as premised on dependency and therefore premised also on inequality, it is inevitable that there will be myriad power relationships existing at various levels. Although it is possible to argue that in certain ways adults are also dependent on children (parents can be emotionally dependent on children, some depend on them for physical care, in the past parents often depended on children for economic reasons) it would be hard to argue that overall children are anything except disempowered. Again, this changes, and certainly children can and do resist, but the balance of power undoubtedly lies with those designated in charge of the protection of children, whether parents, care workers, priests or teachers.

Protected by state policies and state agencies, protected by parents, teachers and priests: protection is the rationale for all our policies relating to children and their extensive period of dependency in western culture. But protection, like human beings themselves, has a flip side, a dark side. Inherent in protecting roles, as we have seen, are power and control and the wherewithal to act out one's own unconscious desires and rages on to others. Children, generally well looked after and protected, are none the less extremely vulnerable as a result of their own dependencies, isolation, silencing and disenfranchisement.

Of course it is possible to look at it in a completely different way and say that, given all these factors, how remarkable it is that so many children grow up to live relatively full and responsible lives. How remarkable, perhaps, that so many children grow up at all. Surely this is a testament to the *positive* side of parenting and of adult concern for children. It is important to bear in mind the depth of feeling most parents hold for their children regardless of material circumstances. The human capacity for love has been and undoubtedly remains the salvation of the majority of people who have been through difficult circumstances. It should also be considered seriously that in order to be able to survive in a complex and ruthless world overprotection might also be damaging to children. Having to deal with a certain amount of pain, conflict and injustice is, surely, part of being human. An essential part of the myth of childhood is that childhood should be totally trouble-free, happy, and innocent. If that were to be the case, how ever would children negotiate entry to the cut-throat, violent, greedy adult world of the present day? Rather than set impossible goals for parenting, is there not some sense in aiming instead for acceptance of, greater toleration of, the dark and irrational aspects of all of us, adults and children alike? If we were to accept these, rather than to reject and project them on to others, there might be fewer angels, but there would also be fewer devils.

Surely one of the changes in recent years with the development of postmodernist theory has been a challenge to the old idea of a unified self. Freud's theory of the unconscious should have laid that one to rest decades ago. People have different aspects to their selves; arguably we are all fragmented. This means none of us is always rational and we do not by any means always behave with conscious, clear and rational motives, though our capacity to rationalise our irrational and contradictory acts is indeed stunning. If we are to confront the whys and wherefores of children's pain and suffering, then it is necessary to try and understand both adults and children at both conscious and unconscious levels. We need to steel ourselves to come to terms with both the 'divine child' within our own psyches as well as the monsters who live there too.

# 4

## WHAT DO CHILDREN REPRESENT?

A few years ago I went back to upstate New York and worked at a university where I taught a course on children and childhood. Early in the course I showed a series of slides, one of which was a picture of a girl prostitute in Taiwan sitting on a motorbike and smiling. The students were puzzled by this because, they said, they had always thought prostitution must be a sad and difficult way of life. 'What makes you think it isn't?' I asked. Because she's smiling, they replied. I spent the rest of the class – indeed, much of the rest of the course – trying to explain that photographic images – *any* images or representations, whether pictorial or written – are set up, constructed *by* someone, *for* someone with the intention of conveying a particular idea or impression. In whose interests was it, I suggested they consider, for her to be seen as smiling? We talked about the *meaning* of motorbikes and how they suggest speed, sexual excitement, youth, and how, as a means of transportation, they are cheap. Could those qualities also be applied to the girl? Where was the photo most apt to appear: in a soft porn magazine, a travel brochure or a family photograph album? Who, in other words, was looking at her through the camera and for what purpose? Many of the students still insisted that photographs were a slice of reality, a true record of reality, and that it was pointless to make such associations. As Sontag ([1977] 1989, p. 153) comments: 'Reality has always been interpreted through the reports given by images; and philosophers since Plato have tried to loosen our dependence on images by evoking the standard of an image-free way of apprehending the real.'

Representation is not an easy concept to grasp. It suggests that images cannot be accepted as true reflections of their source, but are re-constructed in such a way that they are separate from, distinct from, and other than, those sources. Moreover, as Chaplin (1994, p. 1) argues, 'representation' can be understood as articulating and contributing to social processes. Representation refers both to images and texts, but here I want to focus initially on visual representation. Images are immensely powerful – we remember images much more effectively than we do words – and it is not always easy for people to realise that they are material products that have been constructed by (invisible) others for a specific purpose. Representations 'are not just a matter of mirrors, reflections, key-holes. Somebody is making them, and somebody is looking at them . . . they have a continued existence in reality as objects of exchange; they have a genesis in material production. They are more "real" than the reality they are said to represent or reflect' (Kappeler, 1986, p. 3).

The twentieth century has been witness to a proliferation of images. Unlike our ancestors, wherever we go we are confronted with images: on television, in newspapers, advertisements, hoardings, the cinema. We are arguably now as much watchers as we have in the recent past been readers; we are certainly no longer, in the ways our ancestors were, listeners. Images constantly vie with other images for our attention. What they portray, however, are stereotypes, abstractions, simple narratives for us to try and make sense of in a second or two as they flash briefly on a screen or we flip quickly through a magazine. As Tagg points out: 'What lies "behind". . . image is not reality – the referent – but reference: a subtle web of discourse through which realism is enmeshed in a complex fabric of notions, representations, images, attitudes, gestures and modes of action which function as everyday know-how, "practical ideology"' (Tagg, 1987, p. 305). Images resist interpretation and tend to classify and label complex ideas into overly simple meanings. In this way they are like myths, for they deny ambiguity and contradiction. We, as watchers, do not know the context in which images are constructed, we do not know their history and the net result of this is that their history is denied.

How do we begin to make sense of representations? Charles Peirce put forth a theory of semiotics that outlined the importance of visual art as a form of communication and in this he proposed a typology of signs: *iconic*, *indexical* and *symbolic* (Peirce, 1955, quoted in Chaplin, 1994, p. 88). Chaplin summarises and illustrates these below:

> The *iconic* sign proposes a 'fitness' of resemblance to the object it signifies, as a portrait represents the sitter. The *indexical* sign has a concrete, actual relationship to the signifier – usually of a sequential, causal kind – in the sense that smoke is an index of fire. The *symbolic* sign signifies by virtue of a contract or rule . . . It therefore requires the active presence of the interpretant to make the signifying connection. In this triad, the iconic, indexical and the symbolic signs are not mutually exclusive. Rather, they are three modes of a relationship between signifier and object or signifier and signified which co-exist in the form of a hierarchy in which one of them will inevitably have dominance over the other two . . . While an image of a table may propose a 'fitness' of resemblance to the table it signifies (iconic signal), this is not the only message that the image gives off. It may symbolise upper-class affluence and dinner parties (a large, well-polished, ornately carved table) or it may symbolise poverty and toil in the kitchen (a small, plain, rickety, scratched table). Colour often signifies symbolically. (Chaplin, 1994, pp. 88–9)

Representations of children have been one of the key areas in which imagery generally has burgeoned. Overall, the sheer numbers, the deluge, of images of children have arguably helped to create a myth of a universal child and a universal childhood. Most people, like my students, assume representations of children to be iconic, which at one level, of course, they are. What few realise is the extent to which they are also used symbolically. Images of children are invariably constructed *by adults* to convey messages and meanings *to adults*. The meanings they are used to convey change and vary, although there are certain recurring and central themes: dependency, victimisation/helplessness, loss, nostalgia, innocence, danger, nature.

For example, it is clear from earlier discussions that children as material beings are involved in different relationships of dependency. At a symbolic level, however, children arguably are used to stand for, to represent, dependency itself. Consider, for instance, how frequently children are used in images of nuclear families in advertisements for insurance policies. At an iconic level the image purports to represent a real family. The message conveyed at a more symbolic level, however, is of precious loved ones who are only safe if the father/husband makes careful financial provision for their status and future. The children in such advertisements draw attention to a notion of the family as an institution premised on children's (and women's) dependency, and thus also on inequality that is carefully ordered according to gender and age.

In such representations the man is always taller than the woman, while the boy is almost always older and taller than the girl. They are portrayed as a close-knit group standing outside a large, comfortable home. The audience targeted in such advertisements is undoubtedly middle-class married men whose ideal of the family would presumably correspond to the image in the advertisement. They are designed to trigger such men's wishes to prove their self-worth, their masculinity, by being (or trying to be) wholly responsible financially for their dependants. The people in the advertisements are models unrelated by kinship, the assumed family type they portray one that exists more in government rhetoric and the ideals of middle-class married men than in reality:

> Deeply troubled by such issues as one-parent families, adoption, mixed-race families and – as technology develops – by artificial insemination, *in vitro* fertilisation and – most shocking of all – surrogacy, which separates childbearing from motherhood, the traditional idea of 'family' has been challenged to the point where the concept itself must surely collapse. Yet the narrowest of definitions is aggressively maintained. (Holland, 1992, p. 44)

Such advertisements also carry a clear message about children as the future. Futurity and dependency, as we have seen, are qualities which are frequently represented by children, and which adults use, quite deliberately, to define children and childhood.

Many advertisements also use images associating children with nature and the natural world; this, as discussed previously, is a long-standing association. In the late eighteenth century the shift from a mechanical to a more organicist view of nature ran in parallel with an increasing representation of children as close to nature. In paintings as well as in the newly developing literature written specifically for children, they were often compared to plants and animals. In fairy tales and stories, for example, children were advised to offer the same kind of charity to animals as they would to humans. It is often the case in fairy tales that a child's kindness to an animal turns out to be its salvation, the classic example being the frog who turns into a prince. Even very young children were taught to handle pets carefully. Indeed, 'identifying children with animals' vulnerability, and exploiting children's sympathy for them was developed in the first-person narrative stories with animal heroes that proliferated from this period' (Kinnel, n.d., p. 24).

In painting, images of children with pets became increasingly popular. Consider, for example, Hogarth's early eighteenth-century painting of *The Graham Children* (Figure 1), where all the children are represented as smiling. The oldest girl holds a bunch of cherries; there is also a cat and a caged bird. The children are portrayed as carefree, happy and playful. The way in which the drawing-room is furnished and the children are dressed makes it clear that this is a middle-class family in comfortable, but not affluent, circumstances. The image is carefully composed and ordered, but within that order a certain amount of untidiness is constructed through a coat or cloak and an abandoned toy on the floor near the children. Two of the children (plus the cat) are looking up at the bird rather than at the painter; this draws attention to their affinity with the natural world. The cherries and pets link the children symbolically with nature, but it is a nature that is tamed and contained – caged, like the bird – just as the children themselves are contained within the confines of the family. The emotional response of the viewer is apt to be one of pleasure, comfort, faith in ideas and memories of childhood associated with happiness, fun and security.

It is interesting to compare the Hogarth with a contemporary photograph of a small Brazilian boy that appeared in the *Guardian* a few years ago. In this the boy was sitting on a pavement, or perhaps doorstep, in the street. A dog lay beside him. The context of the street suggested lack of protection, a missing family, despair and poverty. The dog was no well-fed family pet. The boy

*Figure 1 Hogarth,* The Graham Children

was black, naked and seemed dirty. He had a dummy in his mouth and looked unhappy, or perhaps cross. His nakedness emphasised what was 'real', what lay beneath the surface, while his darkness drew attention to misery, dirt, shadow. As Ennew points out 'an association is constantly made between white children who have a correct childhood and black children who have none' (Ennew, 1986, p. 22). The overall impression, the 'reality' constructed by the photographer, drew on the idea of a child symbolising the future, and the message was that the future of Brazil is depressing, uncertain, associated with scavenging, insecurity and vulnerability.

The juxtaposition of the boy and the dog, the human and the natural, was driven home by the caption below the picture: 'A dog's life . . . Brazil's request marks a new sense of urgency as domestic pressures grow' (*Guardian*, 22 December 1988). The actual story had nothing whatsoever to do with the boy himself, he merely gave visual representation to a broader idea. Because arguably we tend to identify with the 'damaged child' at an unconscious level, because we all feel (whether we recognise it or not) that we have been neglected or hurt as children, such an image acts quickly and directly on our emotions and the image thus helps to reinforce feelings of concern over a wider political issue that only affects children themselves obliquely.

Thus children are frequently used to represent futurity, but of course the *content* of that futurity varies widely. One such photograph (see Figure 2), for example, showed Cambodian boys playing gleefully in the sea; the article was about a forthcoming election. The message was presumably that such democratic changes spelled out a brighter future, one where greater freedom and pleasure might become possible. Children, of course, are frequently used by (usually male) politicians in photographs to convey similar messages of hope and a brighter future (as well as representing the politician as a 'family' man).

Similarly, when children are used to represent nature, the content of the messages may vary considerably. In 1984 the National Anti-Vivisection Society had an advertisement, for instance, that

*Figure 2  Cambodian boys cool off in Tonle Sap river*
Source: *The* Guardian, *1 June 1993*

used the photograph of a baby as if it were an animal about to be experimented on. There are wires attached to the baby and it is clearly in pain. It is also naked, without any protection. The caption reads: 'The law still allows people to squirt weedkiller in a baby's eyes, inject it with poison, grow cancers on its back, burn its skin off, expose it to radiation and eventually kill it, in unreliable experiments . . . So long as it's only an animal' (*Guardian*, 12 December 1984). The message here is that animals are really like children and deserve to be treated with similar care and kindness as we would want to treat children.

In contrast, a 1989 advertisement for ActionAid showed two images juxtaposed: one of a domestic cat, clearly a pet, the other of an African girl, obviously living in poverty. Underneath the cat was the message: £20.00 a month; underneath the girl was the message: £10.00 a month (*Guardian*, 2 March 1989). Here the message is that Third World children are seen as less valued than animals and a demand is made to try and view these children as at least as good as our own pets. Historically, representations of colonised children have differed markedly from those of white children. In the early twentieth century, Beinart (1992) notes, at a time when infant welfare in Britain was associated above all with the imperialist desire to produce a healthy race for war and colonial expansion, photographic representations of African children were usually incidental. With reference to Henry Martin's photographs of the Gold Coast in 1902 she notes African children

> appear among a group who have brought in headloads of rubber, cocoa and palm kernels . . . one picture shows a long row of naked children . . . a favourite group pose of the period (suggesting) a lack of understanding of family structure, a desire to show them as physical specimens rather than members of inter-related groups. (Beinart, 1992, p. 222)

Steve Baker points out that: 'Western society continues to draw heavily on symbolic ideas involving animals and . . . the immediate subject of those ideas is frequently not the animal itself, but rather a human subject drawing on animal imagery to make a statement about human identity' (Baker, 1993, p. ix). Baker explores reasons why animals seem to play such a vital role in the construction of human identity. Partly he sees this as a loss of the animal's symbolic power and mystery, but also he argues that the label of 'animal' is used to project certain human characteristics, whether desired or rejected, from one group of people on to another:

> Western society more than any other emphasizes the 'otherness' of the non-human. By drawing a sharp dividing line between human and non-human, a vast gap is created between *subject* (the free acting human agent) and *object* (the passive acted-upon thing). This notion is related to the notion that we, as Homo Sapiens, are unique among the animal species ... We perceive ourselves as belonging to a totally different order: the realm of *culture*, while all other beings and inanimate things are only *nature*. (Noske quoted in Baker, 1993, p. 79)

Children are used in the same way to carry qualities that adults cannot tolerate in themselves.

Children, Baker suggests, are important as *liminal* beings bridging culture and nature who at the same time remind us of our animality. Because we tend to hold contradictory feelings about our own animality, and over time attitudes to these have varied widely at a cultural level, we are also apt to hold contradictory feelings about children. This is reflected in the different ways in which children are associated with nature in representations. Sometimes they are represented as innocent or pure, while at other times damaged or endangered children are used to represent a natural environment increasingly seen as under threat. In other instances unkempt 'out of control' children are associated with 'beasts', with being 'no better than animals'.

## Paintings

Historically, paintings have been an important form of representation. As discussed earlier, Philippe Ariès first drew attention to the salience of artistic representation of children in understanding the social and historical construction of the concept of childhood. The meanings attached to 'child' and 'childhood', he argued, change and vary across time. Ennew, however, points

out that the word 'child' prior to the fifteenth century implied
only kinship and status; it did not refer to an age hierarchy. To
take art as representative of all children is thus a mistake: 'these
were the sons and daughters of the nobility. Painters depicted
their own children in charming, domestic portraits which reveal
that children were not always viewed as small adults' (Ennew,
1986, p. 13). Paintings, as much as photographs or advertisements, are made *by* somebody and *for* somebody. They tell a story
as much as they represent any 'reality' and the story they tell is
specific historically and culturally.

Early western art was overwhelmingly religious. Its aim was
arguably never to represent Mary or Jesus in any 'realistic' way,
but to remind and inspire onlookers with the holiness and divinity of those they represented. Painting in the Middle Ages was
virtually by definition symbolic and did not purport to be iconic
or realistic. The representations of children stood for something
other than an embodied child, such as the idea of a holy childhood or the soul:

> The touching idea of childhood remained limited to the Infant
> Jesus until the fourteenth century, when . . . Italian art was to
> help to spread and develop it . . . At this time the theme of a
> Holy Childhood developed and spread. It became more pro-
> fane. Other childhoods were portrayed. From this religious
> iconography of childhood, a lay iconography eventually de-
> tached itself in the fifteenth and sixteenth centuries. (Ariès,
> [1960] 1986, pp. 33 and 35)

From the fifteenth century onwards, however, there was an increasing division in the way children were represented, primarily
as a result of the influence of the humanism of Renaissance art.
For the first time, child portraits became increasingly popular
among the well-to-do. These purported to represent, in a stylised
form, a historically specific child. At the same time, religious
images of children, especially naked boys (*putti*) proliferated.
*Putti*, small naked Eros figures, became prevalent in paintings in
the sixteenth century, having been popularised by Titian:

> like the medieval child – a holy child, or a symbol of the soul,
> or an angelic being – the *putto* was never a real, historic

child . . . This is all the more remarkable in that the theme of the *putto* originated and developed at the same time as the child portrait. But the children in fifteenth and sixteenth century portraits are never . . . naked children. Nobody could visualize the historic child, even when he was very small, in the nudity of the mythological and ornamental child, and this distinction remained in force for a long time. (Ariès, [1960] 1986, p. 42)

Arguably such a division between a 'real' iconic child and a symbolic child made sense at the time because people would never have expected religious representations of children to be realistic; the purpose of religious representations differed from representations of real children, and that was almost certainly clear then. Over time, however, and particularly with the rise of realism and, indeed, the development of photography, the distinction became blurred. Photography, by laying claim to 'scientific objectivity', a claim that has never wholly been refuted, led to a widespread belief that photographs are 'true'. As a result there is now general confusion between the specific and general child, the iconic and the symbolic. Children in advertisements *look* real in a way that children in religious paintings did not. The result of this confusion has been to mythologise the child generally by obliterating and denying difference.

It is interesting to compare and reflect, for instance, on the changing meanings of nudity in representations of children. In 1995 a high-profile media woman was arrested for having taken a photograph of a young female relation naked in the bath. The charge was child pornography, although all charges were dropped. Nudity has now become a highly controversial area with regard to children. The boundary between art and pornography remains, of course, ill-defined and controversial. The meaning of nudity in representations of children has arguably changed very recently so that it has now become equated with sexual abuse. This is presumably a result of the moral panic over child sexual abuse that has dominated the media over the past few years. For many years, however, while there was a taboo on nude representations of real children, nude representations of the Christ Child were ubiquitous (see, for example, Figure 3, *The Virgin and Child* from the studio of Hans Memlinc in the fifteenth century).

*Figure 3 Hans Memlinc,* The Virgin and Child

Leo Steinberg studied the widespread phenomenon of nude representations of Christ in Renaissance art and, in particular, the way in which many focused central importance on the Christ Child's genitalia:

> Renaissance art, both of north and south of the Alps, produced a large body of devotional imagery in which the genitalia of the Christ Child, or the dead Christ, receive such demonstrative emphasis that one must recognise an *ostentatio genitalium* comparable to the canonic *ostentatio vulnerum*, the showing forth of the wounds. In many hundreds of pious, religious works, from before 1400 to past the mid-16th century, the ostensive unveiling of the Christ's sex, or the touching, protecting or presentation of it, is the main action. (Steinberg, 1984, p. 1)

Steinberg's explanation is that nudity was the way that painters at the time used to represent God's descent into manhood: 'The objective was not so much to proclaim the divinity of the babe as to declare the *humanation* of God. And this declaration becomes the set theme of every Renaissance Nativity, Adoration, Holy Family, or Madonna and Child' (Steinberg, 1984, p. 9). Renaissance artists were the first since Christ's birth to use naturalistic modes of representation. It is possible to argue that a naturalist representation of what was intended to be symbolic necessarily blurred the boundary between 'real' and 'symbolic' children.

As an example of how early child portraiture co-existed at both a real and symbolic level, let us consider Frans Hals' portrait of Catharina Hooft with her nurse, painted in 1619–20 (Figure 4). On the one hand, the faces of the child and her nurse we can presume to approximate to how they both looked physically: 'Artists usually attempted to render a good likeness of the face of each subject but felt free to improve on costume or setting' (Calvert, 1982). On the other hand, portraits like this were, of course, commissioned, so it is also likely that any grotesque or unattractive features (if there were any) would have been minimalised or hidden.

Other layers of meaning, however, can be found in this painting. First, the girl is clothed in a miniature version of an adult woman's dress, except for the pair of hanging sleeves suspended from her shoulders 'that looked like two wide ribbons . . . these were the atrophied remnants of the false sleeves that had been popular in the fifteenth and sixteenth centuries. Adults had long since abandoned them, but they were retained for both boys and girls as a symbol of immaturity' (Calvert, 1982). There was at this time little differentiation between girls' dress and that of adult women:

> . . . as a girl would never rise above the subordinate position into which she was born . . . Essentially a girl dressed like a woman, carried the same props, and assumed the same poses. If a girl could be viewed as a miniature adult, the grown woman could be viewed as a more advanced child. Subordination, femininity, and childishness were tightly inter-twined. (Calvert, 1982)

*Figure 4  Frans Hals,* Catharina Hooft with her Nurse

The symbolism of dress is thus of central importance in locating this child as female and subordinate. Her dress, however, is
also distinctly different from that of her nurse, who is dressed in
simple black and white without frills or jewellery. This contrasts
with the finery of the girl, who wears a gold bracelet and necklace
with amber pendant as well as hat, ruff and sleeve cuffs made of
elaborate lace. Though there is obviously an age difference between them, this is not stressed. What *is* emphasised is the wide
gap between them in terms of social status; clothes clearly demarcate the girl's superior status and make it evident she comes from
a wealthy family. Dress, of course, remains an important code
in contemporary culture for indicating who we are, or who we
would like to be. Children in recent years have been particular

targets for fashion and 'designer kids' have become increasingly important as fashion accessories for affluent parents.

It is interesting to note the central importance of the apple in this painting, located as it is almost at the centre of the image. Portrait painters used props extensively to symbolise key aspects of those represented; in adult portraiture male props such as ledgers, batons or the Bible indicated occupation or achievement, while children, and especially girls, tended to be represented with 'natural' props such as fruit. The apple, of course, carries a wealth of meaning in connection with women generally, and sexuality and the Fall in particular.

The message conveyed by the apple here seems to relate not to Catharina Hooft's status as an infant so much as to her future status as a woman who, although of high social status, will still be marked by the curse of Eve. Her facial expression is both baby-like and somewhat beguiling, even knowing. Now small and apparently innocent, the painting seems to say, sin is just around the corner and with it all the problems of temptation and corruption. The somewhat pained and sad expression of the nurse, and the fact that it is she who holds the apple, conveys her knowledge, as a mature woman, of what is in store for her young charge, regardless of social status. This portrait does not, therefore, dwell on the subject's age so much as on her social position and her gender. In terms of gender she is ultimately like her nurse, but socially she is a world apart. These factors, rather than age, were the crucial determinants of the girl's life chances as seen at the time.

Compare the Hals portrait with a contemporary photograph of a girl of similar age, also with an apple (Figure 5). This shows a Lebanese girl, almost naked, with a missing foot and extensive shrapnel wounds to her body. Beside her is an ignored doll. She holds an apple. Here the girl is used to represent the idea of the innocent victim betrayed by war. She is damaged, maimed and scarred. The doll lies cast aside like the child's life. But why the prominence of the apple? Is it meant to carry similar connotations to those in the Hals' portrait? To some extent I think it is; significantly, it has been bitten into. It may also be associated in our minds with the poison apple and the Snow White story. Both ultimately suggest innocence (bitten into and) betrayed. Where the Hals portrait may be seen as representing both the prosperity

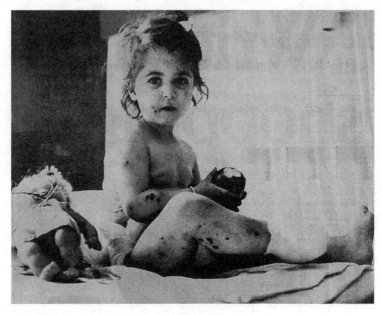

*Figure 5  Lebanese girl and apple*
Source: *The* Guardian, *11 April 1989*

of a particular family as well as the theme of the sin and corruption of womanhood, the 'enemy' in the photo of the Lebanese girl
is external to her, but it is not, ultimately, unconnected with
religion.

Child portraiture can reveal a great deal about wider attitudes
to children and childhood as well as to more specific themes.
Karin Calvert studied 900 American portraits from the period
1670–1870, depicting in total 1330 children below the age of
seven. She found paintings combined a good likeness of the subjects' faces with an array of settings, props, costumes and poses
often borrowed from other paintings or prints: 'The painting of
children could thus be a complex combination of reality, local or
borrowed motifs, and imagination' (Calvert, 1982).

Before 1750, Calvert discovered, family portraits presented the
group as having two complementary components: a dominant
group of men and breeched boys, and a subordinate group of

women and children in petticoats. Both girls and boys wore petticoats until the age of seven (and nothing was worn underneath so that they could urinate easily on the ground) as a sign of subordination and submission. Although there were small differentiations between girls and boys until that age, for example, collars tended to be different, costumes were virtually identical. At the age of seven, however, boys were breeched and from then on their dress was totally different from that of girls. Breeching continued as an important ritual for boys into the twentieth century, at least in some social groups. The following account is by Samuel Mountford, who was born in Birmingham in 1907 and was one of 12 children:

> My first recollection of life was when I was breeched ... I remember standing on the table all dressed up in white blouse, velvet trousers with shoulder straps, white ankle socks, patent black shoes and bow tie. My word, I did look posh, and I felt posh. All the folk in the terrace came in to inspect and wish me all happiness in life, and of course presented me with presents and, as was customary, a silver coin ... I think my age would be two to three years. (Burnett, 1982, p. 5)

Boys, as Ariès pointed out, were the first specialised children. They began attending school in large numbers from the late sixteenth century and their dress by the end of the eighteenth century differentiated them both from women/girls and from adult males. In portraits the props and clothes for boys testify to their distinct path into maturity, masculinity and authority.

Calvert (1982) argues that the portraits she studied reveal little sense of childhood as being a special social group characterised by play or playfulness until the eighteenth century: 'A child was merely an adult in the making, and childhood, as a period of physical and spiritual vulnerability, was a deficiency to be overcome.' There seems to be universal agreement that the eighteenth century marked a watershed in terms of a new concept of the meaning of 'child' and childhood. As discussed earlier, it was at this time that literature for children first flourished, that toys became commercially produced, that education became increasingly widespread. This new childhood, however, was defined in

*Figure 6  Goya,* The Family of the Duke of Osuna

terms of, and applied to, the more well-to-do sectors of society.
The idea of a universal child with a universal childhood did not
become fully accepted until the present century.

Consider a family portrait from the late eighteenth century,
Goya's *The Family of the Duke of Osuna* (1788) (Figure 6). The
family group is clearly demarcated by boundaries based on age
and gender. The father stands at the centre, supporting both wife
and daughter. His clothing is the most strongly coloured and the
most ornate. There is a sword at his side, symbolising authority,
strength, masculinity, and probably also indicating military
connections.

The two daughters are dressed almost identically to the
mother, with slight variations in the collars and size of buttons.

Each girl clutches a fan, symbolising idle femininity. The mother seems to be holding a letter. One girl leans against the mother while the other's hand is held by her father. Both, in other words, are represented as dependent, unable to stand alone. In contrast, the sons, although apparently younger than the daughters, are unsupported, more independent. One has a pull-along toy, the other a pipe. Both are active toys. Toys were rarely represented in portraits before 1770. Girls' toys were overwhelmingly domestic (dolls, fans, pets) while boys had more active toys such as drums, pipes and hoops. In this painting the boys seem active and playful, but the girls are not. Here too we see the boys dressed in specialised clothing, unlike earlier custom. They wear special suits – skeleton suits – that are different both from their father's costume and from that of the girls. Skeleton suits first appeared in both Europe and the USA in the late eighteenth century:

> Trousers were the common uniform of some subordinate classes of men, including laborers, sailors, and European peasants. A young boy's trousers therefore symbolized his subordination to the men of the family, but the vocabulary of submission was now borrowed from the dress of lower-class males rather than that of upper-class women. Boys as young as three or four were dressed in skeleton suits, recognising their masculinity long before they reached maturity . . . [it] separated young boys from the mass of women, girls and very small children in petticoats, and placed them in a special category. The skeleton suit drew equal attention to the wearer's age and sex, for it was worn neither by miniature men nor by asexual children but by boys. It also divided the development of a boy into three clear stages: three or four years of infancy in frocks, about six years of boyhood in the skeleton suit, and another four or five years of youth in a modified adult costume. (Calvert, 1982)

Childhood, in other words, was not only becoming more distinct and specialised but was articulated most clearly through boyhood.

Note in this painting the presence of domestic pets: the cat in front of one daughter, the dog peering out from between the petticoats of the two girls. They are represented as closest to the girls rather than the boys, probably referring to the common view, linked to the idea of the Great Chain of Being, that women were closer to animals and nature than were men. The idea that children were particularly close to nature arguably depended on a specific emotional attitude to childhood (Kinnel, n.d., p. 19). The child as seen by the Romantics and differentiated from, for instance, the child as seen by the Evangelicals, was premised on the intensity of feeling the child evoked in adults:

> Blake's *Songs* are chiefly remarkable for their intensity, with the individual's misery speaking for a generation of children. Coleridge and Wordsworth similarly elevated their involvement with individual children to an overarching philosophical concept of childhood. Feeling was no longer an untrustworthy arbiter in dealing with children: it could be considered as an appropriate framework within which their upbringing and education were worked out. (Kinnel, n.d., p. 19)

The Romantic elevation of feeling to a moral construct was distinctly different from the evangelical perspective that regarded children as in strict need of adult control rather than being allowed any emotional freedom or spiritual autonomy.

Although the divergent discourses of the Romantics and the Evangelicals continued, overall the increasing association between children and nature, concomitant with a more benevolent and increasingly idealised view of nature itself, led to a greater freedom accorded to (middle-class) children. In portraiture girls until around the age of 12 are increasingly represented in less constrained clothes. Their dresses become markedly more simple and free-flowing than those of women. They are often represented in gardens or similar natural settings so that by the nineteenth century the garden becomes a metaphor for childhood itself (natural, yet carefully cultivated and controlled). The garden was often contrasted with the wilderness, darkness and danger where the 'other' lurked, as represented, for instance, by the gypsies that Maggie Tulliver visits in George Eliot's ([1960] 1979) *Mill on the Floss*, or indeed, by the whole of Africa and the 'primitive' in nineteenth-century imperialist discourse.

In Gainsborough's *The Painter's Daughters Chasing a Butterfly* (c. 1755) (Figure 7) the two little girls are in loose frocks, running

*Figure 7 Gainsborough,* The Painter's Daughters Chasing a Butterfly

freely through a natural outdoor setting. This is in marked contrast with other earlier portraits, such as *The Graham Children* (Figure 1) or *The Family of the Duke of Osuna* (Figure 6), where children were represented within the parameters of an interior of a home strictly ordered by parents with clear boundaries of age and gender. It is interesting to note, however, that given the subject of this painting it would certainly not have been commissioned; this may well have given artists a chance to represent children as *they* wanted to. The girls are implicitly likened to nature generally and butterflies in particular: ephemeral, free, soon to change into something quite different. This reveals a

*Figure 8  Millais,* Sweetest Eyes were Ever Seen

distinct shift in attitudes to children at the time, showing the specialisation of childhood, but here in particular the speciali-sation of girlhood. Within that notion of specialness are new ideas about otherness, loss, evanescence. Unlike the portrait of Catharina Hooft, there is no suggestion of sin or knowingness; the emphasis is entirely on innocence, but that innocence also makes them Other in a way that Catharina Hooft is not.

These qualities eventually led to an increasing senti-mentalisation of childhood. Millais' *Sweetest Eyes were Ever Seen* (Figure 8), for instance, continues in the nineteenth century the association of children, and notably girls, with nature and gar-dens. The girl's clothes in this are casual, free and her hair hangs loose. She appears soft, flowing. On the verge of pubescence,

however, these qualities are about to be transformed and ultimately lost, cut, like the flowers she holds in her basket.

Similar sentimental representations of girls (and to a lesser
extent, boys) recur over and over throughout the nineteenth, and
into the twentieth, centuries. From the late nineteenth century,
however, they become increasingly evident in advertisements,
such as the classic 'Bubbles' advertisements where nature, purity,
innocence and transience are portrayed in a sentimental way and
used to sell a wider and more diverse variety of products than
ever before. Such representations, however, mark the merging of
difference in childhood into a far more universal notion of child
and childhood, at once an abstraction and an idealisation premised on denial of difference.

## Family Photographs

That children connote different qualities and meanings in advertisements, news photographs and cultural representations seems
clear. Less clear, perhaps, is the ways in which adults use children
in personal and family photographs. What could be more a representation of reality, of important milestones in a child's – and its
family's – life than snapshots of birthdays, parties, holidays?

There has been an ongoing debate since Daguerre invented
photography in 1839 as to whether photography is 'art' and
whether or not it is 'scientific' in its claim to represent reality.
Photographs have been used, for instance, as evidence by the
police. Late nineteenth-century campaigners against poverty and
homelessness, such as Jacob Riis, used photographs as visual
evidence in their campaigns, often with great effect. Others, such
as Stieglitz, a pioneer American photographer (1864–1946), insisted that photography was as much art as any painting. As
Chaplin remarks:

Photography tends to disturb the distinction between 'visual
art' and other social categories of visual representation; but so
does the politicised concept of culture itself, for this treats both
'photography as reportage' and 'fine art photography', for example, as cultural production. Semiotic theory also tends to
blur the boundary between art and 'non-art', since it focuses on

communication as a social process, and treats visual art as one form of communication. (Chaplin, 1994, p. 80)

Photography has become readily accessible to everyone since the early twentieth century. Perhaps its very accessibility has made any claims to 'art' more controversial. Family photography has enabled virtually everyone to be able to take numerous pictures of themselves, their children, their holidays and to preserve these as memories, archives, mini-museums. In no other historical period has this been possible. Sontag ([1977] 1989) suggests that now it is the images we collect that have become more important than memories. Snapshots, in a sense, have *become* our memories, yet are also external to them. We take them to remember, but we also take them for the future, for our children's and their children's memories. Integral to this is the ubiquitous claim of photographs that this family was *happy*. Hence the supreme importance of the command to smile, to say 'cheese'.

As Holland argues, however, family photographs, as well as being 'an act of faith in the future' also pose a number of challenges to 'different pasts, as memory interweaves with private fantasy and public history' (Holland, 1991). Family photographs can never be just memories alone because they represent a number of people and pasts, disconnected points that we try to reconstruct and organise into some sense of order and meaning. They are constructs of what the photographer (usually the father) wanted to record of his family, what he wanted to prove about his family and what he would like it to have been: 'The children's party may bring tantrums, but the pictures will show laughter. The holiday may be spoilt by rain, but it will be the sunny days that make it to the family album' (Holland, 1991, p. 2). In this way,

> at a time when the family group . . . is fragmented and atom-
> ised, images continue to be produced which reassure us of its
> solidity and cohesion. The compulsive smiles in the snapshots
> of today insist on the exclusive claim of the family group to
> provide satisfying and enduring relationships, just as the calm
> dignity of earlier pictures emphasised the formality of family
> ties. (Holland, 1991, p. 1)

My father loved to take, develop, and preserve photographs. Perhaps it gave him a sense of control over the chaos that characterised our family just below the surface, much of which he himself caused. Perhaps it was his fascination with science and technology. Perhaps he was desperately trying to cover up his transgressions by creating a body of evidence that bore witness to a happy family. Interestingly, however, I have discovered a number of photographs he took which, at least in my interpretation, suggest the opposite.

There are two photographs of a dinghy my father built which was wrecked in a hurricane in 1953, and which we found strewn over the local golf course after the hurricane subsided. Father had christened it *Repulsive II*; there had been an earlier *Repulsive* and it was all a pun on the more stalwart ship *Repulse*. The name, the text, of the boat was a joke, but jokes, of course, can be read as powerful statements from the unconscious. In the first photo (Figure 9), which he took, my sister and I are both in the remains of the boat, so that beneath us is framed the message 'Repulsive Two'. Yet I seem to resist this construction; I am resisting his (camera's) gaze, perhaps after early experiences of being forced to pose for less savoury photographs. Armed with my own Brownie, I confront his (camera's) gaze with my own, so that I reflect back to him his own process that leaves him invisible, but in control. By so doing I am drawing attention to the process itself and the power relations it disguises. Like him, I do not show my face.

The second photo (Figure 10) was taken by me and, unusually, included my father. Here was *my* chance to construct a souvenir, a statement, for posterity. In it I have made my parents hold up the stern of the boat in front of their lower bodies, including their genital area, thereby labelling *them* as 'Repulsive Two'. My sister and one of our cats get off relatively lightly. I do remember insisting at the time that my parents should also hold a small doll of mine. What, I wonder now, did that mean, what did it represent? Was it my idea of a lost baby? I do not know. What interests me most in both these photographs is my resistance, my refusal to comply with their version of who we were. On the other hand, I was also cast repeatedly as the rebel, the 'black sheep', the problem child, so in one way

*Figure 9 Family photograph: Repulsive II (i)*

*Figure 10 Family photograph: Repulsive II (ii)*

*Figure 11 Family photograph: mother and daughters*

perhaps my actions here did conform to my script in the family drama.

In another photograph (Figure 11), father has taken a group shot of my mother, sister and myself sitting together in what at first sight would seem a close and intimate representation of mother and daughters. It was taken outside our house in Vermont. I am not quite six years old. My mother is in the centre, smiling, but with a smile I think that lacks conviction. I suspect it was requested. My sister, also smiling, wields a gun. This seems to be pointing just short of my head and probably just short of Father's, too. She does not meet his gaze at all, but stares meaningfully at her weapon, dreaming perhaps of growing older and reaching an age when she could buy real bullets and blow us all to smithereens. I, on the other hand, do meet Father's (camera's) gaze, but refuse to comply with a smile. Instead I seem to be busy strangling the cat. I think more probably I was, literally, clinging to the cat; pets were immensely important to us as children for they were, in their way, consistent, and offered comfort and warmth without betrayal. Of course I do not know what was really going on then, no doubt different things were going on for each of us. Perhaps Father was once more constructing a joke, a spoof of happy family groups. Or perhaps we were resisting his genuine attempt to make our family appear happy. For me there does seem to be a truth in these pictures in the way they convey contradictory messages; there is power and resistance, fun and terror all jumbled together. Perhaps there was a battle going on for a dominant representation of our family.

## Myths, Stories and Fairy Tales

Clearly between 1800 and 1900 some enormous transformations took place which altered in significant ways the meanings of children and childhood. By 1900 the concept of 'the' child was clear and was being increasingly enshrined in legislation: compulsory and free education, for instance, and within a few years, provision of school meals and health inspection were given by rights to all children. At the close of the eighteenth century, however, although childhood was increasingly being defined in terms of bourgeois domestic ideology, it did not yet encompass all children. At this time there still remained a marked divergence between middle-class children and the children of the poor, a difference that was predicated on dependency: 'Childhood for the poor in the seventeenth century and for most of the eighteenth century was perceived as a time for involvement into habits of labour . . . it was assumed that the children of the poor should have an economic value for their parents. Such views went unchallenged until the nineteenth century' (Cunningham, 1991, p. 3).

Although debates on child labour, dependency and education during the nineteenth century focused generally on 'children' and 'childhood' – the rhetoric was universalised – implicitly the focus was entirely on working-class children. Again and again working-class children were seen as transgressing middle-class ideals of childhood dependency, innocence and purity. Children who worked were not dependent, children who worked with adults were seen as susceptible to moral corruption of the worst sorts, children who spent much of their time on the streets transgressed middle-class ideology of the home and the realm of the private.

Criticisms of working-class families and parenting were framed in terms of 'the order of nature', synonymous with middle-class domestic ideology. It is a good illustration of Barthes' ([1972] 1987) argument that myths are created out of historical complexities by claiming certain categories to be 'natural'. As Cunningham (1991, p. 83) points out: 'In the order of nature parents, and particularly fathers, would labour for the support of their young children; the latter would certainly have a role in supporting the family economy according to their age and abilities, but the primary responsibilities should lie with parents.' The Evangelicals, and Lord Shaftesbury in particular, in their attempts to fend off what they saw as the evils of Chartism and Socialism, regarded child labour, especially in factories, as distorting the natural order of both nature and England (Cunningham, 1991, p. 87). Increasingly, they pointed the finger of blame at working-class parents rather than at the factory system itself. The state, they argued, needed to step in only if and when parents failed. Such precepts, of course, underlie to this day our social policies on children and family where implicit middle-class assumptions are that state intervention is appropriate only in working-class families. Hence, as discussed before, the furore over the interventions of state agencies into middle-class families in Cleveland.

The rapid changes that occurred during the late eighteenth and early nineteenth centuries through industrialisation, urbanisation, an unprecedented demographic growth and the political upheavals of the American and French Revolutions were certainly key factors in a shifting perception of 'nature', the rural, and a resultant sense of loss and alienation:

> The more adults and adult society seemed bleak, urbanised and alienated, the more childhood came to be seen as properly a garden, enclosing within the safety of its walls a way of life which was in touch with nature and which preserved the rude virtues of earlier periods of the history of mankind . . . the child was 'the other' for which one yearned. (Cunningham, 1991, p. 3)

The fear of perceived socioeconomic and political turmoil created a sense of disorder and disruption that arguably resulted in fears of chaos and pollution. Fears of this sort are common during periods of rapid social change, as Douglas (1966) has shown, and lead above all to obsessive concern over boundaries and boundary-maintenance. Much of this concern for order that resulted from such fears was undoubtedly articulated in, and represented by, overwhelming concern with 'the family' and the place of children within it at a time when the family largely stood for the idea of social order.

The new middle classes were promulgating and consolidating their domestic ideology of a well-ordered household with clear boundaries of gender, age and authority. Children were essential to this ideal, but in the strict role of well-disciplined dependants who were subject to parental authority within the clearly defined, private, confines of the bourgeois home. Consolidation of this domestic ideology meant a concomitant universalisation of the values on which its foundations stood. Children and childhoods that failed to conform with these ideals, therefore, were increasingly viewed as not only deviant, but pathological. By universalising childhood, as the middle classes tried to do during the course of the nineteenth century, they also simplified and ultimately mythologised the idea. Crucial to this process was the denial of the validity of different childhoods and a concerted campaign to both rescue and destroy such differences: 'The fear was that the children [of the poor] represented as disorderly and dirty, were a threat to the future of the race unless something was done' (Cunningham, 1991, p. 4).

During the late eighteenth and early nineteenth centuries, then, attention focused on the children of the poor generally, and the issue of children at work specifically. This was also a time when other key issues included slavery, 'civilisation' versus the 'primitive', and animals and nature (particularly after Darwin). In other words, the 'other' was of prime concern. Difference lies at the root of otherness because it threatens order and control:

> When . . . the sense of order and control undergoes stress, then doubt is cast on the self's ability to control the internalised world that it has created for itself, and anxiety appears which mirrors the earlier affective coloring of the period of individuation. We project that anxiety onto the other, externalizing our loss of control . . . When . . . a group makes demands on society, the status anxiety projected by those demands characteristically translates into a sense of loss of control. Thus a group that has been marginally visible can suddenly become the definition of the other. (Gilman, 1985, p. 20)

Such a group was the chimney sweeps, who suddenly became the focus of a fierce and far-reaching debate about children, work, childhood and the future. It was no coincidence that blackness was central to the debate, for it raised issues about race, empire and otherness. Gilman points out that blackness has long been a root-metaphor for otherness, and that otherness can accommodate a number of different groups simultaneously juxtaposed and brought into association. In the late eighteenth century, for example, blackness was associated with revolution as well as with foreignness, the proletariat, and the child (Gilman, 1985, p. 34). Sweeps, though few in number, were symbolically important. First, because their blackness associated them with dirt, negritude, slavery and work, but also in a contradictory way because in reality they were white and British. Second, they transgressed class boundaries because they entered and worked in the houses of the wealthy. Though apparently there to clean, they also brought pollution in, and were living reminders to the well-to-do not only that childhood was not universal, but also that slavery was problematic.

The general outrage felt about English boys who were forced to work as sweeps did not, however, extend to girls – also English and also frequently black/dirty – who worked as domestic servants in middle-class homes.[1] The home allegedly 'protected' them from harm, though the sexual dangers they lived in from middle-class male predators within the household were often great. Domestic servants, however, were not visible in the same way as sweeps, who were both inside and outside, bridging the public and private through the flue, itself a liminal place between two realms which the Victorians were obsessed with trying to keep separate.

The flue can be seen as a kind of secret, vaginal passage between outside and inside, public and private, from which the middle-class home gives birth to a dirty working-class boy, as represented in Kingsley's *The Water Babies* (published in 1863). The notion of boundaries was central to the Victorian middle classes, especially those between private and public, home and work. Sweeps necessarily transgressed those boundaries, thus causing disquiet in a way that working-class domestic servants (who remained within the household, ostensibly 'protected' by a middle-class head of household) did not.

Jonas Hanway first brought the conditions of sweeps to public attention in the 1770s with the publication of his book, *A Sentimental History of Chimney Sweepers*. In this he argued that children are sacred, and condemned the sale of children into chimney sweeping on the grounds of humanity, reason and Christianity. From this time on the child labourer came to be represented as both victim and slave, representations we continue to see in, for example, advertisements for Third World charities and children used to represent poverty generally. In contemporary images of this sort the children are still represented as overwhelmingly dark, showing the continued analogy between blackness and human misery.

From the late eighteenth century onwards, then, there was an increasing tendency to perceive childhood as a special state 'in which innocence and freedom from care should flourish and be protected' (Cunningham, 1991, p. 63). During this period children were also often seen as close to the idea of the 'Noble Savage' because of their alleged closeness to nature and because of the then popular law of recapitulation. In the law of recapitulation, ontogeny repeats phylogeny, that is, the child is believed to recapitulate in its individual development the stages of development of the whole human race. This 'image of the good savage as childlike served . . . to perpetuate and justify European rule' (Cunningham, 1991, p. 101). Similar associations are apparent to this day, as in the photograph of naked boys swimming in the article about forthcoming elections in Cambodia (Figure 2).

The representation of poor boys as 'Street Arabs' from the middle of the nineteenth century drew on similar themes in response to fear about disorder. Because middle-class definitions of childhood were premised on the idea of children as necessarily dependent and unable to fend for themselves, the independence of these self-reliant working-class boys posed a direct threat to middle-class domestic ideology. Originally such 'Street Arabs' were perceived as dangerous, but later came to be regarded as appealing objects of pity in need of rescue. Throughout the nineteenth century the association between poor working-class children, 'foreigners' (Arabs, savages), slaves and blackness linked the otherness of class with slavery, poverty and empire. All were grouped together as 'other'.

From the mid-nineteenth century, children generally, and working-class children specifically, become increasingly represented in a sentimental way, with their alleged 'weakness' and otherness stressed in the image of victim. Evangelical concern from the 1860s shifted to the goal of rescuing 'waifs and strays', who were perceived as innocent victims of cruel parents. This trend was arguably bolstered by an increasing middle-class tendency for adults to idealise their own childhoods. Grieving for the perceived loss of childhood as if for a lost Eden, links were made between the idea of childhood and those of self and interiority. In an increasingly secularised world, childhood thus began to take on what was virtually a religious connotation: 'Childhood began to play a part similar to that which Ruskin sketched out for women and the home; it was both a place of refuge . . . and a source of renewal which would enable the adult to carry on . . . childhood was a substitute for religion' (Cunningham, 1991, p. 152).

Arguably much of the dichotomy in external representations of poor children and middle-class children, by implication corresponding to 'bad' and 'good' children, dark and light, began to be internalised within individuals themselves. Within such a framework the notion of childhood became analogous with heaven as immortalised in a golden age of children's literature – written, of course, by adults – that included Kingsley, Carroll, Alcott, Barrie, Potter and Milne (Cunningham, 1991, p. 152). Steedman (1995) discusses these developments at length, as outlined in Chapter 3, drawing particular attention to the growing idea of, and concern with, interiority. She connects this with new ideas about 'the child', the development of cell theory and theories of the unconscious. The theme of a lost child/hood, both psychologically and culturally, became increasingly important and were used repeatedly in representations of 'the child' in literature, both for children and for adults.

The late seventeenth and early eighteenth centuries had witnessed the beginning of literature written specifically for children by adults. Plumb (1975, p. 81) argues that 'the new children's literature was designed to attract adults, to project an image of those virtues which parents wished to inculcate in their offspring, as well as to beguile the child'. Adults, in this way, were actively involved in the social construction of childhood by developing a body of literature ostensibly focused on children alone, but in many ways more concerned with what adults wanted children to be. Fairy tales were originally tales shared by everyone, adults and children alike, and part of a rich, and ancient, oral tradition. August Nitschke, for example, showed that *Cinderella* originated towards the end of the Ice Age (Zipes, 1979, p. 172). In the late seventeenth century groups of writers, especially aristocratic women, met in salons and began to edit and write down fairy tales specifically for children. As a result, they were transformed into *moral*, didactic tales. Perrault and the Brothers Grimm were at the forefront of this.

In the mid-eighteenth century John Newbery and his family produced a huge range of children's books, from simple instruction books in the 'Three Rs' to classics adapted for young readers, and books on science, history and geography. Morality tales were favourites – at least, those were what parents chose to buy for, and read to, their children. By the early nineteenth century, however, the emphasis on morality in children's literature shifts from a love of nature and the importance of compassion to a much darker and gloomier note under the influence of Wesley and the Evangelical revival. Corpse-viewing, for instance, was a favourite theme (Plumb, 1975, p. 83).

As Rose argues, however, in the case of Barrie's *Peter Pan* (first published 1904/05), such literature was really more aimed at adults and adult desire for the child and their own lost childhood than it was at children themselves: 'children's fiction sets up the child as an outsider to its own process, and then aims, unashamedly, to take the child *in*' (Rose, 1984, p. 2). Children's literature, she argues, is all about what the adult desires: 'Suppose . . . that Peter Pan is a little boy who does not want to grow up, not because he doesn't want to, but because someone else prefers that he shouldn't. Suppose . . . that what is at stake in *Peter Pan* is the adult's desire for the child' (Rose, 1984, p. 3).

Children's innocence, according to Rose, is not, therefore, about either a non-existent or a repressed sexuality, but about our own fears that children's sexuality – as outlined by Freud as bisexual, polymorphous and perverse – are, in fact, our own (Rose, 1984, p. 4). Making the child 'other' distances this disquieting idea by emphasising and indeed constructing a childhood manufactured to represent children as 'special' in their otherness and difference from adults, even though, paradoxically, we too were children once. It is arguably this tension that nourishes much of the adult's desire for the child, a theme that will be considered in more detail in Chapter 6.

By the beginning of the twentieth century, then, there was a myth, a story, of a universal childhood which all children were entitled to, regardless of social class. This childhood was held up as a time of innocence, dependence and happiness that somehow existed in a world outside of the harsh realities of life – as in, for example, a garden. This co-existed as a myth, in images and texts, both culturally and psychologically. In the process of being mythologised all contradictions of class, gender, race and physical difference were minimised to the extent of almost total denial. Aberrations from this ideal, this myth, continued and continue.

The black child and the poor child are still treated as other, in some way deviant or pathological from the white middle-class child that has dominated representations for the past century, or else the difference itself is minimised, rendered invisible.

## A Story of the Nation?

Cunningham (1991, p. 228) argues that this narrative of the universal child was, in fact, 'a story of the nation'. The struggles of Shaftesbury and others for reform of labour laws, for universal education and so on were told throughout the twentieth century as a narrative of progress that rescued the child, educated it, purified it; the narrative is one where the child represents the story of nationhood. This equation of child with nation can be seen to continue today. Consider, for example, the airlift of Sarajevo's wounded during the siege of 1993. While Europe stood by and watched the genocide and destruction, the British government attempted to stage what was arguably a publicity stunt by organising an RAF rescue of 20 casualties, requesting, however, that these should be children. Media attention focused on one five-year-old girl, Irma Hadzimuratovic, who had suffered spinal, abdominal and head wounds in a mortar attack that killed her mother in Bosnia. Airlifted to Great Ormond Street Hospital, media attention focused for days on her maimed and damaged body as a symbol of war-torn Bosnia and as a humanitarian gesture from a government that was otherwise doing remarkably little to stop the suffering of thousands of others left behind unaided. As such she stood as both symbol and distraction. Her death two years later attracted relatively little media attention, for her usefulness as a symbol had by then disappeared.

Another myth of childhood that could be read as analogous to nationhood is the story and career of Shirley Temple. In her autobiography (Black, 1989) she recounts how Hollywood mythologised her image by reconstructing her personal past. Shirley Temple was born in 1928, a time of recession and increased polarisation of American society where Steinbeck's *Grapes of Wrath* (first published 1939) co-existed uneasily with the golden age of Hollywood. In the era of Prohibition and gangsters, America was increasingly divided and perceived as in a state of severe crisis.

By the time Shirley Temple was just over three years old, and beginning her career in film, there were over 12 million unemployed in the USA.

Though she began dancing lessons at three, film producers insisted that it must never be acknowledged that she had had to learn to dance: 'Shirley must be recreated as a natural phenomenon, someone without formal training' (Black, 1989, p. 39). As she grew taller, producers tried to disguise this by keeping her skirts short and dressing her much younger than she really was. When she was five, Sheehan of Fox Studios had her birth certificate altered to make her a year younger. Increasingly the creation of the myth of Shirley Temple involved the denial of her specific traits as an individual (obliterating, for instance, her love of slingshots) and the construction of an image of a 'natural' child who was innocent, happy, talented and 'cute'. Part of this process was the creation of a symbol that could be seen as standing for the nation as a whole. Shirley Temple was a virgin, untainted, pure and thus whole – in a way that the USA was not at that time. White, Anglo-Saxon, young, innocent and energetic, she represented an ideal of American society of the time that can be seen as symbolising (the desire for) American unity and the hope of the New Deal.

There were also other stories besides nationhood, however, that emerge from the discourses of children and childhood in the nineteenth and twentieth centuries. There are stories about independence/dependence, a story about the self and interiority, a story about loss and a lost world, both psychologically and culturally. Such stories surrounding the child persist, surviving and flourishing in representations of children today. The myth survives both in culture and within ourselves and our own sadness and quest for a 'lost child'. Evidence for this is apparent in a plethora of films about, and focused on, childhood and children, as well as in a complex array of therapies and self-help publications purporting to help individuals recover their 'lost child'. Overwhelmingly such manifestations are commercialised and used to sell a wide range of products and services. In this process our feelings of loss and yearning associated with the image of the lost child are frequently manipulated and constructed by both the media and the advertising industry.

# 5

## Are Children Innocent?

The government in Britain has drawn up criteria for pre-school education and stipulated that by the age of five children should know the difference between right and wrong. In the Bulger trial teachers and psychiatrists testified that Venables and Thompson knew the difference between right and wrong; one head teacher even claimed that all four year olds entering school have this moral sense. But, as Blake Morrison pointed out, 'four-year-olds also believe in the man in the moon . . . if children of 10 do know right from wrong, why not juries of 10-year-olds?' (*Independent*, 29 May 1994). Furthermore, if children are so clear as to the difference between right and wrong by the age of ten, why do we not permit them to decide for themselves whether or not to smoke, drink alcohol or have sexual relationships? There seems to be a clear case here of double standards in terms of adult definitions of children's morality. Children's innocence, in the sense of knowledge of adult morality, is clearly liable to a wide range of different, sometimes conflicting, definitions by adults.

Knowledge (and ignorance) of adult sexuality and sexual relations is another sense in which the concept of innocence is frequently applied by adults to children. In the case of sexual abuse, knowledge and experience of adult sexuality can first be forced upon children by (some) adults, and then used by them to define such children as no longer children. Experience of adult sexuality seems now to be taken as the boundary that distinguishes childhood from adulthood, regardless of the age at which it is experienced by children. Is it possible for a child to be morally innocent but legally guilty? Or can a child be legally innocent, but sexually corrupt? There are no clear answers to these questions; meanings of innocence vary and change and also encompass concepts such as helplessness, purity, naiveté.

Innocence has long been linked with Christianity. Originally associated with Herod's Slaughter of the Innocents – in which all boys below the age of two were condemned to die – after Christ's birth (Matthew 2:16), innocence had an early connection with children. Hayward points out that even this connection has, however, changed and been influenced, indeed constructed, 'by the changing place of childhood in matters of theology and spirituality' (Hayward, 1994, p. 67). From the late fourth century, he argues, an increasing amount of stress was laid on the suffering of the Holy Innocents, which became a requirement for their martyrdom. Later, priority was given to *innocentia* as an exhortation to humility and active virginity (Hayward, 1994, p. 86). In Isaiah (9:6) Christ is himself called a child, and to become like a child was a central tenet of Christ's message. Baptism is the crucial act by which a child, born in sin, *becomes* innocent. Innocence in this doctrine is not innate, but acquired.

In Latin *in-nocere* meant either 'not to hurt' or 'not to be hurt', thus embracing both the active and passive voices of the verb 'to harm'. In Middle English it was used to mean 'silly' or to describe an idiot, simpleton or half-wit (*Shorter Oxford English Dictionary*). In the Middle Ages in England, therefore, its meaning was largely to do with a lack of knowledge (though not sexual knowledge) and/or stupidity. It also referred to freedom from guilt before the law. This meaning still holds, of course, as does the Middle English association with naiveté. Further meanings include: doing no evil, free from sin or moral wrong, pure, unpolluted. Inherent in all these layers of meaning are questions as to whether or not, and at what age, a child is capable of, first, adult reason and understanding, and second, adult desire and passion. When exactly does a child cease, or indeed begin, to be innocent?

## Original Sin, *Tabula Rasa*, or Naturally Good?

St Augustine of Hippo first drew attention to the notion of innocence as the antithesis of sin in relation to children in his autobiographical treatise on Original Sin. For Augustine 'the child is a creature of will, a sinner *ab ovo*, and in this no different from adults. Unbaptized, the child was consigned to the flames of hell . . . his innocence a purely negative phenomenon residing in his lack of bodily development but not in his lack of wilfulness' (Pattison, 1978, p. 18). Augustine's emphasis on the corruption of will beginning in childhood meant that reason was 'removed from the supreme position it had held in the mainstream of Greek and Roman thought' (Pattison, 1978, p. 19). By linking childhood with sin and a fallen nature, Augustine gave the human child the only chance of attaining innocence by a second birth in baptism. As Shahar comments:

the prevailing image of the baptized child was one of purity and innocence, on the one hand, and weakness, helplessness, and a lack of reason, on the other . . . The image of the innocent child was inspired by the words of Jesus in the Gospel of St Matthew 18:3–6 and 19:4. The propagation of the cult of the infant Jesus from the twelfth century onwards consolidated this image of innocence and purity. Though born in sin, once baptized, the child was seen as sweet, pure and innocent . . . He was believed to be ignorant of both sexual lust and the meaning of death. (Shahar, 1994, p. 251)

To some extent it can be argued that this view of the child is primarily symbolic and functions as a means of expressing a view of human nature generally, although the implications of it in material, corporeal terms were, and remain, far-reaching. Augustine thus sees the human being as born evil and corrupt with a possibility of *achieving* innocence through Christian baptism and belief. Such achieved innocence, however, is the responsibility of the parents – and the church. It implies that innocence must, ultimately, be enforced.

The Augustinian doctrine of original sin held sway in the christianised West for centuries and is arguably making a comeback at the present time among fundamentalist sects and right-wing groups of various persuasions. Sometimes challenged or denied, it was redefined and reinforced during the Reformation and again during the Wesleyan revival. As Stone comments:

The Reformation – and in Catholic Europe the Counter-Reformation – drive for moral regeneration brought with it an

increasing concern to suppress the sinfulness of children. A
pedagogic movement, which had begun a century earlier with
the Italian Renaissance as a glorification of the purity and innocence of the child, was twisted in the late sixteenth and early
seventeenth century northern religious transplantation into a
deadly fear of the liability of children to corruption and sin,
particularly those cardinal sins of pride and disobedience.
(Stone, 1977, p. 174)

Protestantism stressed the importance of individual responsibility to God in the sense that individuals could not obtain forgiveness from sin just through confession or, as was prevalent in
medieval Catholic Europe, through the purchase of indulgences.
Instead, women and men were exhorted to strive to live out the
precepts of a Christian life on a day-to-day basis. Such emphasis
on the importance of daily and life-long commitment presupposed a rigorous training in Christian values and behaviour:
traits which had to be learned. It is not surprising, therefore, that
the rise of Protestantism, and particularly the rise of Puritanism,
both in Europe and colonial America, brought about new attitudes to childrearing and the importance of childhood generally.
Childhood, it would seem, became a battleground in which
parents fought to inculcate morality and good habits in their
children so that their souls could be saved (Demos, 1970; Greven,
1970).

These tenets undoubtedly had considerable influence on the
beliefs and behaviour of the nascent bourgeoisie from the time of
the Reformation onwards. They increasingly laid stress on the
centrality of both individual morality and the importance of
living in the context of a family as a means (the *only* means) of
achieving that. The sole purpose of sexual relations was argued to
be to bring forth children, although even this was declared as
wicked. Children were believed to be conceived in wickedness;
Richard Baxter, for instance, described his child thus: 'there it lay
in darkness, filth and blood' (Richard Baxter, quoted in Grylls,
1978, p. 24).

Puritan preachers exhorted parents to supervise their children
closely and rigorously from a very early age; play was seen as
dangerous and 'a child's disobedience could count as not only a
domestic offence, but also a species of tyranny and an affront to

the laws of religion' (Grylls, 1978, p. 24). The Calvinists, who believed in predestination and actively sought signs of salvation, stressed early conversion and a rejection of all frivolity as the only way to hope for escape from what was seen as a child's – but also of all humanity's – essentially depraved nature. As mentioned earlier, however, it cannot be assumed that what was preached was necessarily practised. Pollock (1983) argues, for instance, that there is equal evidence to support the thesis that puritan parents were gentle, loving and caring with their children. Most probably then, as now, parental care came in a variety of forms and permutations, and advice from above was not always followed to the letter.

At the same time as doctrines of children's evil were being bellowed from pulpits in Europe and the American colonies, however, other ideas about children and childhood innocence bubbled away relatively unnoticed. Grylls points out that the Christian religion contains the concept of original sin *as well as* the 'seeds of child-idealisation' (Grylls, 1978, p. 29). Different discourses of children and childhood thus apparently co-existed as they co-exist now. From the Middle Ages there were some who maintained a doctrine of innocence, while from the early modern period there were others who began to suggest that children were in some ways wiser than adults (Grylls, 1978, p. 30). This 'primitivism' was identified by Boas, who discovered that there existed – two centuries before the Romantics – arguments against the growing influence of science and scientific rationalism and favoured instead an intuitive knowledge existing in children. In 1628, for instance, John Earle said in his *Microcosmography*: 'In this the child, although still introduced as essentially a grown-up cut down . . . is also the closest approximation to prelapsarian innocence' (quoted in Grylls, 1978, p. 31). At the same time, however, a contemporary asked: 'What is an infant but a brute beast in the shape of a man?' (quoted in Thomas, 1983, p. 43).

Given the co-existence of different discourses of 'the child' and childhood, to make sweeping generalisations about childrearing and childhood can lead to crude reductivism. This has arguably been the case with historians such as Stearns and Shorter, and psychohistorians such as de Mause, who have tended to characterise one century by 'brutality', another by 'tenderness' and so on. If different notions of the nature of the child *co-exist*, what then becomes interesting is to question why one notion becomes dominant at specific times and places and among specific groups.

Children, however, have not always been defined solely in terms of innocence or evil. Theories of science, scientific discourse and rationalism that developed from the late seventeenth century produced different discourses of 'the child' which, like those of innocence and evil, persist today and vie for dominance in cultural definitions of childhood. Locke (1632–1704), for example, argued that the child is a *tabula rasa*, neither good nor bad, but a kind of empty slate on to which parents, society and culture write its personality, traits and life course. Childhood, by this account, is entirely socially constructed; innocence, in the sense of not-knowing, is therefore innate.

Locke's *Thoughts on Education* was published in 1695. In it he argued that perception is passive, merely recording impressions in the outside world. Though he was concerned with education, arguing that it should be an enjoyable process based on the child's interests, and that children should not be forced to learn too much before their power of reason had developed, his main concern was 'with the swift creation, through controlled environment, of the rational adult man. It seldom considered the nature of the child as a child. Treated as a small adult, the child was to be trained out of his childish ways' (Coveney, 1967, p. 40). Order, Nature and Reason remained very much part of eighteenth-century doctrine, although 'the rationalism of acceptance of the early century became by the middle the newer rationalism of discontent, which in time informed the optimisms of the French Enlightenment and the social engineering of the Revolution itself' (Coveney, 1967, p. 38). Concomitant with these changes was the shift in, and conflict of, ideas about nature, with the new organicist view becoming increasing dominant over the old mechanical     one.

Rousseau (1712–78) is generally credited with striking the first blow against rationalism, the prevailing views of nature, and the idea of original sin, although, as mentioned earlier, many of these ideas had in fact been in existence for some time. The crux of Rousseau's thesis is that human beings are essentially good, but are corrupted by society: 'God makes all things good; man meddles with them and they become evil' (Rousseau, [1762] 1992, p. 5). By 'good' Rousseau seems to have meant 'natural' in the sense that we are all born 'naturally' innocent. Corruption could be waylaid through a radical reappraisal of how children were educated and reared. In contrast with Augustine, Rousseau saw humanity as characterised by 'original innocence'. Politically each perspective has very different implications. On the one hand, the idea that sin is innate and innocence must be taught/inculcated implies a strong, hierarchical government, whether at the macro level of the state or the micro level of the family-household. Law in such a system would almost certainly be patriarchal. If, on the other hand, children are seen as 'naturally' innocent, this infers that children themselves should be empowered in whatever ways are deemed necessary to struggle against a corrupt society. Laws in this case would be democratic and egalitarian.

Rousseau's idea of humanity as 'natural' was supported by reference to peasants, 'primitive' people and animals 'all of whom treat their young with a kind of judicious, health-giving neglect. On their model, he urges mothers to feed their children themselves, to abandon their swaddling clothes, to bath them regularly in cold water' (Jimack, 1992, p. xv). With the rapid growth of urbanisation from the end of the eighteenth century, there was increasingly a turning against the urban and a tendency to worship the rural. As industrial capitalism expanded and grew at an unprecedented rate, so there was a turning towards 'nature', craft, and simplicity. As colonialism and the Empire spread across the globe and Britain grew rich with, for example, profits from the slave trade abroad and exploitation of the working classes at home, there was a growing interest in the 'primitive': 'the child as savage became identified with the "Noble Savage" . . . and civilization was seen as the embodiment of corruption rather than a bastion against it. Children were innocent of the sin of the world and required protection from it' (Jackson, 1982, p. 43). But the notion of the protection is itself controversial. As recent crises in our own culture have illustrated, protectors themselves often corrupt those they allegedly protect. Protection suggests keeping children 'innocent' by keeping them ignorant, rather than offering them the necessary information and knowledge to protect themselves. It needs to be considered, therefore, whether in fact children's innocence is, in a real sense, largely created, maintained and defined by adults for their own reasons.

Bridging the more settled world of eighteenth century rationalism and the more turbulent world of the French, American and industrial revolutions, Rousseau was undoubtedly influenced by Locke's sensationalism. Émile, his representation of the ideal boy, is not to learn to read until after he is 12. He must be free to roam outdoors in loose clothing, learning by his own interests and experience in a 'natural' environment. Only in adolescence should he learn to be social, to read and write, and to master a craft. Allegedly free, he is none the less to be carefully guided and coached by an individual tutor – hardly an option available to most children at the time.

Émile's education, moreover, is to be radically different from that of his female counterpart's, Sophie. Sophie is to be trained and encouraged from an early age into domesticity and motherhood – her allegedly 'natural' state. Where Émile's education is to occur outdoors and in the wild, Sophie's is to be indoors and thoroughly domestic. Here we see Rousseau 'naturalising' difference between the male world of outdoor/public space and the female world of indoor/private: one pair of binary opposites that were crucial in defining late-eighteenth and early-nineteenth century middle-class notions of femininity, masculinity, childhood, and the family. Innocence for Rousseau was therefore a 'natural' state that was biologically given, both in relation to the material child and to society as symbolised by the child. Corruption, because it was socially constructed, could therefore be changed.

The initial reception of *Émile* was one of shock. A warrant was issued for Rousseau's arrest and he was forced to flee the country. The book, however, quickly created a climate for a new interest in the child, or more probably, reflected and gave voice to what were already nascent beliefs and trends. What *was* innovative, however, was that Rousseau gave 'an authoritative expression to the new sensibility, and to direct its interest towards childhood as a period of life when man most closely approximated to the "State of Nature"' (Coveney, 1967, p. 42). The centrality of the child and the importance of its perceived alliance with a natural world were themes that were represented and expressed in myriad ways by the Romantics. They remain central to our culture today.

## Representations of Innocence in Literature

Where Rousseau sought to represent the child both as a symbol, representative of humanity's inherent and natural goodness, and as a special category of embodied human being in need of new socio-political concern over rearing and education, Blake's vision of the child can be seen as overwhelmingly symbolic: 'His work was in essence a literature of human salvation. For the eighteenth-century poet William Blake, children were no occasional interest, no vehicle for a mere personal nostalgia. They were for him a symbol of innocence, without which, as a religious artist, he could not have worked' (Coveney, 1967, p. 52). Yet Blake's focus on, and commitment to, God was in no way doctrinal or orthodox. God for Blake lies within us all as a divine and creative potential that can be experienced and expressed through the imagination: 'For Blake the imagination is nothing less than God' (Bowra, 1961, p. 3). Imagination Blake sees as the route to the soul, the divine. The soul, however, manifests two different and opposing sides – 'without contraries there is no progression' – and this is the subject of *Songs of Innocence and Experience: Shewing the two Contrary States of the Human Soul* (see Ostriker, 1985). In this work the figure of the child is central.

Children in *Songs of Innocence* [1789] represent a state of prelapsarian happiness, trust, playfulness and a sense of unity with the universe. For Blake, these attributes are ones shared by all human beings *regardless of age* – they are the 'light' side of the human soul and form a 'childlike vision of existence' (Bowra, 1961, p. 30). Yet innocence can only have meaning in relation to experience; we may experience much of what Blake portrays when we are embodied children, but ultimately experience spoils, or threatens, imaginative play and 'mercy, pity, peace, and love' tend to lead to fear, greed, envy, cruelty and the ultimate destruction of love. Both aspects are within all of us, but experience does not ultimately mean we cannot access feelings associated with the light aspect of the soul, as symbolised by the child: 'Blake does not write at a distance of time from memories of what childhood once was, but from an insistent, present anguish at the ugly contrasts between the childlike and the experienced conceptions of reality' (Bowra, 1961, p. 30).

The images in *Songs of Innocence* are generally pastoral, rural and playful. In *Songs of Experience* [1794], where many of the poems of *Innocence* are mirrored with the same title, we find poverty and cruelty in a more urban landscape. The lamb of innocence has become the tiger of experience. While the images can be taken as symbolic of a soul made barren by experience, they also indicate outrage at socioeconomic conditions which thwart and pervert and can ultimately destroy imagination, the creative spirit, and thus human freedom and potential.

Comparing, for example, the two poems both entitled 'Holy Thursday', in the first, in *Innocence*, Blake describes children from a foundling hospital being led to St Paul's:

> . . . O what a multitude they seemed these flowers of
>     London town
> Seated in companies they sit with radiance all their
>     own
> The hum of multitudes was there but multitudes of
>     lambs
> Thousands of little boys and girls raising their innocent
>     hands
>
> Now like a mighty wind they raise to heaven the voice
>     of song
> Or like harmonious thunderings the seats of heaven
>     among
> Beneath them sit the aged men wise guardians of the
>     poor
> Then cherish pity, lest you drive an angel from your
>     door
> ('Holy Thursday', *Songs of Innocence*)

The children in this are more akin to angels than to real children; their singing is heavenly; they are radiant lambs; their guardians seem like divine patriarchs rather than grumpy old beadles. They seem otherworldly, ethereal and as such seem to represent the divine in us all, perhaps in the way such experiences may be felt by children who have not yet understood corruption. In this sense it is about the potential within all humans to experience the divine. Compare this poem, however, with the 'Holy Thursday' in *Songs of Experience*:

Is this a holy thing to see,
In a rich and fruitful land,
Babes reduced to misery,
Fed with cold and usurous hand?

Is that trembling cry a song?
Can it be a song of joy?
And so many children poor?
It is a land of poverty!

And their sun does never shine.
And their fields are bleak and bare.
And their ways are fill'd with thorns.
It is eternal winter there.

For where-e'r the sun does shine,
And where-e'r the rain does fall:
Babe can never hunger there,
Nor poverty the mind appall.
('Holy Thursday', *Songs of Experience*)

Here the land is dark, full of poverty, barren and cold. The reference to thorns suggests Christ's betrayal, and the landscape might be compared to Hell or Purgatory – though, because God for Blake is within the human being, it is a human hell devoid of spirit and imagination. It is the dark side of the human soul, ultimately necessary to the light side.

True innocence for Blake can only develop out of experience, and thus the child is very much a symbol of the soul and the soul's potential that lies within us if we can overcome the stultifying effects of fear, greed and envy in a rationalistic, unimaginative material world:

Blake wrote against the fundamentals of English rationalism ... Bacon's experimental method, Newton's materialist physics, and Locke's sensationalism came under his complete anathema. Together they represented the baneful influence of Reason, the power of the abstracted intellect as a force against Life ... Men lay enslaved beneath 'system', and their enfranchisement could only come through a renewed awareness of their original innocence. (Coveney, 1966, p. 53)

Blake insists that we need to know and acknowledge both innocence and evil in this world, but primarily within ourselves, if we
are to achieve the realisation of our innate spiritual and creative
potential. For Blake, the solution to what he saw as an increasingly inhuman and rationalistic world lay in people striving to
find, to rediscover, their own imaginative powers, their own
'inward vision'. Only thus could they – we – find innocence.
Blake's notion of innocence is therefore quite different from Augustine's, which depended on Christian belief and practice, and
which, while clearly a statement about humanity generally, was
also used to define children's 'nature' specifically.

Many of Blake's ideas have been influential in the theories of
twentieth-century archetypal thinkers such as Jung, Hillman and
Moore, who have stressed the importance of the 'shadow' and
the 'underworld' in the human psyche. Freud's theory of the
unconscious, of course, was also seminal to these, but where
Freud stressed the scientific and rational, in particular the notion
of there being innate biological 'drives', archetypal theorists have
focused on the spiritual and creative aspects, and in this sense
their work can be seen more as a direct legacy from Blake, Goethe
and Schiller.

Hillman, for example, argues that Christianity, by making the
Devil/underworld taboo, both stunted potential growth of the
spirit by forbidding us to descend into and welcome the dark side
as part of the whole, and in so doing also keeping the fear alive,
thus negating the light/Christ side. Only by losing Christ, he
argues,

> could the underworld reappear and then as perdition, damna-
> tion and terror. This terror led to a whole new problem: the
> underworld as the devil's realm. To fear the devil (and what
> other reaction is possible in view of this intolerable image?)
> indicated his nearness, which also indicated one was in danger
> of losing Christ. So the devil was established by the fear. The
> devil image still haunts in our fear of the unconscious and the
> latent psychosis that supposedly lurks there, and we still turn
> to methods of Christianism – moralizing, kind feelings, com-
> munal sharing, and childlike naiveté – as propitiations against
> our fear, instead of the classical descent into it, the *nekyia* into
> imagination. (Hillman, 1979b, p. 88)

Arguably both strands haunt us still, witness the confusion and mixed responses to Bulger's murder, where children played the opposing roles of both innocent victim and evil perpetrators: both Christ and the Devil juxtaposed, the one sanctified, the other two demonised. The 'demonic' children are now locked away, their futures not decided by the rule of law but by the intervention of a government obliged to show extreme tactics for a transgression that seemed to defy the core of our notions of what children should be – and thus what we ourselves are. By not allowing for the evil, the dark, the violent within children – and within ourselves – we are always externalising it, always creating monsters and demons, forever denying our own potential growth and wholeness embracing both dark and light, good and evil, innocence and corruption.

Thomas Moore, in his study of de Sade, explores 'the undeniable tendencies of the soul towards the outrageously dark' (Moore, 1990, p. 5) where 'the mythology of de Sade can be seen . . . as a particular instance of the pathologizing need of the soul'. De Sade, he contends, specifically targeted innocence, as well as and as part of Christianity, drawing attention to the way in which innocence and corruption constellate and depend on each other in all of us. This is represented in de Sade by the innocent Justine and the corrupt libertine:

> Justine's innocence inflames the libertines. The more she exposes her naiveté, the more they want her . . . Innocence inspires inspection. What kind of heart could be so innocent? The libertine enquires . . . Inspection itself, of any kind, partakes of the libertine's cruelty . . . What seems harmless inspection can easily turn into sadistic torture. Media delight in inspecting innocence betrayed, has become so common and 'natural' in our world today that we take it for granted and are unaware of the pain our efforts bring to earth, to society, and to individuals. (Moore, 1990, pp. 38–40, passim)

Moore sees de Sade's message as one that is very much needed in contemporary society: 'Feelings of guilt invite us to consider innocence with a look at our own cruelty. As a symptom, feeling guilty sustains innocence, but it also invites responsibility' (Moore, 1990, p. 42).

Perplexity, horror and fascination constantly haunt us over representations of violence, cruelty, serial murders, children who kill, women who kill, and sexual abuse of all kinds. Increasingly, and quite understandably, parents respond by incarcerating children in the home, forbidding them to play outside without adult supervision, driving them to school and extracurricular activities well into adolescence in such a way that the home has for many become akin to a prison. Several incidents in recent years, and in particular the tragic massacre of schoolchildren at Dunblane Primary School in 1996, have prompted fears about danger in schools and the need for more protection, and we may well see an increase in security and prison-like protection at schools. Violence *within* schools also seems to be increasing, especially in those areas where selective education operates, and one or two schools in an area become centres for pupils not acceptable in a selective school, such as occurred in the Ridings school in Halifax, Yorkshire, in the autumn of 1996. Teachers have become increasingly subject to violent attacks by students.

Protection, however, is a two-edged sword. We do need to question the extent to which protection of innocence/innocents also keeps children disempowered, ignorant and thus ultimately more vulnerable. Moreover, for many the dangers lie more within the home than outside it. Danger is forever projected outwards: outside, on to city and suburban streets, on to psychopaths, on to the mentally ill, on to different religious and ethnic groups. While, of course, there *is* danger outwards, rarely do we question at an individual or family level where the darkness lies, rarely do we seek to question where cruelty and corruption lie and lurk within ourselves.

Innocence for William Wordsworth (1770–1850) was deeply rooted in the 'natural' and physical world. Where Blake did not write from his own specific 'self', or even so much from his specific world[1] and certainly not from specific children, Wordsworth was to write from his personal experiences. Innocence for Blake, as epitomised by the symbol of the child, stands for the potential of humanity for love, creativity and freedom. For Wordsworth, however, the child is something quite different, for he represents it as part and parcel of his own child*hood* as remembered by an adult looking back in time. Central to this 'child' is a sense of oneness with both his own physical body and the physi-

cal world that surrounded him in childhood, which he also links
to a sense of the divine. It is from this that the child's unique
innocence springs:

Oh! Many a time have I, a five years Child,
A naked Boy, in one delightful Rill,
A little Mill-race sever'd from his stream,
Made one long bathing of a summer's day,
Bask'd in the sun, and plunged, and bask'd again
Alternate all a summer's day, or cours'd
Over the sandy fields, leaping through groves
Of yellow grunsel, or when crag and hill,
The woods, and distant Skiddaw's lofty height,
Were bronz'd with a deep radiance, stood alone
Beneath the sky, as if I had been born
On Indian Plains, and from my Mother's hut
Had run abroad in wantonness, to sport,
A naked Savage, in the thunder shower.
(Wordsworth, *The Prelude*, I, 291–300 [first published in 1805])

It is not just the child's joy in nature and his own body that is
apparent here; this is a *recollection*, and as such draws on the past
from the adult's perspective of childhood as a 'lost Eden'. The
child here is a memoried child, re-interpreted by the adult, reconstructed, and arguably idealised in that process. In this way it is
made both personal (and arguably distorted by memory) and
universalised. He is both talking about memories about himself
as a boy *and* making statements and generalisations about childhood innocence and the 'nature' of the child on a wider basis.
This hearkening back to a prelapsarian childhood which then
becomes the basis for wider generalisations about childhood lies
at the core of the more sentimental view of the child that was to
develop from the nineteenth century onwards. It also bears witness to the increasing trend towards interiorisation, in which
adults were more and more looking inwards, as well as back-
wards in time, to their own personal childhood.

It is also interesting to note how Wordsworth compares the
child in this passage to a 'naked Savage' on 'Indian Plains'. Since
the explorations and discoveries from the fifteenth century onwards there had been a growing interest in the notion of the

'Noble Savage' which was believed to represent what people had been like prior to 'civilisation' (and colonialisation). Such 'Noble Savages' were seen as encapsulating an essence of humanity and were used, for instance, in Haeckel's 'law of recapitulation'. Earlier, Shakespeare explored this idea in the character of Caliban in *The Tempest*. In this century, Boas drew attention to the traits of cults of primitivism which have at different times focused on Women, the Child, the Folk, and the Noble Savage:

> They were all supposed to have some, if not all, of the characteristics which had been attributed to the Noble Savage. Above all there was a kind of intuitive wisdom in them as contrasted with learning . . . a keener appreciation of beauty, not of course the beauties of the academy but of something called Nature . . . there was a greater sensitivity to moral values . . . a general anti-intellectualism which had been growing since sixteenth century . . . [and] happened synchronously with the advancement of the natural sciences. (Boas, 1966)

The child, Boas argues, becomes easily substituted for the chronologically primitive, unspoiled by the artifices of civilisation. There is a theme in primivitism of innate wisdom and thus a parallel anti-intellectualism 'which . . . has developed almost step by step with the progress of natural science' (Grylls, 1978, p. 30). This stress on intuition, feeling and 'natural innocence', which can be seen as both essentialist and anti-intellectual, is often used in representations of the child.[2] Images of Native Latin American children, for example, are often exploited to represent messages about the destruction and/or beauties of the rainforests. Much New Age discourse, inherently anti-intellecutal, relies heavily on the ideas of 'the child' and a primitivism characterised by 'back to nature'.

In Wordsworth primitivism frequently goes hand in hand with a veneration of 'nature' and the animal world. Consider, for instance, these lines from *Tintern Abbey*:

> . . . like a roe
> I bounded o'er the mountains, by the sides
> of the deep rivers, and the lonely streams,
> Wherever nature led: more like a man

Flying from something that he dreads than one
Who sought the thing he loved. For nature then
(the coarser pleasures of my boyish days,
And their glad animal movements all gone by)
To me was all in all ...
(Wordsworth, *Tintern Abbey*)

Innocence here is implicitly defined as natural, and this natural innocence is animal, instinctual, totally rooted in the body. The child experiences fear as an animal would, and is above all *unaware* of the beauty of the place, of the inevitability of time and ageing, of adult knowledge. It is an innocence that has its own knowing, but a knowledge akin to that of a deer, not in any way akin to adult knowledge that could reflect on, analyse and make sense of the experience.

This idea that the child has a different kind of knowing, an otherness that sets it apart from the adult world, was examined some hundred years after Wordsworth by the Swiss psychologist Jean Piaget. Although Piaget's work has been to a great extent discredited, particularly his theory that there are set ages at which children reach various stages, the theory none the less raises important issues about childhood innocence in relation to knowledge:

> Imagine a being, knowing nothing of the distinction between mind and body. Such a being would be aware of his desires and feelings, but his notions of Self would undoubtedly be much less clear than ours ... he would experience much less the sensation of the thinking self ... the feeling of a being interdependent of the external worlds ... the psychological perceptions ... would ... be entirely different from our own. Dreams ... would appear to him as a disturbance breaking in from without. Words would be bound up with things and to speak would mean to act directly on these things. Inversely, external things would be less material and would be endowed with intentions and will. (Piaget, 1973, p. 9)

Moreover, Piaget argues that up to the age of ten or eleven 'there is confusion between thought and body ... [and] there is confusion between the sign and the thing signified, the thought and the thing thought of . . . the child cannot distinguish a real house . . . from the concept or mental image or name of the house' (Piaget, [1929] 1973, p. 71). Whether or not he was wrong about the specific ages and stages, the question as to how much children know and understand of the adult world, adult morality, and adult behaviour remains central, and contentious, to the idea of innocence.

This was a theme considered with great insight by Henry James in his novel *What Maisie Knew*. Maisie is the child of divorced parents who use her in their various amorous entanglements, exposing her to all kinds of adult corruption and squalid behaviour in the process. James explores the extent to which this exposure to adult corruption threatens her innocence – in the sense of her knowledge: from the beginning 'either from extreme cunning or from extreme stupidity, she appeared not to take things in'. Maisie's moral innocence appears to be protected by her innocence in the sense of not-knowingness. Her development, her maturing, is marked by gradual awareness of corruption: 'It was to be the fate of this patient little girl to see much more than she at first understood, but also even at first to understand much more than any little girl, however patient, had perhaps ever understood before' (James, [1908] 1980, p. 15).

The issue of understanding is thus crucial. It is pivotal to debates as to whether, and when, children can testify in court. But it is not just about the difference between 'truth' and 'falsehood' and children's ability to differentiate the two. Adults at times quite deliberately misrepresent fiction as truth to children – Father Christmas and the Tooth Fairy being classic cases in point. Arguably there is a sense in which adults deliberately blur the boundary between truth and falsehood as part of their own mental representation of what they want childhood to be and how they want *their* idea of innocence to characterise children generally. Postman (1985), for example, has bemoaned the 'disappearance' of childhood as a result of children being exposed extensively to adult television. But if Piaget's theory has some cogency, and if James were right, then children make their own sense of the adult world in their own time, and exposure to such knowledge and behaviour, however corrupt, may not have any direct impact on their understanding and behaviour in relation to it.

The issue has more to do with the ability to think as an adult, whether or not such thought is actually 'true' or 'false'. Edmund Gosse, for example, showed in his autobiographical work, *Father and Son*, how his father was unable to grasp or accept that his young son perceived and made sense of the world differently from himself:

> My father's religious teaching to me was almost exclusively doctrinal. He did not observe the value of negative education, that is to say, of leaving Nature alone to fill up the gaps which it is her design to deal with at a later and riper date . . . He was in a tremendous hurry to push on my spiritual growth, and he fed me with theological meat which it was impossible for me to digest. Some glimmer of a suspicion that he was sailing on the wrong tack must . . . have broken in upon him when we had reached the eighth and ninth chapters of Hebrews, where, addressing readers who had been brought up under the Jewish dispensation . . . the apostle battles with their dangerous conservatism . . . Suddenly by my flushing up with anger and saying, 'O how I do hate that Law,' my Father perceived, and paused in amazement to perceive, that I took the Law to be a person of malignant temper from whose cruel bondage, and from whose intolerable tyranny and unfairness, some excellent person was crying out to be delivered. I wished to hit Law with my fist, for being so mean and unreasonable. (Gosse, [1907] 1989, pp. 92–3)

It would seem that children see the same things as adults, but do not always make the same interpretations of them. As the Opies found in their seminal studies of children's culture and play, children make sense of their own world in their own way (Opie and Opie, 1969). From discussing how adults perceive and represent childhood innocence, then, we come to the silence of children themselves and whether concepts such as 'innocence' or 'corruption' can have any meaning for them with regard to their own experiences. Always, however, such themes are explored by the adult looking back through the distorted mirror of memory.

Certainly I have no memories of feeling innocent. I can remember feeling hurt, betrayed, confused. Some of this, I think, may have been as much a result of enforced secrecy as it was of actual abuse. If I had been able to talk about what had happened to me and the feelings I experienced of pain, fear and grief without dread of punishment, I do not think the scars would have been so severe or lasted as long as they did. Innocence was not an issue to me at the time; I cannot remember a sense of having 'lost' either my innocence or my childhood. That came later, when I was a middle-aged adult.

Memory was central for Wordsworth in relation to his feelings about the loss of childhood. The child for him, looking back through memory, has become 'other':

> . . . I cannot paint
> What then I was . . .
> That time is past
> And all its aching joys are now no more,
> And all its dizzy raptures
> (Wordsworth, *Tintern Abbey*)

We have here what was to become a template for 'the child' and childhood innocence in the nineteenth and twentieth centuries: other, idyllic, prelapsarian, something that we once were, or owned, and which is now forever lost. Loss is the overriding theme and emotional focus of this poem; it is a loss informed by melancholic yearning. Innocence here is represented as both 'natural' and 'animal' and thus opposite to knowledge and reason. Wordsworth, while drawing to some extent on Blake's vision of the child, redefines it in a primitivist way that laid the foundations for sentimentalisation and was crucial to the ongoing process of interiorisation.

Between the poetry of the Romantics and the novels of Dickens lay only a few decades, but a sea change in society, polity and economy. Urbanisation, industrialisation and the population itself had all grown at unprecedented rates. Waves of migrants from country to town helped to swell the rapidly expanding cities and towns where disease, overcrowding, poverty and filth proliferated and became more visible than ever before. The hold of the traditional church was in decline, yet Wesleyanism and Evangelicalism were on the increase. People were marrying younger, the birth rate soared, the death rate began to decline with the waning of plagues and epidemics. Children were everywhere, but were most noticeable in city streets. Child labour, most visibly that in mills and factories, helped to swell the profits of the nascent industrial bourgeoisie. The child became a focus for acrimonious debates about child labour, freedom, slavery, as well as becoming the subject of an increasing amount of literature, both for children and about children. Children were well and truly on the Victorian agenda both as embodied beings and as representations of wider ideas and themes, the two, then as now, often conflated and confused.

Where Wordsworth's children can be seen as 'wild', growing up in the countryside and in close association with nature, more akin to animals and the 'Noble Savage' than to adults, the children represented by Dickens were much more domestic and urban beings. Girls appear as characters in their own right, usually represented as either stupid and devious (Mercy and Charity in *Martin Chuzzlewit*, for example), or as pure, angelic and devoid of any trace of wickedness, much less sexuality (Sissy Jupe, Little Nell, Florence Dombey). Both girls and boys are represented by Dickens as 'other', as special, and as 'spiritually wiser than adults, better equipped by nature as seers, prophets and guides' (Grylls, 1978, p. 35).

Dickens' children, unlike those of Blake, are children in and of society. Overwhelmingly representing the redeeming powers of feeling, they grapple with forces of evil: greed, utilitarianism and rationalism *in extremis*: 'goodness is always characterised through individuals remarkable for their generous flow of human feeling' (Coveney, 1967, p. 113). They tend to be born heroes in their emotional innocence and then victimised by a ruthless and uncaring society as represented by adults or, as for example in *Dombey and Son*, parent(s). Dombey in his greed and self-centredness corrupts little Paul by not acknowledging or allowing childhood to be carefree, innocent, different, and, above all, a time for love and joy. In this sense Dickens' children are the heirs of Rousseau.

Unlike Blake and Wordsworth, however, Dickens equates childhood innocence not only with emotion and purity, but also with death and pathos: 'With Dickens' children, we find both the pathos and the idealisation – and sometimes, perhaps, the squalid as well. We feel his emotions rush towards the image and accumulate about it, until his children become sometimes no more than the accumulated presence of his own self-pity' (Coveney, 1967, p. 159). Here is clear evidence of the Christian tradition originating in the Holy Innocents that associates children with death. Where Wordsworth and Blake used children to represent joy, life and delight in the natural world, and indeed, at least for Blake, in human potential, Dickens' children are often characterised by morbidity. Paul Dombey's death, for instance, is given great attention without the reader ever really knowing why – except that, by dying, he facilitates a new life in a kind of parody of Christ. The message ultimately is that children can be sacrificed, are sacrificed, indeed, need to be sacrificed, in order to achieve a better social world. Sacrifice is, of course, a central tenet of Christianity.

The theme of sacrifice is one that also characterises George Eliot's novels, most notably in *The Mill on the Floss* [1860]. Maggie Tulliver is a lively, passionate, imaginative and intelligent little girl who is far more interested in books and stories than she is in her appearance or her 'femininity'. Eliot presents her as at once innocent in her sincerity and deep feelings, and at the same time as carrying the seed of original sin in her passion for, and fascination with, the wild and undomesticated aspects of self and life, as symbolised by the attic and the gypsies. Her character is anomalous amid the narrow conventions and boundaries of provincial bourgeois society with its strict and limiting definitions of norms and standards for women. As her father comments: 'She's twice as 'cute as Tom. Too 'cute for a woman, I'm afraid . . . It's no mischief while she's a little un, but an over 'cute woman's no better nor a long-tailed sheep' (Eliot, [1860] 1979, p. 60). As a child such an anomaly can be passed over as innocent and harmless, yet with maturity, if not abandoned, it leads to downfall, destruction and ultimately death. If Maggie Tulliver, representing all intelligent and spirited girls and women, wants to fit in with society, she has to sacrifice her own self.

Maggie Tulliver's delight in the natural world as a child is almost Wordsworthian, but from the beginning it is clear she also carries the *potential* for sin and tragedy. The message is not unlike that conveyed by the *Portrait of Catharina Hooft* (see Figure 4) discussed in Chapter 4. Eliot seems to suggest that childhood – or girlhood – though by no means always a happy time, still carries moments of joy as well as the potential for pain and evil. In Maggie's case this potential is implicitly sexual, which was certainly a core belief in Victorian culture, where the madonna figure was frequently juxtaposed with, defined in relation to, the whore.

Victorian women – respectable Victorian women – were idealised as asexual, domestic and pure, and such ideals were also applied to children. As a girl, Maggie can be seen as innocent, yet her innocence is conditional and precarious, resting on her need to deny passion, intelligence and love (Eros) as soon as she leaves girlhood. Yet these are her very character traits and, by being unable to deny them as demanded by society, she is destroyed. Sexuality is in this way never an issue for boys, whether in Eliot's novels or Dickens' or other contemporaries. Eliot, through the character of Maggie Tulliver, thus highlights and problematises the gendering of childhood – and, indeed, the gendering of innocence – and represents the dilemmas this poses, and posed, for girls and women who were both defined by, and at the same time denied, their sexuality.

Just as women have long been stereotyped as madonnas or whores, so little girls have been typecast as either little angels (sugar and spice and all things nice) or as little vixens, Lolitas and flirts. Innocence for girls seems therefore more precarious because of sexual traits and expectations projected on to them by adults from a very early age. Consider, for instance, Belotti's findings about flirtatiousness in infant girls and boys:

> Flirtatiousness at one year and even beyond is common to both sexes. Eibl-Eibesfeldt describes it as an innate behaviour pattern of approach and flight which has become a ritual inviting pursuit . . . As boys grow older, this kind of behaviour gradually disappears. In girls it persists precisely because of the reactions it receives from adults. The girl's flirtatiousness is solicited and encouraged, since she is seen as being already so 'feminine'. In the case of the boy, his attempts at flirtatiousness are not accepted, and he is taught other patterns of behaviour. (Belotti, 1975, p. 54)

Where Dickens divided his girls between good ones and bad ones, Eliot's Maggie Tulliver carries the seeds of both, and thus problematises the notion of innocence, particularly in its sense of being defined as opposite to evil.

Mark Twain [1885] also used the character of a 'bad' child to represent and explore notions of innocence in *The Adventures of Huckleberry Finn*, though innocence in this book, presumably because Huck is a boy, carries no connotations of sexuality as it does for Maggie Tulliver. Twain, like Blake, Dickens and Wordsworth, used a child to represent the heart, or soul, in the nineteenth-century debate of head versus heart. Though it is possible to analyse Huck as a character in his own right, an individual who experiences acute moral dilemma, his problem can be seen as a more general exploration of the notion of innocence in relation to issues such as slavery and money, which resonate in a tension between the river and the 'sivilization' of the towns.

There is a third place, however, that is central to this book: the woods. It is here that Huck escapes from 'sivilization' to be 'free', with echoes of the ideals of Rousseau and Wordsworth. Yet it is the woods where his Pap takes him and where, though Huck is able to enjoy fishing and hunting in a kind of romantic primitivism, he is also subject to being brutally beaten and incarcerated by his father. Implicit in this seems to be Twain's critique of romantic primitivism, showing that 'nature' can be not only a source of food and pleasure, but also a site of senseless brutality and violence.

While the river may be natural, the raft is not, and though Huck and Jim live a life on it very different from that of on the shore – a life without money, slavery, clothes or conventional morality – it is none the less a life that is based primarily on a human relationship, and thus on society. Life on the raft represents Twain's view of what he believed people were capable of being; central to this is his concept of innocence, both in the sense of 'not knowing', and in terms of being uncorrupted. It shows his ideal of a morality distinct from conventional morality, yet firmly based on human relationship and love, rather than on an idealised version of nature. This is highlighted in Twain's treatment of Huck, who is in conventional terms a 'bad' boy. He steals chickens and watermelons, disobeys the law on fugitive slaves, spurns school, church and neat clothes. Yet he is innocent in terms of his consistent ability to forgive and see the good in the worst of characters, such as when he feels sorry for the King and Duke after they have been tarred and feathered by the mob.

Huck's central dilemma is whether or not to obey the law and turn Jim in. Twain shows Huck developing a moral conscience which focuses on his growing respect for Jim as an equal human being, in contrast with what he 'knows', has been taught by adults, to be right. In this sense Huck learns *not* to 'know', not to subscribe to social laws and conventions, but to obey his heart rather than his head. The tension between head and heart operates simultaneously at an individual and a symbolic level, hovering between innocence and corruption, the river and the towns. Huck, in this sense, *achieves* innocence through experience when he opts to 'go to hell' against everything he has been taught, so as to save Jim. This learning of innocence through experience seems directly comparable to Blake's ideas in *Songs of Innocence and Experience*. Ironically, it also directly echoes the Christian tenet of attaining innocence through baptism, but with the difference that in order to attain innocence, Huck has to *reject* conventional Christian values.

Twain's treatment of innocence, however, goes beyond the realm of the individual and can be seen as a metaphor for society before its 'corruption' by the Civil War, the coming of the railroads, and the efflorescence of industrial capitalism. Setting the book in ante-bellum America, when the steamboats were still a central part of a frontier and 'innocent' society, gives the novel an extra layer that seems to echo Huck's age – on the threshold of puberty, still sexually innocent, about to plunge into the chaos, excitement and corruption of adult masculinity. By narrating in the voice of the innocent, the child, Twain also achieves an irony that suggests at some level that this innocence itself, while always a worthy goal, is also transient and, as the river flows on and boys become men, is also liable to eventual change and corruption.

If innocence in *Huckleberry Finn* is more transient, more ambiguous, we can see this happening to a far greater extent in Henry James' [1907] masterpiece, *The Turn of the Screw*. Here ambiguity over innocence and corruption, implicitly sexual, is at the core of the work. Controversy has long raged as to whether it is the children, eight-year-old Flora and ten-year-old Miles, who have been corrupted by two former disreputable servants who died under strange circumstances, or whether it is in fact the governess, the 20-year-old daughter of a vicar, who is susceptible to terror (as the only one who sees the apparitions), and is herself going mad. There are sexual innuendoes which can either be read as suggesting her 'hysteria' as triggered by her attraction to the children's absent uncle, or could imply some kind of sexual abuse by the dead servants.

Edmund Wilson (1988) argues that the governess hallucinates the ghosts and there is strong sexual symbolism in the male ghost who appears on the tower, the female on the far side of the lake, and the scene where Flora fits a wooden mast to the base of the boat. Other critics have labelled the governess as a 'vampire' (Gorley Putt, quoted in Wilson, 1988, p. 19) and Miles a victim of 'emotional cannibalism'. Fraser, a psychiatrist, sees Miles' insistent wish to be among boys as expression of homosexual yearnings and indicative of Henry James' paedophiliac desires; the horror of Peter Quint he interprets as James' horror of his own sexual attraction to little boys (Fraser, quoted in Wilson, 1988, p. 20).

Others, however, argue that it is the children who are corrupt. Why else would Miles have been expelled from school? Why does he steal the letter? Why is he prowling outside at night? Christine Brook-Rose, however, in *A Rhetoric of the Unreal*, argues convincingly that 'ambiguity is the essential attribute of a tale of the fantastic and therefore the issue is never intended to be resolved' (quoted in Wilson, 1988, p. 23). It is this ambiguity which throughout creates the tension and causes the reader to reflect on the very nature of children. Is it possible for children of eight and ten to be corrupt? Can a child retain innocence regardless of what evil they may have inflicted, or indeed, have had inflicted on them? And, if so, what exactly is the nature of this innocence? Is it the ability to fully comprehend evil, as Piaget might suggest? Or is the issue of innocence one that only relates to adult projections on to children, adult ideals of what they would like 'the child' to be? James attempts no answer to these questions, but merely provokes reflection. The book therefore encapsulates much of what still remain core questions relating to issues of innocence and childhood.

Children themselves, like Miles and Flora in the book, are silent on the issue. Miles and Flora say remarkably little; all the verbal and imaginative action occurs through the narrator's reading of the governess's account, within which is scarce dialogue with the children. It is a narrative of a young adult wrestling with what *she* thinks and feels about the children, and what it is possible for children to be and do. As the daughter of a vicar, there is a suggestion that this dilemma is also a religious, or spiritual, one. I find Wilson's theory that it is her desire for the absent uncle less than cogent in its attempt to impose a Freudian interpretation on the text, for it is *the children* on whom the words, images, struggle and desire focus. Again and again she calls them beautiful, angelic, and constantly wants to be with them – 'protecting' them – but also implicitly wanting to possess them:

> There was something in this beautiful little boy, something extraordinarily sensitive, yet extraordinarily happy, that, more than in any creature of his age I have seen, struck me as beginning anew each day. He had never for a second suffered. I took this as a direct disproof of his having really been chastised. If he had been wicked he would have 'caught' it, and I should have caught it on the rebound . . . I could reconstitute nothing at all, and he was therefore an angel (Wilson, 1988, p. 168)

The sexual yearning seems clear in this passage, whether we take it as the governess's yearning for Miles (not Flora) or as a disguise for James' yearning for little boys. It is noteworthy, however, that this passage is followed immediately by the appearance of the ugly and terrifying face at the window who 'had come for some one else'. When the governess places her own face where the apparition's had been, surely this implies that the ugly side, looking through to beauty with such yearning, is *hers*? And, of course, also James'. The homoerotic yearnings are disguised by the complexities of narration: a governess's story told by a male narrator as written by a male author.

There is a battle here between good and evil in the context of the boy's beauty and the desire it evokes in the adult which is linked to the appearance of an ugly and disreputable face. It is interesting to note how in earlier debates it had been the governess who incurred the wrath of critics, with her alleged 'hysteria' forced into a Freudian mould in which she was blamed for corrupt desire. But the uncle has little substance and all the passion expressed is for the children – and the feelings that result from this as represented by the ghosts. The structure of the work disguises and distances adult desire for children. But the question of whether or not the children themselves can be, or have been, corrupted, remains.

This question, of course, is still as controversial now as it was in James' day. To what extent can a young human being perceived by adults as beautiful and innocent be capable of inflicting pain on others? Surely ultimately the issue is about adult notions of beauty, innocence, desire – and childhood. There is plenty of evidence that children can be brutal, violent and cruel. Roddy Doyle's (1993) novel *Paddy Clarke Ha Ha Ha*, for example, conveys this, as do the many instances of child bullies, and the rare ones of children who kill. Adult denial of violence in children surely has to do with the ways in which adults have represented children and childhood, the ways in which they have projected on to them their own ideals and muddled memories of what they would like children and childhood to be – or to have been.

Whether or not, and at what age, children *understand* adult morality – with all its contradictions – is another question. Children perceive and know, it would seem, in different ways from adults, although it is unclear exactly how, or indeed when this changes. Innocence has been, and remains, one of the main ways in which this difference has been defined, idealised and represented by adults. Because innocence is synonymous with ignorance, therefore, there is a real sense in which adults seeking to 'protect' what they define as innocence results in prolonging dependency, ignorance and disempowerment in children.

# 6

## CHILDREN'S SEXUALITY: WHY DO ADULTS PANIC?

My father gave my sister a book on Freud for her thirteenth birthday. My mother, however, was furious and screamed and shouted at him, saying that it was totally inappropriate. His action, and her reaction, fascinated me, because for all the covert abuse that went on in our family, rarely had I witnessed such overt anger and confrontation as this. What was so terrible about Freud, I wondered, that could provoke such intense feelings? I (aged ten) saved up all my pocket money and went to the drugstore to buy my own copy of Freud. But the local drugstore had no Freud, only Adler. Still, the blurb on the back said Adler *knew* Freud and had worked with him, so I bought it. I couldn't make head nor tail of it. Where was the scandal, the shock, the titillation? All I could glean was obscure talk about power. What a waste of money, I thought. Later, I managed to sneak a read of my sister's Freud when she was away for the day. Somewhat more interesting, with references to penises and faeces, I still had trouble understanding what all the fuss had been about.

Reflecting on this event in later years, and giving my mother the benefit of the doubt, I thought perhaps her outrage had been connected with her wanting to protect my sister at a time in her life when issues about sexuality would have been particularly sensitive. But that didn't really seem to apply to our ménage, nor to my mother's love of D. H. Lawrence and Henry Miller. I could only conclude that her anger had something to do with Freud's theory of the Oedipus complex. In this he denied his earlier acceptance of women's accounts of being sexually abused by male relatives, mostly fathers and step-fathers, and concluded they were all the women's fantasies. Almost certainly a ploy to protect his practice in *fin-de-siècle* Vienna – not a time or place that would have accepted such shocking revelations – Freud not only betrayed the trust and integrity of his own women patients, but also of thousands of women throughout the twentieth century whose accounts of abuse were persistently dismissed as fantasy by analysts and therapists who subscribed to Freud's theory.[1] How well such a theory suited men like my father who could treat and mistreat daughters as they chose without any fear of recrimination! What a clever, sneaky birthday present, as if he were telling my sister, as she stood precariously on the threshold between childhood and adolescence, that everything that had gone on between them was just her (twisted) imagination, her own sick fantasies.

Physiological sexual maturity has in recent times often been seen as marking the boundary between childhood and adulthood, intimating that there is a radical difference that changes a person irretrievably, and that this change is rooted in, defined by, sexual maturity. In spite of Freud's insistence that children are sexual beings, they are still rarely regarded as such, and there are now, more than ever, a plethora of rules and regulations that define sex as the exclusive realm of adults. Transgression of such rules, as we have seen, jeopardises a child's chance to even be considered as a child. 'On both sides of the moral barricade,' Jackson points out, 'sexuality is singled out as a special area of life, as sacred or taboo, as elevating or degrading' (Jackson, 1982, p. 2). In the creation of children as 'other', as special, which has arguably been ongoing for at least the past 200 years, much of this otherness has been premised on an exclusion from knowledge of adult sexuality:

> It is the sexual 'innocence' of children that above all else distinguishes them from adults . . . Our children are asexual, apolitical, vulnerable, dependent, incapable of taking part in serious adult pursuits not because that is the way children naturally *are* but because that it [*sic*] the way they are treated. (Jackson, 1982, p. 28)

Children, then, are generally defined as *a*sexual.

## What is Sexuality?

Sexuality is one of those terms we all use frequently yet seldom stop to consider what different shades of meaning might be contained within it. I think it can usefully be divided into the following broad categories: first, the biological, physical aspects, which include the body and its sensations, its ability to reproduce, and sexual acts; second, the social and political aspects, which include sexual identity and sexual relationships; third, the psychological aspects which include fantasies and desire, both conscious and unconscious. There is arguably a fourth category which spreads its net over the other three: pleasure.

The biological aspects of sexuality relate first to embodiment, and embodiment differs between women and men, adults and children. It is not physically possible for a girl to bear a child or a boy to impregnate a girl or woman until they are sexually mature in a physiological sense, which is almost always long before such acts become socially and legally acceptable. Reproduction, however, is only one aspect of sexuality, and only one aspect of embodied sexuality. It is in, or via, the body that sexual acts are carried out and experienced, and these include not only heterosexual intercourse, but also buggery, fellatio, cunnilingus, bestiality, masturbation.

The body is the vehicle through which we experience pain and pleasure, although arguably much of this is in fact a result of the psychological aspects of fantasy and desire. Freud argued that from birth children experience sexual pleasure, in a similarly diffuse way, throughout their bodies and various orifices: they are, he said, 'polymorphously perverse'. By this he meant that the pleasures a baby experiences come from many different sources: from being fed, for instance, or being held, but also from being tickled or sung to, from playing with its feet, fingers or genitals, from having its nappy changed or moving its bowels. None of these early pleasures is sex-specific, nor do they depend on who performs them. They are basic physical experiences, however, that lie at the root of all our subsequent sensual and sexual pleasures.

What was outrageous about this theory at the time (and remains so, arguably, for many still) is that the logical conclusion to it is that it reveals how heterosexuality and exclusively genital sex are neither natural nor essential, but are instead socially constructed, that is, singled out as more acceptable than other forms of sexual acts. In this way Freud 'gave back' to children their sexuality, defined in terms of corporeal experience, but also in the process suggesting that adult sexuality is constructed rather than innate and is not linked to reproduction (a point de Sade had made a hundred years earlier). This aspect of his theory, however, was to a great extent obfuscated by his insistence on the existence of biological 'drives', which, as discussed earlier, he regarded as innate forces within all human beings. This results in the anomaly that adult sexuality is socially constructed, but from innate biological forces. These anomalies were challenged by the French psychoanalyst Lacan.

While retaining many of Freud's central tenets, Lacan challenged Freud's more problematic theory of 'drives' and argued instead that subjectivity and sexuality are essentially *symbolic* constructions arising from the child's acquisition of language, the supreme symbol-system. Where the two central themes to Freud can be seen as, first, sexuality, and second, the unconscious, 'Lacan can be seen to add the powerful insights of semiology . . . Lacan's understanding of the unconscious, sexuality, desire, and identification, implies these are sites for the production and transgression of meaning' (Grosz, 1990, p. 3). For Lacan, the unconscious is structured like language, governed by the two central poles of linguistic functioning: metaphor and metonymy. Sexual drives, according to Lacan 'are the consequence of the absorption of the drive by systems of cultural meaning, by representations (we desire objects not to gratify our needs, but because they mean something, they have value or significance' (Grosz, 1990, p. 4). Sexuality, Lacan argues, is not, as Freud maintained, a product of instincts or biology, but a result of signification and meaning; specifically, 'sexuality is the consequence of the interaction of the material inscription of desire on and with the child's body' (p. 13).

Building on Lacan's reinterpretation of Freud, the theory of infantile sexuality has been further developed by feminists such as Irigaray (see Whitford, 1991), Kristeva (see Moi, 1986) and, to some extent, Chodorow (1978), who have paid more attention to the crucial pre-Oedipal period of early infancy when all babies, girls and boys alike, form their first and closest relationship, which is almost invariably with the mother or a female carer. This means that little girls have to learn, as they develop and reach the Oedipal period, to shift their love object from a woman to a man. Heterosexuality, and monogamous heterosexual relationships, in other words, had to be, and have to be, learned, and for girls the learning process is more complex because it is triadic, and thus often more difficult and contradictory than it is for boys, who simply have to shift the object of their desire from one woman (the mother) to another. Moreover, the logical conclusion to this is that sexuality is not only precarious, but also liable to challenge, change and choice.

Irigaray claims, however, that the biological aspect *is* important for women, for whom sexual pleasure can be, and is, experienced all over the body in a diffuse way, rather than, as assumed by Freud, only in specifically 'erogenous' zones. Women are not, she argues, characterised by 'lack' as Lacan would have us believe, but instead by a plenitude of sexuality: 'Woman has sex organs just about everywhere. She experiences pleasure almost everywhere . . . the geography of her pleasure is much more diversified, more multiple in its differences, more complex, more subtle, than is imagined' (Irigaray, quoted in Sayers, 1986, p. 44).

Such arguments take us, however, more into the realm of the social and political aspects of sexuality. Society and its legal and normative systems lay fairly clear rules as to what is acceptable and unacceptable in terms of sexual acts and sexual relationships. The law tells us when we can have sexual relationships, with whom, and when we can marry or divorce. It defines and delineates incest, rape and sexual violence. Such laws change and vary. Incest, for instance, did not become a crime in Britain until 1908, while bestiality has been a crime for centuries. Laws have always prescribed and proscribed sexual relationships and acts in terms of age groups; historically the reason for much of this was the overriding importance of virginity for the daughters of the propertied and politically powerful. Crucial financial and political transactions often rested on the intact hymens of daughters as prospective brides.

Stereotypes of gender, masculinity and femininity are generated in the realm of society, and it is also within the realm of the social that sexual identities are made and presented. Sexual identity can often conflict with sexual acts, as well as with desires. A growing number of cases of sexual abuse of children show, for instance, that Catholic priests, whose *sexual identity* is one of celibacy, perform *sexual acts* with children. Their *sexual fantasies*, however, might concern something altogether different. Men who present themselves as respectable and married 'family men' have been involved in acts of buggery and rape with children of both sexes. In 1995 Rosemary West was convicted of murdering a number of young women, many of whom she had sexual relations with. She was, however, 'happily' married and, it would seem, very much in love with, her husband Frederick West.[2] Power is a crucial aspect to many, if not most, sexual relationships, but especially those between adults and children.

It is often commented that sexuality really operates almost exclusively in the mind. If it were innate, if we were driven solely by biological instinct, then sexual acts would be performed whenever and wherever the urge pounced upon us, as it were, whether at the supermarket, an opera performance, a petrol station or in the classroom. Such behaviour, however, is relatively rare and when and if it does occur is usually quickly labelled as deviant or pathological. Images and fantasies of such occurrences, and indeed, far more outlandish ones, however, would seem to flit through the minds of the majority of the population quite regularly. Some of these are conscious, many are unconscious.

Unconscious desires and fantasies, according to Freud, are those we experienced as infants and small children, and they were arguably strong urges to possess, to link with, to be married to, our mother and later, for most girls, our father. Because we found such feelings overwhelming at the time, and because we learned they were socially unacceptable, they were, if we accept Freud, repressed into our unconscious minds. There they still lurk, barely recognised by our conscious minds, but still affecting who we are attracted to, how we experience relationships, sexual acts, desire and pleasure in myriad unacknowledged ways.

For Lacan, however, sexuality is better understood in relation to *desire* and to the origins of desire. He considered the pre-Oedipal period as crucial and, in particular, what he calls the 'mirror phase'. This is the point at which the infant, somewhere around the age of six months, begins to realise it is separate from the mother, having previously assumed it and the mother were one. When the infant begins to recognise its mother's absence, and absence generally, it first becomes aware of a sense of *lack* and with this comes an incipient awareness of separation, inside/ outside, subject/object, and self/other. As Grosz comments:

> From this time on, lack, gap, splitting will be its mode of being. It will attempt to fill its (impossible, unfillable) lack . . . This gap will propel it into seeking an identificatory image of its own stability and permanence (the imaginary), and eventually language (the symbolic) by which it hopes to fill the gap. (Grosz, 1990, p. 35)

At the same time, then, as the baby first becomes aware that its mother is not always there when it wants her to be, it begins to feel a sense of lack, of being split, and from this develops gradually an awareness that one object can stand for another: its first understanding of difference and of symbolism.

All these developments are essential to the baby's subsequent acquisition of language, but most important, are central to the formation of *desire*. The infant's realisation that it is in fact separate from the mother leads to a feeling of despair at this (imagined) loss, this lack. The baby yearns to be one again, to be reunited with the mother it (thinks it) lost. This deep sense of loss and yearning remains, but because it is prelinguistic, unconscious, it is never understood for what it in fact is, or was. Subsequent acquisition of language means a child can ask for and demand what it thinks it wants, but beneath the surface of such requests for, for example, water, sweets or toys, is this deeper unacknowledged yearning for what it feels it lost, that is, the mother. This yearning, this desire, remains with us all our lives, but in the unconscious. It is at the root of desire and, while desire can be, and often is, expressed in sexual fantasies, acts and relationships, it is far more diffuse than this. Childhood desire and experience, then, can be seen as the foundation to adult sexuality. Sexuality in the broad sense of the term is thus a determining characteristic of children and childhood. Why, then, does the idea of sexuality in children seem to occasion such horror, such panic, in adults?

## The Cleveland Crisis

The Cleveland crisis over child sexual abuse (see note 5 to Chapter 2) erupted in 1987. It can be seen as a crisis because it raised crucial issues about, first, the relationship between state agents/agencies and parents over children; second, to what extent children's testimonies, particularly regarding the transgressive behaviour of their parent(s), is reliable as court evidence, and at what age specifically children can understand the difference between right and wrong, and tell the 'truth'. It is worth remembering that children are brought up to respect, honour, believe their parents; if a parent abuses a child sexually that child is almost inevitably sworn to secrecy by the offending parent; a child is thus placed in an invidious position if questioned by an outside agent as to whether abuse by a parent/step-parent took place. It also raised important questions about just how widespread such behaviour in fact is in families, how it should be diagnosed and dealt with, whether the abused child or the offending parent should be removed from the family, and what the balance should be between children's rights and parents' rights. It has often been referred to as a moral panic. Cohen defined 'moral panic' as when

> a condition, episode, person or group of persons emerges to become defined as a threat to societal values and interests; its nature is presented in a stylised and stereotypical fashion by the mass media; the moral barricades are manned by editors, bishops, politicians and other right-thinking people. (Cohen, 1980, p. 9)

Yet during the spring of 1987 there was great confusion as to who was threatened and who was threatening. It was more of a moral panic about morality in the sense that, at least initially, neither a folk devil nor a clear-cut victim was apparent. The children who had been allegedly abused seemed to be the obvious victims, yet very quickly 'the family' – including the fathers, who were, in a third of the cases, the perpetrators – came to be seen as the victim. The professionals – all of whom were women – who had initially set out to rescue the children were labelled as the real folk devils and were increasingly pilloried by the tabloid press. None of this happened, however, without a struggle, and even in the end considerable confusion remained.

The confusion embraced children, fathers, mothers, the police, social services, doctors, politicians, the media – and the anus. This was not a case, however, of 'perverts' corrupting innocent children through anal rape, nor was it a case of girls being victimised by genital rape or sexual interference. It concerned instead married men, whose sexual identities were by definition heterosexual, but who were buggering both girls and boys (in a ratio of 2:1). The average age of the children was 6.9 years. Many of the men were the fathers or step-fathers of the children. As Campbell (1988) said, the crisis was arguably to a great extent about male sexuality – and, indeed, about masculinities – rather than it was about children or families.

The perpetrators, the men, transgressed boundaries between homosexual acts and heterosexual identity, thus challenging conventional cultural definitions and representations of heterosexual masculinity. The revelation that this practice was apparently quite widespread threatened the notion of sexual difference between men and masculinities. This, as much as the transgression of age boundaries (one which had been transgressed many times before without attracting anything like the horror that it did in Cleveland) could be seen to be at the core of the resultant confusion in the media. It eventually became translated as 'the family' versus 'the caring professionals', which was certainly a long shot indeed from the reality of respectable married men buggering little girls and boys.

If we take the body as a metaphor of society, it can be seen as representing a bounded system. Bodily boundaries represent any boundaries which are threatened or precarious (Douglas, 1966, p. 115). Thus 'all margins are dangerous. If they are pulled this way or that the shape of fundamental experience is altered. Any structure of ideas is vulnerable at its margins . . . the orifices of the body . . . symbolise its specially vulnerable points' (Douglas, 1966, p. 121). During the Cleveland crisis, the supreme orifice of investigation and controversy was undoubtedly the anus.

The anus is the place of discharge of unwanted matter from the body: the back passage, the back door, the exit *par excellence*. Whereas the mouth is associated both with taking in and giving out, the anus is primarily associated with expelling what is in, what is unwanted, what is unacknowledged in a process that can be seen as comparable to the psychological process of projection. The anus, however, is also an orifice for sexual pleasure that has been generally associated with male homosexuality, although the act of buggery is, and has been, practised by men of all sexual identities.

Forensic scientist Michael Green urged Dr Wynne, one of the doctors involved in the Cleveland case, to inspect children's bottoms on the grounds that *at least 10 per cent* of heterosexual adults practise anal intercourse (Campbell, 1988, p. 23). Anal dilatation as an indicator of anal penetration had been used in forensic pathology for years; Dr Wynne and her colleague Dr Hobbs were the first to apply the test, however, to *paediatrics*. This was both innovative and transgressive, because 'for the first time the science of sexual crime was applied to the world of children' (Campbell, 1988, p. 21). It was acknowledged not just that 'normal' men practised 'abnormal' sex, but that it was practised on children, both girls and boys alike. Where were the boundaries here of age, of gender, and of sexual identity?

Perhaps the most challenging aspect of all was that there were no other clear-cut social categories by which the perpetrators could be type-cast, stereotyped and scapegoated as 'other'. The perpetrators were overwhelmingly white, primarily middle-class or respectable working-class, men. It was, in other words, the hegemonic group that was transgressing social boundaries and social categories – transgressing, that is, its own rules. The threat, then, must have been largely to do with a fear of a breakdown of *all* social categories, all hierarchy, all boundaried order. Accepted norms and codification of adult sexuality were threatened by this apparent androgyny and polymorphism – threatened, in other words, by *children's* sexuality as 'polymorphously perverse', not yet contained by strict boundaries of monogamous heterosexual identity and acts.

Boundaries between adults and children in relation to sexuality and sexual desire were therefore threatened in a number of ways. First, there was the transgression of the boundary between homosexual and heterosexual acts among men: a threat to boundaries of masculinities. Second, there was the issue of the anus itself which, because it is a universal and ungendered orifice, transgressed boundaries between women and men: androgyny was the threat here. Third, because the acts and relationships were between adults and children they transgressed accepted age boundaries, thus threatening a crucial division between social groups in the social hierarchy. Finally, because many of the acts and relationships were between step/fathers and step/children, they transgressed boundaries between family members, and thus transgressed the ideal, rhetoric and hierarchy of the family.

Core categories by which society and social relations are defined, classified and ordered were thus destabilised. Hence, arguably, the mad scramble by the media and local politicians, the clergy, and so forth, to deflect the issue, to transform it into something else. Stuart Bell, for instance, a Labour MP, argued that the crisis was all about a threat to 'the family', although he never stipulated whose family, or what kind of family, was threatened. Arguably he was appealing to the long-established rhetoric of 'the family' as a symbol of social order based on hierarchy and organised by clear delineation of age and gender, rather than to the reality of real family-households, only a minority of which now match the 'nuclear family' ideal of married couple with 2.4 children. In an age-old tradition, the messenger got the blame for the bad news: it was paediatrician Marietta Higgs, herself a mother of five, who was represented by the press over and over again as single, foreign, deeply suspicious in her reasons for 'interfering', and ultimately the cause of the whole problem.

Let us, however, return to the anus. It is not only the orifice of defecation and unwanted matter, not only an erotic zone usually associated with homosexual masculinity, but it is also dark, pungent and associated with secrecy, the unknown, and the unspoken. From behind, unseen – surely there are other associations here with the shadow, with darkness, with the devil, and with the unconscious? The shadow, as already discussed, can be seen to represent our hidden and unacknowledged aspects that we project out on to other individuals and groups, who serve in turn as scapegoats for everything we do not want to own or acknowledge in ourselves.

Reflecting on the Cleveland crisis in terms of what it represented at a more symbolic level is thus important in trying to make sense of the huge panic it aroused among adults and the media. Taking the debate further, it is possible to suggest that, drawing on the symbolism of the anus, it could be seen to represent a whole 'excremental culture'. Excremental culture characterises the contemporary western world, according to postmodernist theorists such as Kroker and Cook (1988), by its characteristics of disposability, rubbish, immediate and meaningless gratification. Objects of desire are picked up, used, and thrown away in quick succession, whether they are cars, drinks, clothes, houses – or children. The child, once seen as representing purity, innocence and a hopeful futurity, now becomes a sullied, consumed, penetrated victim, an object of meaningless desire and gratification which, once realised, is thrown away. Representations of abused children or Third World children almost always draw on these images of the 'discarded', dirtied, useless child.

In such a scenario the anus, once a focus of rigid parental control as a means to self-discipline and adult authority, now becomes instead the focus of adult desire, an object to be invaded, used and consumed in a mockery of any notion of purity, care or innocence. The supreme irony, as de Sade was well aware, is that it is these very qualities of innocence and purity that are desirable in the first place. Purity and innocence are attractive to adults, primarily men, because their defining characteristics of the unexplored, the new, the uncolonised, the untainted make them want to inspect, test and ultimately destroy. *Quae negata, desiderata* – 'what is forbidden is what we desire'. Desire and power are close allies.

Child sexual abuse could thus be seen as symbolic of consumerism run riot in a culture that values only momentary pleasures. Once consumed, the child, like pizza wrappers or cheap clothes, can be thrown away, discarded in a rubbish-heap society. Once used, invaded (or not), the child's anus then becomes an object for further investigation and invasion by the medical world. It becomes an object of interest in its own right, divorced from the rest of the body and psyche to which it belongs, and is then observed, measured, photographed and published for scrutiny by adult 'experts' who then decide a child's fate on the basis of the state of its anus, according to current medical and social work discourse. In such a process it is as if the child becomes its anus, and the anus of the child in turn represents an excremental culture.

## Body/Mind

Symbolism of the body thus can reveal a great deal about wider attitudes. Bodies, however, have only recently become a focus of interest to sociologists and historians, who tended in the past to exclude them from consideration on the grounds of 'biological determinism'. Birke, however, has argued that biology and society/culture cannot be so easily separated and that, rather, they tend to interact on each other. Bordo and others have also drawn attention to the importance of seeing the body as socially determined as much as it is biologically determined; certainly we cannot see it as *outside* society and culture (Birke, 1992; Bordo, 1993).

Since at least the time of ancient Greece there has been a tension in western culture and philosophy between the perceived binary opposition of desire and reason, spirit and matter, form and ecstasy. Represented by the gods Apollo and Dionysos, this tension has largely been located in the dialectic between body and mind. Assimilated by Christianity, the body/mind dualism became central to the moral dilemma of the sinfulness of the flesh in opposition to the (potential) purity of the soul. Children were important to this debate because they were seen as primarily creatures of the flesh, only *potential* adults, inhabiting bodies as yet unregulated by more spiritual, or indeed rational, awareness. Representing futurity, their present state was ambivalent. Despite Christ's injunction to 'become as little children', however, from Paul onwards children became essentially equated with sin, especially sin of the flesh. This was both a result of the sin inherent in adult coition, and in their own right as products of sin. This became explicit, as discussed earlier, in the works of St Augustine.

This opposition between body and mind, passion and reason, is, and has been, strongly gendered. It is women who have been equated with the body, with passion, and with irrationality. Children, both girls and boys, are subsumed within the female/body aspect of the pairs of binary opposites, although boys emerge from this aspect to take up their place in the 'positive' aspect of mind/reason/masculine. The process by which they do this, and the age at which they do this, not to mention the anxiety it incurs among the adult population, form the focus of much of the history of childcare and child development, in which the term 'child' has generally masked – and still does mask – the gendered specificity of 'boy'. Girls become women and stay within that side of the binary pairing anyway, although there is controversy as to exactly when and how this change occurs. Arguably it is much more blurred between girls and women than it is between boys and men; the different clothing in Goya's portrait of *The Family of the Duke of Osuna* illustrates this point well (see Figure 6). In contemporary culture, dominant representations of childish women – skinny, boyish, with short haircuts – are portrayed as the epitome of desirability.

Binary opposition is also expressed in spatial terms of high/ low and up/down, and this bi-polarity is often reflected in the body itself as well as within culture generally (Stallybrass and White, 1986). The head can be seen to represent the 'high' – the mind, the spirit – and is equated with reason, clarity, purity and masculinity. The lower regions of the stomach, genitals and anus then represent the 'low' – the material, the dirty, the irrational and the feminine. In this context, it is interesting to consider the phrase that children grow 'up'.

A new concern with just what it meant to 'grow up', with particular reference to the body of the child, developed from the sixteenth century. Protestantism not only proscribed and pre-scribed appropriate behaviour with relation to God, money, com-munity and family, but also put the body firmly on its agenda as an area in need of strict control and rational delimitation. The idea of individual responsibility to God and the inability to seek forgiveness for sin through confession or indulgences, as Catho-lics were able to do, put a new onus on to Protestant individuals in their relation to their own bodies.

Elias shows how in the second quarter of the sixteenth century a new concept of *civilité* arose, which was concerned primarily with outward bodily propriety. His theory is that increasing con-trol of affectivity and growing intimacy of bodily functions led to a shielding of the body which, by way of compensation, opened up a world of fantasies and emotions increasingly hidden from others. Elias (1978, p. 53) sees the 'decisive antithesis ex-pressing the self-image of the West during the Middle Ages' as that between Romano-Latin Christianity on the one hand, and paganism, heresy and Greek Christianity on the other. *Civilité,* linked to Romano-Latin Christian ideology, emerged in the period of nascent capitalism, specifically with the publication of Erasmus' *De Civilitate Morum Puerilium* (On civility in children) in 1530 (Elias, 1978, pp. 53–4). The book ran into 130 editions, 13 of them published as late as the eighteenth century. (See Erasmus, 1991.)

Erasmus laid down clear rules about appropriate bodily carriage, dress, gestures, eating habits, spitting, nose-picking and so on. It is interesting to note, however, the existence of an anonymous poem from about 1480 that offered similar advice to children; here are some excerpts from it:

Little children, here ye may lere,[3]
Much courtesy that is written here.
Look thine hands be washen clean,
That no filth in thy nails be seen.
Take thou no meat till grace be said
And till thou see all things arrayed.
Look, my son, that thou not sit
Till the ruler of the house thee bid . . .

The morsels that thou beginnest to touch
Cast them not in thy pouch.
Put not thy fingers in thy dish,
Neither in flesh, neither in fish;
Put not thy meat into the salt
(Into thy cellar that thy salt halt)
But lay it fair on thy trencher[4]
Before thee, that is honour . . .

Pick not thine ears nor thy nostrils,
If thou do, men will say thou com'st of churls . . .

Nor spit thou not over the table
Nor thereupon – for it is not able.
Lay not thine elbow nor thy fist
Upon the table whilst thou eat'st . . .

When thou eatest gape not too wide,
That thy mouth be seen on every side . . .

And cast not thy bones unto the floor,
But lay them fair on thy trencher . . .
('Some advice on manners when a child is away from home',
    quoted in Rosen, 1994)

In spite of the title, however, it would seem Erasmus' book was
directed at adults as much as at schoolchildren, although Elias
argues that it resulted in an increased differentiation between
adults and children:

> The more 'natural' the standard of delicacy and shame appears
> to adults and the more the civilized restraint of instinctual
> urges is taken for granted, the more incomprehensible it be-
> comes to adults that children do not have this delicacy and
> shame 'by nature'. The children necessarily touch again and
> again on the adult threshold of delicacy and – since they are not
> yet adapted – they infringe the taboos of society, cross the adult
> shame frontier, and penetrate emotional danger zones which
> the adult himself can only control with difficulty. (Elias, 1978,
> p. 167)

Thus the sixteenth century was marked, among other emerging
categories of boundaries and differentiation, by an increased differentiation between adult and child. This was problematised
around the issue of 'the natural', as well as between 'upper and
lower' ranks of society. It focused, moreover, on and around
bodily behaviour. Control of bodily functions and a new propriety became increasingly important in parallel with new ethics of
saving, spending and investing money.

The concern of Erasmus, with his notion of *civilité*, focused not
only on the body in general but on bodily orifices and their
various emanations in particular: the mouth, the nose, the anus
and the genitalia were all central to his writing. Taking the body
as a symbol of society in which all margins are dangerous,
Erasmus' concern with the protection of orifices can thus be seen
as symbolic of social preoccupations with exits and entrances, as
well as with the creation and re-creation of social order and social
hierarchy.

Falk argues:

> The stronger the cultural Order and the community bonds . . .
> the more 'open' is the body both to outside intervention and to
> a reciprocal relationship with its cultural/social context . . . the
> less rigid the cultural Order and the weaker the community
> bonds, the more intertwined are the boundaries of the self with
> those of the individual body . . . the constitution of the subject
> takes the form of an individual self . . . articulating the inside/
> outside distinction primarily at the boundaries of the indi-
> vidual self, and thus the body surface. (Falk, 1994, p. 12)

A tension between high and low can thus be seen to run through
culture, and arguably this was particularly marked during the
early modern period and the nascent development of capitalism.
The body is symbolically central to this process, and, in particular, as Elias maintains, the social control of bodily functions, the
public regulation of bodies 'is a restructuring of personality with
enormous "consequences"' (Elias, 1978, p. 89). To restructure
personalities by regulating bodies involves primary attention
paid to children and their developing bodies and minds as the
future of society itself. In this sense, the rise of Protestantism
generally, and Puritanism in particular, *had* to focus its attention
on children. It is possibly this, rather than Ariès' contention that
childhood was 'discovered' that could help to explain the new
concern with and interest in childrearing which developed from
the sixteenth century onwards.

The Puritans put great emphasis on the salvation of the soul
through continual striving towards good works and the suppression of sin. The inculcation of these traits on their children, however, was focused to a great extent on their bodies. Preachers
exhorted parents to 'beat the devil out' of their children from the
earliest age, crawling was forbidden, play was suspect. Children
were coming under increased surveillance, their bodies the battleground between innocence and sin. Puritan parents believed it
to be their religious duty to ensure their children lived wholly
sin-free lives; to try and achieve this meant implementing a revolutionary new approach to childrearing, one which involved
closer supervision, more attention to, and control of, bodily functions. To an increasing extent, this also resulted in a growing
separation from adult work life and thus a new notion of children

as dependants who were separate, different and 'special'. Despite the rhetoric of preachers, however, this did not necessarily mean a more brutal approach to childrearing:

> We were bred tenderly, for my mother naturally did strive to please and delight her children, not to cross and torment them, terrifying them with threats, or lashing them with slavish whips . . . reason was used to persuade us, and instead of lashes, the deformities of vice were presented unto us. (Margarite Cavendish, c. 1620, England, quoted in Pollock, 1987, p. 182)

The shift might be seen more as one that strove to care for the soul and the perceived necessity for its purity, yet the body was the gateway to this.

Foucault argues that an increasingly rationally 'administered' society came about as a result of the increasing control of people through bodies, and especially through the medicalisation of bodies. The body was becoming an object of power to be identified, controlled and reproduced (Turner, 1984). History, he contends, is inscribed on the body through various means of power and knowledge. The primary shift with the development of capitalism was from punishment of the body *per se* to control of the soul or psyche. Foucault sees the shift occurring as rather later than does Elias, arguing that the seventeenth century 'was a time of direct gestures, shameless discourse, and open transgressions, when anatomies were shown and intermingled at will, and knowing children hung about amid the laughter of adults: it was a period when bodies "made a display of themselves" ' (Foucault, 1978, p. 3).

The effects of the Reformation and the Counter-Reformation were to put more and more emphasis on individual responsibility to God, as well as on careful self-examination and self-discipline. Within these developments, the body was central as both an object of knowledge and an object to be under surveillance at all times. Discipline, then 'is a technique of power, which provides procedures for training or for coercing bodies . . . The instruments through which disciplinary power achieves its hold are hierarchical observation, normalising, judgement, and the examination' (Smart, 1985, p. 85). Thus power and visibility are inextricably linked. Central to this development was an increasing focus on the issue of sexuality: for pedagogues, with the spread of education for boys from the sixteenth century onwards, for clerics, and more and more for scientists, especially those specialising in medicine.

Sexuality was part of a wider debate on issues between the state and the individual: 'Sex became an issue, and a public issue no less; a whole web of discourses, special knowledges, analyses and injunctions settled upon it' (Foucault, 1978, p. 26). Seventeenth-century moralists, for example, 'increasingly campaigned against multiple occupancy of beds and bedrooms and the habit of leaving children with servants for long periods of time' (Jackson, 1982, p. 44). Sexuality became both more secretive and, paradoxically, more discussed:

> The Middle Ages had organized around the theme of the flesh and the practice of penance a discourse that was markedly unitary. In the course of recent centuries, this relative uniformity was broken apart, scattered, and multiplied in an explosion of distinct discursivities which took form in demography, biology, medicine, psychiatry, psychology, ethics, pedagogy, and political criticism. (Foucault, 1978, p. 33)

According to Foucault, what he calls 'bio-politics' developed in the eighteenth century and can be seen in two different ways. On the one hand, it focused on optimising the body's capabilities, both in terms of economic utility and political docility. Thus diet became an increasing object of enquiry and theorisation as a means of maximising bodily performance (and also profitability). On the other hand, of central importance was an increasing pedagogisation of children's sex that focused in particular on masturbation. A huge moral panic arose around this issue in the early eighteenth century and continued to be a major source of impassioned debate and concern throughout the nineteenth century.

## The Great Masturbation Debate

The publication in 1710 of *Onania, or the Heinous Sin of Self-Pollution* inaugurated the controversy. Beginning with concern over sin, the debate soon became one that centred on illness, health and parental supervision of children. Tissot, a Swiss physician (1728–98) published *Onanism: A Treatise on the Disorders Produced by Masturbation* in 1760. In this, Tissot advocated penetrating the most private aspects of people's lives, arguing that parents 'should oversee children at every possible moment in order to guard against their masturbating tendencies' (Jordanova, 1986a, p. 114). He assumed that parents have the right to know and see all with regard to their children. Here we see evidence of Foucault's theory of the growth of surveillance and 'panopticism' – the close observation of people, especially inmates in asylums, factories and schools, with the express purpose of altering physical modes of behaviour. The following extract illustrates the effects of this; it is by a boy who was raised in an orphanage for middle-class children in the early twentieth century:

> When the shutters were drawn we lay in a terrible darkness. I remember well crouching voiceless with terror at the mysterious creeping whispers of the night. We lay on hard horsehair mattresses resting on a lattice of steel slats joined to an iron frame . . . Our nurse occupied a cubicle in a corner of the dormitory. From it a small porthole gave her a view of us . . . Restless as we were on the long summer mornings before it was time to get up, we were overawed by its power . . . Thou God seest me . . . our respect was augmented by realisation of our vulnerability to the hot sting of the back of a long-handled hair brush to our bare backsides. (Grist, 1974, p. 49)

The reason for such surveillance was usually masturbation, which amounted to an acknowledgement, whether in the eighteenth or twentieth century, that children could be sexually active. This notion, however, was highly problematic, particularly in the eighteenth century, because the new definitions of nature that were emerging at the time argued that children were closer to nature than adults, yet, paradoxically, innocent of adult sexuality. Masturbation thus highlighted the contradictions and confusion in the new categories of thought that were developing, and which were arguably linked both to the growth of bourgeois domestic ideology specifically, and to the rising power of the bourgeoisie generally.

The controversy over masturbation also highlighted more general ideas and problems over prevailing notions of sexuality. Masturbation is by definition self-pleasure. No partner is needed to enjoy it, no legal certificates or religious ritual. Women can do it, boys can do it, girls can do it, men can do it. Sexual pleasure, therefore, can be separated from heterosexual relationships, and certainly from reproduction, not to mention holy matrimony. Yet in Catholic doctrines, sexuality and reproduction had been joined for centuries as part of the same process designed by God. To find pleasure in sexuality without coupling was thus seen as outrageous at the time because it threatened the very concept of God, as well as that allegedly God-given institution, marriage, and its Siamese twin, 'the family'.

The idea of the Christian family was premised on heterosexual monogamy leading to reproduction. To undermine the precepts of this ideal, which was at the time very much in the process of definition and re-definition by the nascent bourgeoisie, threatened social order. It threatened long-established and accepted tenets of Christianity itself. Sexual activity in children, moreover, suggests power, autonomy, and lack of parental control. Masturbation defied clear heterosexual codes, while at the same time undermining rhetoric of the family and notions of childhood innocence. Arguably masturbation therefore also threatened the ideals of dependency and innocence on which middle-class childhood was simultaneously being defined and delineated. Moreover, masturbation threatened the concept of 'child' because it raised debates about the age at which children become adult, and when they could become sexually active. It once again challenged the then prevalent discourse of the special status of children as being closer to the source of life (Jordanova, 1986a, p. 115).

On a more general symbolic level, however, the moral panic over masturbation might also be seen as a cultural crisis reflecting the tension between Hellenic and Hebraic traditions in western culture. Tissot and his followers, both religious and medical, based their arguments on the story of Onan, who was struck down by God for spilling his seed on the ground. Onan's act, however, 'involved no hand-work at all – he ungenerously re-fused to perform the Levirate and raise up children to his de-ceased brother (Genesis 38:9), and it was this, not even the fact of practising *coitus interruptus*, which "displeased the Lord, where-fore he slew him"' (Comfort, 1967, p. 72).

It is interesting to note that in Hellenic culture there was a *god* of masturbation – Pan:

> Masturbation is governed by the goat-God of nature, who 'invented' it, and is an expression of him. This mythological statement says that masturbation is an instinctual, natural activity invented by the goat for the shepherd. It says further that masturbation is significant and divinely sanctioned . . . Masturbation sexualises fantasy, brings body to mind, intensi-fies the experience of conscience. (Hillman, 1979a, pp. xxxiv–xxxv)

Pan was also the god of the nightmare, epilepsy, panic and rape. God of shepherds, fishermen and hunters, he has no clear geneal-ogy, for his pursuits and those he protects are generally solitary. Lecherous, he never pairs 'ever an abandoned child . . . he cou-ples but never wives; he makes music, but the Muses are with Apollo' (Hillman, 1979a, p. xxi). Against the social order, he rules nature in its wild state and can thus be seen to be concerned with loss of control and with instinct:

> When Pan is alive then nature is too, and it is filled with Gods . . . when Pan is dead, then nature can be controlled by the will of the new God . . . As the human loses personal con-nection with personified nature and personified instinct, the image of Pan and the image of the Devil merge . . . Pan never died . . . he was repressed. (Hillman, 1979a, p. xxiii)

Pan, then, could be equated with an older, wilder concept of nature that was increasingly becoming inimical to emerging sci-entific and medical discourses during the eighteenth century. The attack on masturbation can thus be seen as, on the one hand, an attack on old notions of nature and the ideas of sexuality that were inherent in these, in which children were seen as *enjoying* sexual pleasures. On the other hand, it can be seen as symbolising increasing surveillance of bodily functions as part of a culture more and more concerned with, and reliant on, self-control and self-discipline. This new culture of control was one that increasingly accepted only the conscious, rational and positive aspects of humanity. It denied the irrational, the dark, the wild – or rather, it denied these within the dominant social groups and projected these characteristics on to others: the working classes, the 'savages' of the colonised world.

Again, it is possible to see how the redefinition of 'nature' that was occurring from the middle of the eighteenth century onwards was of crucial importance to ideas – and fears – about children's sexuality. The problem was that children were being defined as naturally asexual, while at the same time sexuality was defined as being part of nature. Masturbation was the proof that children *were* sexual, that sexuality was not exclusive to adults (and married heterosexual adults at that). It was evidence of children's dark side, and thus transgressed the increasingly important discourse of innocence. It was evidence that children could be independent, and this transgressed the all-important ideal of children as dependants within a well-ordered bourgeois family. Ultimately, perhaps, it was evidence that Pan, allegedly dead since Christ's crucifixion, was alive and well and in need of not just careful monitoring, but murdering. Instead, he was banished to 'other' darker regions, both in the psychological and in the geographical sense.

Moreover, the panic over masturbation could be seen as evidence of the growing tension between individual and family, or indeed community and state. It might provide evidence for the rigidification of the process Elias discussed in relation to Erasmus' work: an increased armouring of the body against the outside world, evidence of an erosion of rigid structures outside. As such, if Elias is right, the world of fantasy and imagination within the individual become increasingly important. This is indeed what Steedman (1995) argues in *Strange Dislocations*, that growing fascination with 'the child' in Victorian times was a central aspect of the increasing importance of interiority.

During Victorian times, however, the masturbation debate shifted from being a specifically moral one to being a primarily medical one. Doctors increasingly focused on sex as a root cause of nervous disorders:

Educators and doctors combated children's Onanism like an epidemic that needed to be eradicated. What this actually entailed, throughout this whole secular campaign that mobilised the adult world around the sex of children, was using these tenuous pleasures as a prop, constituting them as secrets . . . searching out everything that might cause them or simply enable them to exist. (Foucault, 1978, p. 42)

Foucault, however, ignores the fact that discourses on masturbation were highly gendered; concern was initially over boys and grew to encompass men as well. Masturbation in girls did not become a source of concern until the nineteenth century. Victorian doctors, however, soon advocated a wide variety of restraints and eventually clitoridectomies and infibulation for girls who persistently masturbated. The following is an account from the *New York Medical Record* of 1897 on the mechanical restraint deemed necessary for a young girl:

She had been made to sleep in sheepskin pants and jacket made into one garment, with her hands tied to a collar about her neck; her feet were tied to the footboard and by a strap about her waist she was fastened to the headboard so she could not slide down in the bed and use her heels; she had been scolded, reasoned with and whipped, and in spite of it all she managed to keep up the habit. (Quoted in Comfort, 1967, p. 89)

For girls, masturbation was seen as doubly transgressive because the increasingly dominant discourse of the time was that girls and women were, or should be, asexual. Active sexuality on the part of girls or women was defined as pathological and unnatural.

Foucault maintains that there were in the nineteenth century four main strategies, or discourses, on sexuality. First was the hysterisation of women's bodies; second, the pedagogisation of children's sex, focusing particularly on masturbation; third, the socialisation of procreative behaviour; and, finally, the psychiatrisation of perverse pleasure. For children this meant (although this varied considerably both by social class and by gender – factors to which Foucault pays scant attention) an increased concern with the health and functioning of their bodies, and an increased surveillance of bodies and behaviour by parents, teachers and doctors. For the working classes, such surveillance came later with the advent of social workers, NSPCC officers (the 'Cruelty Men'), health visitors and 'nit-nurses'.[5] Subsumed in all this was a growing conviction that children's bodies – especially working-class children's bodies – belonged as much to the state as they did to their parents.

The net result of these developments for children was that they were increasingly watched, and their increasing visibility to adults meant a decreasing power and independence of their own. Street games were appropriated by public schools, for example, institutionalised and run *by* pedagogues *for* children, rather than leaving children to organise and enjoy their own games for themselves, although the work of the Opies suggests that children did continue to do this, at least to some extent, until very recently:

> Our vision of childhood continues to be based on the adult–child relationship. Possibly because it is more difficult to find out about, let alone understand, we largely ignore the child-to-child complex, scarcely realizing that however much children may need looking after they are also people going about their own business within their own society, and are fully capable of occupying themselves under the jurisdiction of their own code. (Opie and Opie, 1969, p. v)

From the 1840s in Britain the new policemen chased children away from their street games. Compulsory education further drastically reduced children's one-time ability to invent and play their own games in their own street culture. Schools and orphanages were designed both to separate the sexes and to make children as visible as possible. The purpose of such surveillance was, according to Foucault, the all-pervasive fascination with, and fear of, sexuality that ran throughout Victorian discourses and institutional relations like an underground river.

## Desire for Children

Fear, fascination and surveillance fed adult desire for children, it would seem, both as part of the two age groups becoming increasingly separate, and through the development of interiority, integral to which was the search for and yearning for a 'lost' child. It is not surprising, then, that it was during the nineteenth century that child pornography, very much facilitated by the discovery and development of photography, literally 'took off' and became a boom industry. As Ennew (1986, p. 121) points out, 'the fantasy element in child pornography turns upon the concept of childhood. With respect to child pornography, it entails both a symbolic return to the lost childhood of the self (as in paedophilia) and a reprise of the sexual excitement of youth'. Photographs, because they are *objects*, offer the photographer/owner a chance to *possess*, indeed to *control*, the image/object. It would also seem that these developments at the time led to an increasing blurring of boundaries between woman and child, where childish women and womanly girls are both represented as sexually enticing and are held up as ideals of attractiveness to men.

Adult, and particularly male, desire for children has been an increasing source of social concern over the past one hundred years or so. There was, for instance, a major moral panic in the 1880s about child prostitution. The Social Purity movement had been campaigning for raising the age of consent for girls from 12 for some time, but the publication of Stead's article 'The Maiden Tribute of Modern Babylon' in the *Pall Mall Gazette* of 4 July 1885 caused considerable public outcry and shock. It revealed, on the one hand, how despite all the bourgeois rhetoric about the sanctity, innocence and dependency needs of children, working-class children still needed to work from a young age to survive. By focusing their attention, however, on the scandal of girls who worked as prostitutes from an early age – encouraged by such appalling beliefs as that which claimed men could be cured of venereal disease by having intercourse with a virgin – the true extent of how many working-class girls generally were working was diverted to the more outrageous minority group of child prostitutes.

The result of the campaign was a general widening of police powers against brothels and procurers and the raising of the age of consent to 16 for girls in the Criminal Law Amendment Act (Gorham, 1978). Such legislation, however, almost certainly did not change the desire for sexual relations and acts with children. Rather, desire for children has arguably grown with the development of the advertising industry and the media, where children are often represented, sometimes naked, in juxtaposition with consumer goods. Evidence shows that representations of children juxtaposed with consumer goods has in fact spread worldwide. Arguably it has contributed to developments such as sex tourism in areas like the Philippines and Taiwan where prostitution by local girls and women (and increasingly, it would seem, arranged marriages) for western men has become an important sector of the local economy.

Desire, Lacan argues, is ultimately connected with our infantile feelings of lack that arose from feeling we were split from our mother. The yearning remains with us all, but it is unconscious, and as such is diffuse and can be manipulated by others to focus on objects of desire, such as consumer products, that purport to satisfy such misunderstood yearning. This desire for retrieval, for union, is manipulated by advertisers so that a given product is at the same time named and offered as something 'good' that will make you feel better, or more whole, or more successful, and so on. Falk discusses how, for example, Coca Cola was initially marketed in the 1890s as a remedy for headache and as a brain tonic. By 1906 it had become associated with both good health and happiness:

> As naming and representation begin to move away from the actual product and its qualities and towards the act and context of consuming the product, the fundamentally nameless 'it' becomes thematized in the domain of satisfaction and wholeness. This means that the building of the connection between the product and 'goods' turns round: the positive elements no longer refer (primarily) to the qualities of the product . . . but the product is associated with representations of wholeness . . . the depicted 'good' has gained independence from the product and its qualities. (Falk, 1994, pp. 168–9)

The twentieth century has witnessed a burgeoning of images of children that have been, and continue more than ever to be, used to sell a wide variety of consumer goods. Playing on the cultural association between, for example, childhood and purity, little girls are widely used in advertising to sell soap, detergents, adult skin creams, and toilet paper. Drawing on long-established associations with nature, advertisers represent children juxtaposed with rural images to sell 'old-fashioned' products like wholemeal bread or cottage-style kitchen furniture.

This bombardment of images of children in advertising, however, may have resulted not so much in selling the products with which they are associated (though this undoubtedly happens), but in creating instead a deeper desire *for children themselves*. The constant association of children with consumer products can arguably be seen as resulting in children themselves being thought of as consumer goods. Ennew, for instance, points out how common is the use of childish nakedness to advertise consumer products in a frequently gratuitous way, with the result that 'sex offenders in English prisons have been known to send for *Mothercare* catalogues as stimulants for their obsessive fantasies. Childish nakedness is not always innocent in the eye of a beholder' (Ennew, 1986, p. 134). As a result of decades of representations of children in association with myriad consumer products, children have not only become fashion accessories, but also objects of widespread sexual desire.

Advertising, by giving a name and an image to the prevalent and unconscious sense of lack in adults suggests that this image/product is the answer to all one's unhappiness and sense of disconnectedness. While the products and the names of the products vary, the overall frequency and repetition of images of children remain constant. It could be argued that this has a different impact according to gender. Women may be more likely to desire children as fashion accessories, as part of an attractive living style, integral to their ability to bear children, while men are more likely to want to possess children sexually, fascinated, perhaps, by their association with innocence and purity.

Adult panic about children's sexuality can thus be seen in a number of ways. At a psychological level it can be seen to relate to early yearning emanating from a sense of lack at losing the mother; it can also be seen as part of a panic about unconscious desires experienced both as a child for one's parents, and as an adult for children. It can be seen to relate to a general sense of loss that exists both psychologically and culturally, and tends to be manipulated and encouraged by the advertising industry. There seems to be a constant confusion between adults' attitudes to children as sexual or non-sexual beings, and their confusion about their sexual desires when they themselves were children. Jackson comments:

> The psychologist Leah Cahan Schaefer has observed that adults either overestimate or underestimate children's sexual capacities. It is my belief that we frequently do both . . . The paradox that even while underestimating children's sexual potential we overestimate it; even while we insist that children must be 'protected' from sex we treat anything they do or say that seems sexual as if it were motivated by fully-formed sexual interests. Thus, while preventing children from becoming sexually aware, adults often respond to them as if they already were. (Jackson, 1982, p. 78)

The problem seems to lie, then, with the confusion in adults' minds between their own memories of their own 'lost' childhood and the way in which they project myriad feelings of yearning, rage and desire on to other children. Because this process is rarely acknowledged and seldom conscious, it tends to be disguised as 'care' or concern or artistic interest. The true feelings lurk in the shadows, invisible – and thus powerful. The process is made more complex by the ways in which culture, and notably the advertising industry, represents children and mythologises them so that they appear simple, available, desirable, consumable. Again, these feelings are not in the open, but remain implicit, unconscious. When crises or events arise that momentarily seem to reveal the shadow side of adults' feelings about children, their own sexual desires for them, their own covert, hidden and frequently cruel, behaviour towards them, and, indeed, the horror these evoke when they are brought into the light of day, then there is panic.

# CONCLUSION

When I opened the Sunday paper yesterday the front page had a large coloured photograph of a little boy on tip-toes peering into a bright red Porsche. Below that was an article about a cross-cultural custody dispute over a black South African boy who had been fostered by a white woman for whom his biological mother had once worked. To the right of that was an advertisement for a charity, which featured three photographs of little Thai girls – in one a girl was screaming, in the seond a girl was begging, and the final image showed three girls smiling beneath a caption proclaiming they could be saved if I sponsored one today. Inside the paper was an article on how the police in North Wales are refusing to allow outside investigators to inquire into the scandal over an alleged 100–200 sex abuse incidents in children's homes. A few pages after that was an article on the sudden burgeoning of advertisements that use images of embryos and babies; in particular, it discussed the complicated filming of a new television advertisement for a car that portrays 900 infants in rows.

Although real children in *fin-de-siècle* culture are increasingly kept inside, protected from what we perceive to be an increasingly dangerous world, images and narratives of children are everywhere. Interestingly, where seductive women were once used to advertise fast cars, we increasingly see children and babies, indeed embryos, associated with cars. Perhaps it reflects the increased fear of sexuality that has arisen with the AIDS crisis, or maybe they are aimed at appealing to the 'new man's' identity as sensitive, loving, child-like. In the advertisement that uses the human embryo juxtaposed with a car, the verbal message is that the car is almost as secure and comfortable as the womb. Instead

of children being associated with nature here is a new development in which they are linked instead with technology. Embodied babies, of course, *are* increasingly associated with, even
constructed by, technology: IVF, surrogacy, murdered Third
World children whose organs are sold for transplants to affluent
recipients in the West. The image of 900 babies and a car suggests
cloning, assembly-line production, while perhaps the message is:
yes, they're all made in the same way, but each one is still special
to *you*. It also suggests control by the driver/parent, and, at least
in the embryo advertisement, ownership.

Ownership of children remains an issue, even though it is
disguised as 'care and control' or responsibility. There does often
seem to be a real 'tug-of-love' between parents, or foster parents
and biological parents, where different people genuinely love the
child(ren) and want to be close to her or him. But some are still
arguably about money (which need not preclude love of course):
the parents of the adolescent movie star Macaulay Culkin have
been fighting a long and bitter battle for his custody and fortune.
In the case of the black South African boy, local Black Rights
groups sponsored the parents to fight for his custody. Such struggles suggest deeper more disturbing issues about whether 'blood
ties' and the biology of parenthood are, in fact, more important
than social parenting, a comfortable standard of living, and the
chance of a good education. Is love ultimately more important in
a child's survival than nutrition or security? And how can that be
measured, how can it be judged? Who can judge such enormous
issues?

The series of crises and scandals over sexual abuse within
family-households has arguably eroded general trust in 'the family'. Blood, that precious fluid associated for so long with special
ties of intimacy and kinship, not to mention life itself, is now
something of which people are increasingly wary, afraid that it
might be contaminated, polluted. AIDS, BSE, CJD haunt us with
fears of pollution and death. Much of this is reflected in obses-
sions with the body, exercise, fitness and youthful appearance.
Death is feared, but so is blood and so is intimacy. Put another
way, life itself is feared. As a result 'the family', once seen as a
haven in a heartless world, an asylum (in the older sense of the
word, although of course there is a good argument for embracing
both senses) has become not only more precarious, but some-

thing that is arguably viewed with some trepidation. Increasingly, therefore, there has been a turning towards the child, the baby, indeed, more and more, the embryo, as a symbol of hope, trust, innocence and the possibility of a future of which we are in fact terrified. The family, and rhetoric of the family, arguably represented unity and the collective, while the child is individual, isolated. As the family itself becomes increasingly perceived as dangerous, so children are less frequently portrayed in the context of families: the individual has triumphed over the collective. Is this not also what has happened at a social and cultural level? Yet many other images and narratives co-exist: the damaged child, the dangerous 'monster' child, the seductive child.

This plethora of images and different discourses of 'the child' itself reflects a widespread confusion about what the child *is*, what it should be, and what needs to be done. This confusion exists at the three levels on which 'the child' also can be seen to exist: the psychological, the material and the symbolic. We are in a time of rapid change, uncertainty and upheaval. The future seems more frightening than ever and the world itself seems, like children, both dangerous and threatened. The child, in all senses, is at the centre of this confusion and these conflicts.

Much of the controversy over 'the child' in contemporary culture arises because we have confused symbol with memory, memory and symbol with actual children. Consequently our idea of children is based on an over-simplified notion, a myth that can be seen as a result of converging historical developments in ideas, discourses, legislation and our own psychological processes of memory, repression and projection. The myth is alive and believed. It tells us childhood is a special time when children can be free from adult worries (which can also be read as dependent and disempowered), innocent (to a large extent ignorant) and happy (or at least smiling for family photographs when demanded).

We as adults have a heavy investment in perpetuating the myth because if we did not do so our own precarious ideas of having had a happy and special childhood are threatened, and that can shake the very roots of our own sense of self and identity. We struggle to protect children's dependency as well as what we see as their innocence. Part of that struggle is about a desire to maintain our own myth of having once been innocent. Another part relates to the ways in which children's dependency and innocence accord us as adults and parents a great degree of power and control over children. As an advertisement for gas once proclaimed, 'Don't you just love being in control?' And we do.

We seek to protect children's innocence – their ignorance – of adult sexuality and violence, yet we live in a world where violence and myriad representations of violence and sexual acts are endemic. If violence and sexuality are so dangerous, so all-pervasive, should we not be dealing with them *generally*, as social problems affecting everyone, rather than just as they relate to children? Focusing such debates exclusively on children suggests that unknowingly we are using 'the child' as a symbol, confusing it, once again, with real children and what 'the child' represents: nation, humanity, the future. By so doing, we deny our own implication in the causes of the more general problem.

Children do not live in a vacuum. They are not separate from the rest of society and culture, although the myth is that they are, and should be. Such a myth was historically constructed by the middle classes in the nineteenth century and was, to a great extent, partially enforced on their own children through spatial separation of nurseries and nursery regime from the rest of the adult world and, less successfully, on the rest of the population through legislation such as universal education. The idea that all children do, and can, live in a place and time of innocence and joy makes a mockery of the millions who live in poverty, squalor and are subject to abuse. Children have very different childhoods, and these are determined by the gender, class, ethnic group and family-households into which they are born. Children, like adults, are unequal. If we want a year to be The Year of *the* Child, if we want there to be one childhood for all, then we need to tackle *general* problems of economic deprivation, sexual discrimination, racism, patriarchal laws, as well as how representation and symbolisation can disguise these and manipulate our unhappiness, manipulate our desires. This in turn means confronting the morass of irrationality in our own psyches.

Instead we talk of children's rights and a few enactments are made towards that goal. Symbolically such acts are indeed important, for they alert the population to the idea that children can and should have rights. But how many children are aware of such rights? Indeed, how many children were consulted in the framing of such legislation? Can a proclamation of children's rights in any way tackle material deprivation, prejudice, cruelty?

I think one of the most heartening stories I have recently read was about Highfield Junior School in a tough area of Plymouth. Here an enlightened staff has conceded quite substantial power to the pupils themselves. Each class has two representatives to the school council. Each class meets regularly to discuss difficult and important issues to them and the representatives convey this to the council. Pupils interview prospective staff. They invite parents to come and discuss with them issues about their own children's problems. It all appears to work extremely well and smoothly. As the children have become empowered, so bullying has declined. Parents were more willing to discuss their children's problems with other children. The inspectors were impressed (*Guardian*, 1 April 1996). Small steps like these are crucial ways of beginning to empower children so that they can protect both themselves and one another. They are also, of course, vital lessons in democracy, justice and co-operative action. Maybe the pupils speak up more, maybe they are cheekier than some would like, but if so this is a problem for adults, not a problem with children.

We need to ask ourselves carefully just why we want children to remain innocent and what innocence means to us. It can mean freedom from evil and corruption, naïveté, but also ignorance and disempowerment. We need to consider how we benefit from these. Fear for children's safety may also relate to our own fears of losing control over our children. Adult surveillance, control and supervision of children has arguably mushroomed in recent years. Much of this has been fuelled by fear. We fear pollution, chaos, death and, indeed, life. Mary Douglas ([1966] 1988) pointed out how such fears characterise societies in a state of rapid change and upheaval. This certainly is the case. Of course, there is danger for children, just as there is danger for adults. Danger also lies in the family-household. To centre our childrearing habits on fear, however, will arguably lead to a generation of frightened adults. Fear is a useful and fertile ground for abusive and tyrannical governments to flourish. Is this what we want for the future?

Protecting children from the outside, from outsiders, from all apparent danger, thereby rendering them less accessible to others, can also make them far more desirable to men like Thomas Hamilton. There does seem to be a real sense in which whatever we are denied is what we most desire. Facilities such as the free charity telephone service ChildLine have meant that abused and frightened children can talk in confidence to someone about their plight and know that they will be taken seriously – although lack of resources has meant not all of those who need help can have it. But would it not be just as wise, arguably even more so, to provide such services for potential abusers? The problem is not with the children, although it is dealt with as if it were; rather, it is with those who desire children, who want to possess them, be near them, *have* them. Denial that such desires exist, extreme frustration of such desire, can lead to violence and even murder.

Should we not be dealing with causes rather than effects? We shut out 'perverts' and 'oddballs' because they make us feel uncomfortable, remind us of our own irrational and not very nice desires that we struggle to hide and disguise. We do not want to listen to them or see them in our midst. Thus the 'devils', the transgressors, the 'weirdos' are denied even when they cry for help. When they do offend, we stand firm on our moral high ground and demand retribution. In the process, however, real children are destroyed. I think there is a great need to listen to the devils and weirdos both in ourselves and in our midst. I think, somehow, we have to learn to work with them at all levels. Concomitantly we need to trust children themselves and let *them* find ways of speaking, working and becoming empowered. Children are beautiful, they are precious. They not only represent, but they literally are, the future. Perhaps we should spend more time weeding our own back gardens and give them more freedom, where possible, to plant their own in their own chosen way.

# NOTES

## Introduction

1 Thomas Hamilton shot dead 16 children, their teacher and himself in a primary school in Dunblane, Scotland, in March 1996.

2 In Britain, the Married Women's Property Act, 1870, entitled married women to keep their own earnings. The Married Women's Property Act of 1882 allowed women to retain any property they brought into marriage as their 'separate property'.

3 Full enfranchisement for women on a par with that for men was not enacted until 1929 in Britain.

4 This is discussed at greater length in Chapter 1.

5 Harry Hendrick (1990) 'Constructions and reconstructions of British childhood' in James and Prout. Hugh Cunningham also argues along similar lines. His work is discussed in Chapter 4.

6 Recently, however, there have been important changes to this. James and Prout (1990) and the collection by Qvortrup (1994), for instance, have made important contributions to studying children as a social group in their own right.

7 Hartman (1979); Eisenstein (1979). Earlier theorists of patriarchy were Chesler, Ehrenreich and English, Showalter, and Millett, who argued that it was a universal system of older men ruling over women and younger men. Later theorists qualified the concept, e.g. Beechey (1973), Lown (1983), Walby (1986).

8 Rosalind Minsky (1992) has written a very accessible essay that gives a clear account of Lacan's broad arguments.

9 See Florence Rush (1980), *The Best Kept Secret* and Jeffrey Masson (1984) for a fuller discussion of Freud's betrayal of women.

10 This is discussed at greater length in Chapter 3.

# Chapter 1

1   There is a full discussion of these ideas in Chapter 5.
2   See a fascinating analysis of this in Hunt (1970).
3   Stone, Stearns and Shorter all are part of this 'modernisation' school of thought which, broadly speaking, characterises the modern era as more 'loving' than the past.
4   It is interesting to note that eating disorders in the West have escalated over the past few years. While girls and women are starving in Third World countries, western girls and women are increasingly *starving themselves*; 90 per cent of anorexics are women and in recent years girls as young as nine have been reported as suffering from it. It raises important questions as to attitudes towards women's entitlement to nourishment – at all levels.
5   But see Davidoff (1995) for an important essay on this in *Worlds Between*.
6   Over the past 250 years, there have only been 27 recorded cases in Britain of children under 14 years of age killing other children (Sereny, 1995, p. xiii).

# Chapter 2

1   See Archard (1993) for a more detailed discussion of these issues; see also Engels (1986 [1984]), *The Origin of the Family, Private Property and the State*.
2   'Translated into socio-moral and legal ideas, honouring parents has become the law of *patria potestas*, which outlines parental and particularly paternal rights over children. Until quite recently in English law parents could evoke *habeus corpus* to recover custody of their children against their wishes and a now discredited ruling of the Court of Chancery 1883 (re: Agar-Ellis 24 ChD 317) held that paternal rights were paramount over maternal.' (Ennew, 1986, p. 37)
3   See Davidoff and Hall (1987) for an excellent discussion of the relation between capital accumulation, business and family-households in the eighteenth and nineteenth centuries. See also Zelitzer (1985) for a discussion of the changing values put on children from being 'economically priceless' to being 'emotionally priceless'.
4   The Child Support Act 1991 made no distinction between children born in and out of marriage in terms of liability to maintain. It means maintenance is now enforced for all children with its own procedures, rather than as a result of private agreement between parents or as a result of a court order in divorce or separation

proceedings. A fixed formula is applied and results in more being demanded of absent parents. The Child Support Agency calculates and enforces payment. In 1993 it caused a wave of bitter protest by fathers. (See Fox Harding, 1996, p. 120.)

5   Between February and July 1987 125 children from the Cleveland area were diagnosed as having been sexually abused. A key means of diagnosis was 'reflex anal dilatation', a test commonly used by doctors to test if buggery has taken place. Prior to the Cleveland crisis, doctors Wynne and Hobbs found in 1986 that 'more children were being buggered than battered' (Campbell, 1988, p. 25). The diagnoses by Dr Marietta Higgs in Cleveland, however, erupted into crisis when the police refused to act on the doctor's evidence, contrary to police surgeons' forensic literature and the advice of their own professional association that claimed anal dilatation should 'arouse strong suspicions of sexual abuse' (quoted in Campbell, 1988, p. 25). Their rationale for acting as they did was that they could not believe such abuse was taking place on this scale, particularly as many of the alleged abusers were 'respectable' fathers and stepfathers. The crisis was further fuelled by media confusion which culminated in an attack on the (women) paediatrician and social worker, seen as responsible for state 'interference' in the private realms of 'the family'. Little attention was focused on the children who had been allegedly buggered, and even less on the fathers and stepfathers who abused them. In fact, the courts found that in 70 per cent of the cases the diagnoses were correct. Cleveland's Director of Social Services, Mike Bishop, said child abusers 'were often the best liars in the world'. The Butler-Sloss Report, however, which came out in 1994, questioned the certainty of the doctor's diagnosis and criticised the way in which interviews of children had been carried out.

6   It was the decline in mortality *crises*, such as the demise of the bubonic plague, which is generally believed to have been the reason for the decline in what remained a still high mortality rate, at least compared to our times. For a fuller discussion of the Demographic Transition, see, for instance, Wrigley (1969).

7   It is important to note, however, that a high proportion of illegitimate births occur to cohabiting couples. What seems to be more at stake, therefore, is changing attitudes to, and patterns of, cohabitation and marriage.

8   This will be discussed at greater length in Chapter 4.

9   Mary Carpenter (1807–77) was a philanthropist who was very active in the movement for the reformation of neglected children. She founded a 'ragged school' and several reformatories for girls.

10   Thomas Arnold (1795–1842) was an English scholar who became

headmaster of Rugby School in 1828. He introduced substantial reforms that had wide-ranging effects on public school reforms generally.

11 This was as a result of the system of primogeniture, by which the aristocracy transferred lands intact to the eldest son. It meant there was no division of property into ever smaller areas (as was the case in France), but it also meant that younger sons had to make their own way in the world. This they did primarily through entering the professions, particularly those of the army, the law, and the church.

12 The first boot camp in Britain was opened in 1995–96. Modelled on American penal camps for young male offenders, they are characterised by militaristic discipline and strict and strenuous physical training.

13 See Kempe and Kempe's (1978) classic work on this.

## Chapter 3

1 See Chapter 6 for a full discussion of this.
2 This idea is explored in more depth in J. J. Clarke's (1992) *In Search of Jung*, which also has useful references to debates about Jung and postmodernist theory generally.
3 A good starting point for exploring Lacan is Ros Minsky's (1992) essay in *Knowing Women*. It is clear, coherent and accessible. A more elaborate, but also quite accessible, analysis is in Elizabeth Grosz (1990).
4 Although Lacan insisted on this crucial difference between the symbolic phallus and the biological penis, some have argued that the difference is by no means all that clear.
5 The first by Ruth Marchant of South Downs Health NHS Trust, the second by Helen Westcott.

## Chapter 4

1 There was, however, protest about girls and women who worked underground in mines. See, for instance, Angela John's (1980) *By the Sweat of their Brow*.

## Chapter 5

1 Although arguably his writings can be said to be much influenced by the urban artisanate class from which he came.

2   These are also, of course, traits commonly attributed to women by men, although radical feminists also embrace such qualities which they see as central to 'womanhood'.

## Chapter 6

1   As mentioned earlier, Florence Rush and Jeffrey Masson give a good account of Freud's 'betrayal'. The classic text of Freud's that relates to this is *Dora* (1963).
2   Frederick West was accused of sexually assaulting and murdering 13 women, including his own daughter, but committed suicide in prison before going to trial. Rosemary West was convicted on ten counts of murder.
3   'Lere' means 'learn'.
4   A 'trencher' is a plate or dish.
5   See Linda Gordon's (1989), *Heroes of their own Lives* for an excellent account of the relationship between American working-class families and the nascent social services.

# BIBLIOGRAPHY

Alanen, Leen (1994) 'Gender and Generation: Feminism and the "Child Question"'. In Qvortrup et al.

Archard, David (1993) *Children: Rights and Childhood*. Routledge, London.

Ariès, Philippe ([1960] 1986) *Centuries of Childhood*. Harmondsworth, Penguin.

Asper, Kathrin (1988) *The Inner Child in Dreams*. London, Shambhala.

Baker, Steve (1993) *Picturing the Beast: Animals, Identity and Representation*. Manchester, Manchester University Press.

Bardy, Marjatta (1994) 'The Manuscript of the Hundred-years Project: Towards a Revision'. In Qvortrup et al.

Barrett, Michele (1985) 'Ideology and the Cultural Production of Gender'. In Newton and Rosenfelt.

Barthes, Roland ([1972] 1987) *Mythologies*. London, Paladin.

Beechey, Veronica (1973) 'On Patriarchy'. *Feminist Review*, 3.

Behlmer, George K. (1982) *Child Abuse and Moral Reform in England 1870–1908*. Stanford, California, Stanford University Press.

Beinart, Jennifer (1992) 'Darkly through a Lens: Changing perceptions of the African child in sickness and health, 1900–1945'. In Roger Cooter (ed.).

Bellingham, Bruce (1988) 'The History of Childhood since the "Invention of Childhood": Some issues in the eighties', *Journal of Family History*, 13, 2.

Belotti, Elena (1975) *Little Girls*. London, Writers & Readers Publishing Co-operative.

Belsey, Catherine (1985) 'Constructing the Subject: Deconstructing the text'. In Newton and Rosenfelt.

Benedict, Ruth (1955) 'Continuities and Discontinuities in Cultural Conditioning'. In Mead and Wolfenstein.

Bennett, Tony, Martin, Graham, Mercer, Colin and Woollacott, Janet (eds) (1987) *Culture, Ideology and Social Process*. London, Open University Press.

Bentovim, A. and Boston, P. (1988) 'Sexual Abuse: Basic Issues and Characteristics of Children and Families'. In Bentovim, Elton et al.

Bentovim, A. and Vizard, E. (1988) 'Sexual Abuse, Sexuality and Childhood'. In Bentovim, Elton et al.

Bentovim, Elton et al. (1988) *Child Sexual Abuse within the Family: Assessment and Treatment*. London, Wright.

Berger, John ([1972] 1987) *Ways of Seeing*. Harmondsworth, Penguin/BBC.

Berger, John (1980) *About Looking*. London, Readers & Writers.

Bernheimer, Charles and Kahane, Claire (eds) (1985) *In Dora's Case: Freud. Hysteria. Feminism*. London, Virago.

Bettelheim, Bruno (1969) *The Children of the Dream*. London, Thames & Hudson.

Bettelheim, Bruno (1985) *The Uses of Enchantment*. Harmondsworth, Penguin.

Birke, Lynda (1992) 'In Pursuit of Difference: Scientific Studies of Women and Men'. In Kirkup and Smith Keller.

Birke, Lynda, Himmelweit, Susan and Vines, Gale (1990) *Tomorrow's Child: Reproductive Technologies in the 90s*. London, Virago.

Black, Shirley Temple (1989) *Child Star: An Autobiography*. London, Headline.

Boas, George (1966) *The Cult of Childhood*. London, The Warburn Institute.

Bordo, Susan (1992) 'Anorexia Nervosa: Psychopathology as the Crystallization of Culture'. In Crowley and Himmelweit.

Bordo, Susan (1993) *Unbearable Weight: Feminism, Western Culture and the Body*. Berkeley, CA, University of California Press.

Boswell, John (1989) *The Kindness of Strangers: The Abandonment of Children in Western Europe from Late Antiquity to the Renaissance*. London, Penguin.

Bowra, Maurice (1961) *The Romantic Imagination*. Oxford, Oxford University Press.

Bradbury, Bettina (1982) 'The Fragmented Family: Family Strategies in the Face of Death, Illness, and Poverty, Montreal, 1860–1885'. In Parr.

Bradley, Ben S. (1989) *Visions of Infancy: A Critical Introduction to Child Psychology*. Oxford, Polity.

Brooke, Iris (1930) *English Children's Costume since 1775*. London, A & C Black.

Burn, James Dawson (1978) *The Autobiography of a Beggar Boy* (edited by David Vincent). London, Europa Publications.

Burnett, John (ed.) (1982) *Destiny Obscure: Autobiographies of Childhood, Education and Family from the 1820s to the 1920s*. London, Allen Lane.

Butler, Marilyn (1981) *Romantics, Rebels and Revolutionaries. English Literature and its Background 1760–1830*. Oxford, Oxford University Press.

Calvert, Karin (1982) 'Children in American Family Portraiture, 1670–1810', *William and Mary Quarterly*, Special issue on the Family in Early America, 3rd series, xxxix, 1, January.

Campbell, Beatrix (1988) *Child Sexual Abuse: the Cleveland Case*. London, Virago.

Campbell, Colin (1987) *The Romantic Ethic and the Spirit of Modern Consumerism*. Oxford, Blackwell.

Chaplin, Elizabeth (1994) *Sociology and Visual Representation*. London, Routledge.

Chisholm, Lynne, Buchner, Peter, Kruger, Heinz-Hermann and Brown, Phillip (1990) *Childhood, Youth and Social Change: A Comparative Perspective*. Basingstoke, Falmer Press.

Chodorow, Nancy (1978) *The Reproduction of Mothering*. Berkeley CA, University of California Press.

Clark, Anna (1987) *Women's Silence, Men's Violence: Sexual Assault in England 1770–1845*. London, Pandora.

Clark, Gillian (1994) 'The Fathers and the Children'. In Diana Wood (ed.).

Clark, Linda (1981) 'The Socialization of Girls in the Primary Schools of the Third Republic', *Journal of Social History*, 15, 4, Summer.

Clarke, J. J. (1992) *In Search of Jung*. London, Routledge.

Clarke, John, Hall, Stuart, Jefferson, T. and Roberts, Brian (1987) 'Sub Cultures, Cultures and Class'. In Bennett et al.

Cohen, Stanley (1980) *Folk Devils and Moral Panics: The Creation of the Mods and Rockers*. Oxford, Blackwell.

Comfort, Alex (1967) *The Anxiety Makers. Some Curious Preoccupations of the Medical Profession*. London, Nelson.

Connell, Robert (1987) *Gender and Power*. Oxford, Polity.

Constantine, L. L. and Martinson, F. M. (eds) (1981) *Children and Sex: New Findings, New Perspectives*. Boston, Little Brown & Co.

Cooter, Roger (ed.) (1992) *In the Name of the Child: Health and Welfare, 1880–1940*. London, Routledge.

Corr, Helen and Jamieson, Lynn (1990) *Politics of Everyday Life. Continuity and Change in Work and the Family*. London, Macmillan.

Coveney, Peter (1966) 'Introduction to Huckleberry Finn'. In Twain, Mark, *Huckleberry Finn*, Harmondsworth, Penguin.

Coveney, Peter (1967) *The Image of Childhood: The Individual and Society: A Study of the Theme in English Literature*. Harmondsworth, Penguin.

Coward, Ros and Ellis, J. (1987) 'Structuralism and the Subject: A Critique'. In Bennett et al.

Crowley, Helen and Himmelweit, Susan (1992) *Knowing Women*. Oxford, Polity.

Culler, Jonathan (1983) *Barthes*. Glasgow, Fontana.

Cunningham, Hugh (1991) *The Children of the Poor: Representations of Childhood since the Seventeenth Century*. Oxford, Blackwell.

Davidoff, Leonore (1995) *Worlds Between: Historical Perspectives on Gender and Class*. Oxford, Polity.

Davidoff, L. and Hall, C. (1987) *Family Fortunes: Men and Women of the English Middle Class 1780–1850*. London, Hutchinson.

Davies, Tony (1987) 'Education, Ideology and Culture'. In Bennett et al.

Davin, Anna (1982) 'Child Labour, the Working-Class Family, and Domestic Ideology in 19th Century Britain'. *Development and Change*, 13, 633–52.

Davin, Anna (1990) 'When is a Child Not a Child?'. In Corr and Jamieson.

Demos, John (1970) *A Little Commonwealth: Family Life in Plymouth Colony*. New York, OUP.

De Mause, Lloyd (1976) 'The Evolution of Childhood'. In de Mause.

De Mause, Lloyd (ed.) (1976) *The History of Childhood*. London, Souvenir Press.

De Salvo, Louise (1989) *Virginia Woolf: The Impact of Childhood Sexual Abuse on Her Life and Work*. Boston MA, Beacon Press.

Dodgson Collingwood, S. (1898) *The Life and Letters of Lewis Carroll*. London, T. Fisher Unwin.

Douglas, Mary ([1966] 1988) *Purity and Danger: An Analysis of the Concepts of Pollution and Taboo*. London, Ark.

Douglas, Mary (1970) *Natural Symbols: Explorations in Cosmology*. London, The Cresset Press.

Doyle, Roddy (1993) *Paddy Clarke Ha Ha Ha*. Secker & Warburg.

Driver, Emily and Droisen, Audrey (eds) (1989) *Child Sexual Abuse: Feminist Perspectives*. London, Macmillan.

Drotner, Kirsten (1988) *English Children and their Magazines 1751–1945*. London, Yale University Press.

Dunn, Patrick P. (1976) '"That Great Enemy is the Baby": Childhood in Imperial Russia'. In de Mause.

Edwards, Susan S. M. (1981) *Female Sexuality and the Law*. Oxford, Martin Robertson.

Eisenstein, I. R. (ed.) (1979) *Capitalist Patriarchy and the Case for Socialist Feminism*. London, Monthy Review Press.

Elias, Norbert (1978) *The Civilizing Process*. Oxford, Blackwell.

Eliot, George ([1860] 1979) *The Mill on the Floss*. Harmondsworth, Penguin.

Engelbert, Angelika (1994) 'Worlds of Childhood: Differentiated but Different Implications for Social Policy'. In Qvortrup et al.

Engels, Friedrich (1986 [1984]) *The Origin of the Family, Private Property and the State*. London, Penguin.

Ennew, Judith (1986) *The Sexual Exploitation of Children*. Oxford, Polity Press.

Ennew, Judith (1994) 'Time for Children and Time for Adults'. In Qvortrup et al.

Erasmus, Desiderius (1991) *Collected Works of Erasmus*. Toronto, University of Toronto Press.

Erikson, Erik (1977) *Childhood and Society*. Bungay, Triad/Granada.

Falk, Pasi (1994) *The Consuming Body*. London, Sage.

Ferguson, Moira (ed.) (1987) *The History of Mary Prince, A West Indian Slave, Related by Herself* (first published in 1831). London, Pandora.

Fever, Fred (1994) *Who Cares? Memories of a Childhood in Barnardo's*. London, Warner Books.

Fildes, Valerie (1988) *Wet Nursing: A History from Antiquity to the Present*. Oxford, Blackwell.

Ford, Boris (ed.) (1982) *From Blake to Byron*, Vol 5 of the New Pelican Guide to English Literature. Harmondsworth, Penguin.

Foucault, Michel (1972) *The Archaeology of Knowledge*. London, Tavistock.

Foucault, Michel (1977) *Discipline and Punish*. London. Allen Lane.

Foucault, Michel (1978) *The History of Sexuality*, Vol 1. London, Allen Lane.

Fox Harding, Lorraine (1996) *Family, State and Social Policy*. Basingstoke, Macmillan.

Fraser, Antonia (1966) *A History of Toys*. London, Weidenfeld & Nicolson.

Freud, Sigmund (1963) *Dora: An Analysis of a Case of Hysteria*. New York, Collier.

Frønes, Ivar (1994) 'Dimensions of Childhood'. In Qvortrup et al.

Fuss, Diana (1990) *Essentially Speaking: Feminism, Nature and Difference*. London, Routledge.

Gamarnikow, Eva et al. (1983) *Gender, Class and Work*. London, Heinemann.

Gathorne-Hardy, Jonathan (1972) *The Rise and Fall of the British Nanny*. London, Hodder & Stoughton.

Gay, Peter (1984) *The Bourgeois Experience: Victoria to Freud, Vol I: Education of the Senses*. New York, Oxford University Press.

Gay, Peter (1985) *Freud for Historians*. Oxford, Oxford University Press.

Gay, Peter ([1988] 1989) *Freud: A Life for our Time*. Basingstoke, Macmillan.

Gilbert, Sandra M. and Gubar, Susan (1979) *The Madwoman in the Attic: The Woman Writer and the 19th Century Imagination*. New Haven, Yale University Press.

Gillis, John R. (1981) *Youth and History: Tradition and Change in European Age Relations 1790–Present*. London, Academic Press.

Gilman, Sander L. (1985) *Difference and Pathology: Stereotypes of Sexuality, Race and Madness*. Ithaca, Cornell University Press.

Girard, René (1977) *Violence and the Sacred* (translated by Patrick Gregory). Baltimore, John Hopkins Press.

Gittins, Diana (1982) *Fair Sex: Family Size and Structure, 1900–1939*. London, Hutchinson.

Gittins, Diana (1985 and 1993) *The Family in Question*. Basingstoke, Macmillan.

Gittins, Diana (1994) *Dance of the Sheet*. Nether Stowey, Odyssey Press.

Godfrey, F. M. (1956) *Child Portraiture*. London, The Studio Publications.

Gordon, Linda (1989) *Heroes of their Own Lives*. London, Virago.

Gorham, Deborah (1978) '"The Maiden Tribute of Modern Babylon" Re-examined: Child Prostitution and the Idea of Childhood in Late Victorian England', *Victorian Studies*, 21, 3.

Gosse, Edmund ([1907] 1989) *Father and Son*. Harmondsworth, Penguin.

Gould, Graham (1994) 'Childhood in Eastern Patristic Thought: Some Problems of Theology and Theological Anthropology'. In Diana Wood (ed.).

Gray, Robert (1987) 'Bourgeois Hegemony in Victorian Britain'. In Bennett et al.

Green, R. L. (ed.) (1953) *The Diaries of Lewis Carroll*, Vols I and II. London, Cassell & Co.

Greven, Philip (1970) *Four Generations: Population, Land and Family in Colonial Andover, Massachussetts*. Ithaca, Cornell University Press.

Greven, Philip (1977) *The Protestant Temperament: Patterns of Child Rearing, Religious Experience, and the Self in Early America*. New York, Alfred Knopf.

Grist, Donald (1974) *A Victorian Charity*. London, R. V. Hott.

Grosz, Elizabeth (1990) *Jacques Lacan: A Feminist Introduction*. London, Routledge.

Grylls, David (1978) *Guardians and Angels: Parents and Children in 19th Century Literature*. London, Faber & Faber.

Gullestad, Marianne (ed.) (1996) *Imagined Childhoods: Self and Society in Autobiographical Accounts*. Oslo, Scandinavian University Press.

Hall, Stuart (1987) 'Cultural Studies: Two Paradigms'. In Bennett et al.

Hartmann, Heidi (1979) 'Capitalism, Patriarchy and Job Segregation by Sex'. In Eisenstein.

Hayward, Paul A. (1994) 'Suffering and Innocence in Latin Sermons for the Feast of the Holy Innocents, c. 400–800'. In Diana Wood (ed.).

Hendrick, Harry (1990) 'Constructions and Reconstructions of British Childhood: An Interpretative Survey, 1800 to the Present'. In James and Prout.

Herman, Judith Lewis (1981) *Father–Daughter Incest*. Cambridge MA, Harvard University Press.

Heywood, Colin (1988) *Childhood in 19th Century France: Work, Health and Education Among the Classes Populaires*. Cambridge, Cambridge University Press.

Hillman, James (1979a) 'An Essay on Pan'. In Hillman and Roscher.

Hillman, James (1979b) *The Dream and the Underworld*. New York, Harper & Row.

Hillman, James (1990) 'On Mythical Certitude', *Sphinx* 3.

Hillman, James and Roscher (1979) *Pan and the Nightmare*. Dallas, Spring Books.

Hinshelwood, R. D. (1989) *A Dictionary of Kleinian Thought*. London, Free Association Books.

Holland, Patricia (1991) 'The Old Order of Things Changed'. In Spence and Holland.

Holland, Patricia (1992) *What is a Child? Popular Images of Childhood*. London, Virago.

Houston, Susan E. (1982) 'The "Waifs and Strays" of a Late Victorian City: Juvenile Delinquents in Toronto'. In Parr.

Hoyles, Martin (ed.) (1979) *Changing Childhood*. London, Writers & Readers Cooperative.

Hughes, M. V. ([1934] 1989) *A London Child of the 1870s*. Oxford, Oxford University Press.

Humphries, Steve, Mack, Joanna and Perks, Robert (1988) *A Century of Childhood*. London, Sidgwick & Jackson.

Hunt, D. (1970) *Parents and Children in History: The Psychology of Family Life in Early Modern France*. New York, Basic Books.

Hyde, H. Montgomery (1964) *A History of Pornography*. London, Heinemann.

Ignatieff, Michael (1985) 'Torture's Dead Simplicity'. The *New Statesman*, 20 September.

Illich, Ivan D. (1971) *Deschooling Society*. London, Calder & Boyars.

Illick, Joseph E. (1976) 'Child-Rearing in 17th Century England and America'. In de Mause.

Jackson, Stevi (1982) *Childhood and Sexuality*. Oxford, Blackwell.

Jacobs, Janet (1990) 'Reassessing Mother Blame in Incest', *Signs*, 15, 3, Spring.

James, Allison and Prout, Alan (eds) (1990) *Constructing and Reconstructing Childhood*. London, Falmer Press.

James, Henry ([1907] 1988) *The Turn of the Screw*. Harmondsworth, Penguin.

James, Henry ([1908] 1980) *What Maisie Knew*. Oxford, Oxford University Press, World's Classics paperback.

Janus, Sam (1981) *The Death of Innocence: How our Children are Endangered by the New Sexual Freedom*. New York, Wm. Morrow & Co.

Jenkyns, Richard (1980) *The Victorians and Ancient Greece*. Oxford, Basil Blackwell.

Jense, An-Magritt (1994) 'The Feminization of Childhood'. In Qvortrup et al.

Jimack, P. D. (1992) 'Introduction'. In Rousseau.

John Angela V. (1980) *By the Sweat of their Brow: Women Workers at Victorian Coal Mines*. London, Croom Helm.

Johnson, Orna R. (1981) 'The Socio-Economic Context of Child Abuse and Neglect in Native South America'. In Korbin.

Jones, Ann Rosalind (1985) 'Writing the Body: Toward an Understanding of *l'écriture féminine*. In Newton and Rosenfelt.

Jordanova, Ludmilla (1986a) 'Naturalizing the Family: Literature and the Bio-Medical Sciences in the Late Eighteenth Century'. In Jordanova (ed.).

Jordanova, Ludmilla (ed.) (1986b) *Languages of Nature: Critical Essays on Science and Literature*. London, Free Association Books.

Jordanova, Ludmilla (1987) 'Conceptualising Childhood in the 18th Century: The Problem of Child Labour', *British Journal for Eighteenth-Century Studies*, 10.

Jordanova, Ludmilla (1989) 'Children in History: Concepts of Nature and Society'. In Scarre (ed.).

Jung, C. G. and Kerenyi, C. ([1949] 1985) *Science of Mythology: Essays on the Myth of the Divine Child and the Mysteries of Eleusis*. London, Ark Paperbacks.

Kaplan, Cora (1983) 'Wild Nights: Pleasure/Sexuality/Feminism'. In *Formations of Pleasure*. London, Routledge Kegan Paul.

Kappeler, Susanne (1986) *The Pornography of Representation*. Oxford, Polity.

Kelly, Liz (1988) *Surviving Sexual Violence*. Oxford, Polity.

Kempe, R. and Kempe, C. (1978) *Child Abuse*. Suffolk, Fontana/Open Books.

Kerenyi, C. (1982) *The Gods of the Greeks*. London, Thames & Hudson.

King, Michael (ed.) (1981) *Childhood, Welfare and Justice*. London, Batsford.

Kinnel, Margaret (no date) 'Childhood and its Image Makers: English Children's Literature 1760–1830' Document C/1723 HSS in the Cambridge Group Library.

Kirkup, Gill and Smith Keller, Laurie (1992) *Inventing Women: Science, Technology and Gender*. Oxford, Polity.

Korbin, Jill E. (ed.) (1981) *Child Abuse and Neglect: Cross Cultural Perspectives*. Berkeley, University of California Press.

Kovarík, Jirí (1994) 'The Space and Time of Children at the Interface of Psychology and Sociology'. In Qvortrup et al.

Kroker, Arthur and Cook, David (1988) *The Postmodern Scene: Excremental Culture and Hyper-Aesthetics*. Basingstoke, Macmillan.

Landon, George P. (1979) *Approaches to Victorian Autobiography*. Athens OH, Ohio University Press.

Langness, L. L. (1981) 'Child Abuse and Cultural Values: The Case of New Guinea'. In Korbin.

Lee-Wright, Peter (1990) *Child Slaves*. London, Earthscan.

Leonard, Diana (1990) 'Persons in their own Right: Children and Sociology in the UK'. In Chisholm et al.

Lessing, Doris (1988) *The Fifth Child*. London, Paladin.

LeVine, S. and LeVine, R. (1981) 'Child Abuse and Neglect in Sub-Saharan Africa'. In Korbin.

Lown, Judy (1983) 'Not so Much a Factory, More a Form of Patriarchy: Gender and Class During Industrialisation'. In Gamarnikow et al.

Lyman, Richard B. Jr (1976) 'Barbarism and Religion: Late Roman and Early Medieval Childhood'. In de Mause.

Lyotard, Jean-Francois (1979) *The Postmodern Condition: A Report on Knowledge*. Manchester, Manchester University Press.

MacLeod, David I. (1982) 'At Your Age: Boyhood, Adolescence and the Rise of the Boy Scouts in America', *Journal of Social History*, 16, 2, Winter.

MacLeod, Mary and Saraga, Esther (1988) 'Challenging the Orthodoxy: Towards a Feminist Theory and Practice', *Feminist Review*, 28, Spring.

Makrinioti, Dimitra (1994) 'Conceptualisation of Childhood in a Welfare State: A Critical Reappraisal'. In Qvortrup et al.

Marcus, Steven (1970) *The Other Victorians: A Study of Sexuality and Pornography in Mid-Nineteenth Century England*. London, Weidenfeld & Nicolson.

Martindale, Andrew (1994) 'The Child in the Picture: A Medieval Perspective'. In Diana Wood (ed.).

Marvick, Elizabeth W. (1976) 'Nature Vs. Nurture: Patterns and Trends in Seventeenth Century French Child-Rearing'. In de Mause.

Masson, Jeffrey Moussaieff (1984) *Freud: The Assault on Truth: Freud's Suppression of the Seduction Theory*.

May, Robert (1980) *Sex and Fantasy: Patterns of Male and Female Development*. New York, W. W. Norton.

McDonell, Diane (1986) *Theories of Discourse: An Introduction*. Oxford, Basil Blackwell.

McIntosh, Mary (1988) 'Introduction to the Issue: Family Secrets as Public Drama', *Feminist Review*, 28, Spring.

McLaughlin, Mary M. (1976) 'Survivors and Surrogates: Children and Parents from the Ninth to the Thirteenth Centuries'. In de Mause.

McLure, Ruth (1981) *Coram's Children: The London Foundling Hospital in the Eighteenth Century*. New Haven, Yale University Press.

McRobbie, Angela (1987) 'Settling Accounts with Sub-Cultures: A Feminist Critique'. In Bennett et al.

Mead, Margaret (1955a) 'Children and Ritual in Bali'. In Mead and Wolfenstein.

Mead, Margaret (1955b) 'Theoretical Setting – 1954'. In Mead and Wolfenstein.

Mead, Margaret and Martha Wolfenstein (eds) (1955) *Childhood in Contemporary Cultures*. Chicago, University of Chicago Press.

Meens, Rob (1994) 'Children and Confession in the Early Middle Ages'. In Diana Wood (ed.).

Mendelievich, Elias (1979) *Children at Work*. Geneva, ILO.

Merivale, Patricia (1969) *Pan the Goat-God: His Myth in Modern Times*. Cambridge MA, Harvard University Press.

Miedzian, Myriam (1992) *Boys will be Boys. Breaking the Link between Masculinity and Violence*. London, Virago.

Miles, Rosalind (1994) *The Children we Deserve: Love and Hate in the Making of the Family*. London, Harper & Collins.

Miller, Alice (1985) *Thou Shalt Not be Aware: Society's Betrayal of the Child*. London, Pluto.

Miller, Alice (1987) *For Your Own Good: The Roots of Violence in Child-Rearing*. London, Virago.

Minsky, Ros (1992) 'Lacan'. In Crowley and Himmelweit.

Moi, Toril (ed.) (1996) *The Kristeva Reader*. Oxford, Blackwell.

Moogk, Peter N. (1982) '*Les Petits Sauvages*: The Children of Eighteenth-Century New France'. In Parr.

Moore, Thomas (1990) *Dark Eros: The Imagination of Sadism*. Dallas, Spring Publications.

Nash Smith, H. (1985) 'Introduction'. *The Adventures of Huckleberry Finn*. Harmondsworth, Penguin.

Nåsman, Elisabet (1994) 'Individualization and Institutionalization of Childhood in Today's Europe'. In Qvortrup et al.

Nava, Mica (1988) 'Cleveland and the Press: Outrage and Anxiety in the Reporting of Child Sexual Abuse', *Feminist Review*, 28, Spring.

Nead, Lynda (1988) *Myths of Sexuality: Representations of Women in Victorian Britain*. Oxford, Basil Blackwell.

Nelson, Janet L. (1994) 'Parents, Children, and the Church in the Earlier Middle Ages'. In Diana Wood (ed.).

Newton, Judith (1989) '*Family Fortunes*: "New History" and "New Historicism"', *Radical History Review*, 43, January.

Newton, Judith and Rosenfelt, Deborah (eds) (1985) *Feminist Criticism and Social Change*. London, Methuen.

Oldman, David (1994) 'Adult–Child Relations as Class Relations'. In Qvortrup et al.

Olson, Emelie A. (1981) 'Socio-Economic and Psycho-Cultural Contexts of Child Abuse and Neglect in Turkey'. In Korbin.

Opie, Iona and Opie, Peter (1969) *Children's Games in Street and Playground*. Oxford, Oxford University Press.

Ostriker, Alice (ed.) (1985) *William Blake: The Complete Poems*. London, Penguin.

Otto, Walter F. (1981) *Dionysus: Myth and Cult* (translated by R. B. Palmer). Dallas, Spring Publications.

Ovenden, Graham and Melville, Robert (1972) *Victorian Children*. London, Academy Editions.

Padgug, R. A. (1979) 'Sexual Matters: On Conceptualizaing Sexuality in History', *Radical History Review*, 20, Spring/Summer.

Parr, Joy (ed.) (1982) *Childhood and Family in Canadian History*. Toronto, McClelland & Stewart.

Parr, Joy (1994) *Labouring Children: British Immigrant Apprentices to Canada, 1869–1924*. Toronto, University of Toronto Press.

Parton, Nigel (1985) *The Politics of Child Abuse*. London, Macmillan.

Patterson, Thomas (1989) 'Post-Structuralism, Post-Modernism: Implications for Historians', *Social History*, 14, 1, January.

Pattison, Robert (1978) *The Child Figure in English Literature*. Athens GA, University of Georgia Press.

Phádraig, Máire Nic Ghiolla (1994) 'Day Care – Adult Interests versus Children's Needs?'. In Qvortrup et al.

Piaget, Jean ([1929] 1973) *The Child's Conception of the World*. St Alban's, Paladin.

Pinchbeck, I. and Hewitt, M. (1973) *Children in English Society*, Vol. 2. London, Routledge & Kegan Paul.

Plumb, J. H. (1975) 'The New World of Children in Eighteenth-century England'. *Past and Present*, 67, 64–93.

Pollock, Linda (1983) *Forgotten Children. Parent–child Relations from 1500 to 1900*. Cambridge, Cambridge University Press.

Pollock, Linda (1987) *A Lasting Relationship: Parents and Children over Three Centuries*. London, Fourth Estate.

Postman, Neil (1985) *The Disappearance of Childhood*. London, Comet/ W. H. Allen.

Qvortrup, Jens (1994a) 'Childhood: An Introduction'. In Qvortrup et al.

Qvortrup, Jens (1994b) 'A New Solidarity Contract?'. In Qvortrup et al.

Qvortrup, Jens, Bardy, Marjatta, Sgritta, Giovanni and Wintersberger, Helmut (eds) (1994) *Childhood Matters. Social Theory, Practice and Politics*. Aldershot, Avebury Publishing.

Raine, Kathleen (1970) *William Blake*. Oxford, Oxford University Press.

Riley, Denise (1983) *War in the Nursery: Theories of Child and Mother*. London, Virago.

Robertson, Priscilla (1976) 'Home as a Nest: Middle Class Childhood in Nineteenth-Century Europe'. In de Mause.

Rose, Jacqueline (1984) *The Case of Peter Pan or the Impossibility of Children's Fiction*. London, Macmillan.

Rosen, Michael (ed.) (1994) *The Penguin Book of Childhood*. London, Viking.

Rousseau, Jean-Jacques ([1762] 1992) *Émile* (translated by Barbara Foxley). London, J. M. Dent & Sons.

Ruggiero, Guido (1980) *Violence in Early Renaissance Venice*. New Brunswick NJ, Rutgers University Press.

Rush, Florence (1980) *The Best Kept Secret: The Sexual Abuse of Children*. New Jersey, Prentice Hall.

Said, Edward W. (1994) *Culture and Imperialism*. London, Vintage.

Samuel, Raphael and Thompson, Paul (eds) (1990) *The Myths we Live By*. London, Routledge.

Samuels, Andrew (1985) *Jung and the Post-Jungians*. London, Routledge Kegan Paul.

Scarre, Geoffrey (ed.) (1989) *Children Parents and Politics*. Cambridge, Cambridge University Press.

Schama, Simon (1987) *The Embarrassment of Riches: An Interpretation of Dutch Culture in the Golden Age*. London, Collins.

Sereny, Gitta ([1972] 1995) *The Case of Mary Bell. A Portrait of a Child who Murdered*. London, Pimlico.

Serrano, A. and Gunzburger, D. (1983) 'An Historical Perspective of Incest'. *International Journal of Family Therapy*, 5, 2, Summer.

Sgrita, Giovanni (1994) 'The Generational Division of Welfare: Equity and Conflict'. In Qvortrup et al.

Shahar, Shulamith (1994) 'The Boy Bishop's Feast: A Case-study in Church Attitidues towards Children in the High and Late Middle Ages'. In Diana Wood (ed.).

Sherwood, Mary ([1818] 1977) *The History of the Fairchild Family*. London Garland Publishing Inc.

Shorter, Edward (1975) *The Making of the Modern Family*. London, Fontana/Collins.

Shostak, Marjorie (1990) *Nisa: The Life and Works of a !Kung Woman.* London, Earthscan.

Showalter, Elaine (ed.) (1986) *The New Feminist Criticism: Essays on Women, Literature and Theory.* London, Virago.

Sidel, Ruth (1987) *Women and Children Last: The Plight of Poor Women in Affluent America.* New York, Penguin.

Simpson, Eileen (1987) *Orphans: Real and Imaginary.* London, Weidenfeld & Nicolson.

Skeggs, Beverley (1991) 'Postmodernism: What is all the Fuss About?'. *British Journal of Education,* 12, 2.

Smart, Barry (1985) *Michel Foucault.* London, Tavistock.

Smith, Emma (1954) *A Cornish Waif's Story* (told to A. L. Rowse) London, Odhams Press.

Sontag, Susan ([1977] 1989) *On Photography.* New York, Doubleday.

Soyinka, Wole (1991) *Aké.* London, Minerva.

Spence, Jo and Holland, Patricia (eds) (1991) *Family Snaps: The Meaning of Domestic Photography.* London, Virago.

Stainton Rogers, Rex and Stainton Rogers, Wendy (1992) *Stories of Childhood. Shifting Agendas of Child Concern.* Hemel Hempstead, Harvester Wheatsheaf.

Stallybrass, Peter and White, Allen (1986) *The Politics and Poetics of Transgression.* London, Methuen.

Stearns, Peter (1975) *European Society in Upheaval.* London, Macmillan.

Steedman, Carolyn (1982) *The Tidy House.* London, Virago.

Steedman, Carolyn (1990) *Childhood, Culture and Class in Britain. Margaret McMillan, 1860–1931.* London, Virago.

Steedman, Carolyn (1995) *Strange Dislocations: Childhood and the Idea of Human Interiority 1780–1930.* London, Virago.

Steedman, Carolyn, Urwin, Cathy and Walkerdine, Valerie (eds) (1985) *Language, Gender and Childhood.* London, Routledge Kegan Paul.

Stein, Robert (1973) *Incest and Human Love.* Michigan, Jungian Classics Series.

Steinberg, Leo (1984) *The Sexuality of Christ in Renaissance Art and in Modern Oblivion.* London, Faber & Faber.

Stone, Lawrence (1977) *The Family, Sex and Marriage in England 1500–1800.* London, Weidenfeld & Nicolson.

Strathern, Marilyn (1992) *After Nature: English Kinship in the Late Twentieth Century.* Cambridge, Cambridge University Press.

Tagg, John (1987) 'Power and Photography – a Means of Surveillance: the Photograph as Evidence in Law'. In Bennett et al.

Tagg, John (1988) *The Burden of Representation: Essays on Photographies and Histories.* London, Macmillan.

Tate, Tim (1991) *Children for the Devil: Ritual Abuse and Satanic Crime.* London, Methuen.

Thane, Pat (1981) 'Childhood in History'. In King.

Thomas, Keith (1983) *Man and the Natural World: Changing Attitudes in England 1500–1800*. Harmondsworth, Penguin.

Trilling, Lionel (1959) 'Huckleberry Finn'. In Harold Beaver (ed.) *American Critical Essays*. London, OUP.

Tucker, M. J. (1976) 'The Child as Beginning and End: Fifteenth and Sixteenth Century English Childhood'. In de Mause.

Turner, Bryan S. (1984) *The Body and Society*. Oxford, Blackwell.

Twain, Mark ([1885] 1966) *The Adventures of Huckleberry Finn*. Harmondsworth, Penguin.

Van Franz, Marie-Louise (1972) *The Feminine in Fairy Tales*. Dallas, Spring Publications.

Vittachi, Anuradha (1989) *Stolen Childhood: In Search of the Rights of the Child*. Oxford, Polity.

Walby, Sylvia (1986) *Patriarchy at Work: Patriarchal and Capitalist Relations in Employment*. Cambridge, Polity.

Walther, Luann (1979) 'The Invention of Childhood in Victorian Autobiography'. In Landon.

Walvin, James (1982) *A Child's World: A Social History of English Childhood 1800–1914*. Harmondsworth, Penguin.

Walzer, John F. (1976) 'A Period of Ambivalence: Eighteenth Century American Childhood'. In de Mause.

Warner, Marina (1989) *Into the Dangerous World*. London, Chatto & Windus.

Weedon, Chris (1987) *Feminist Practice and Poststructuralist Theory*. Oxford, Blackwell.

Whalley, Joyce and Chester, Tessa (1988) *A History of Children's Book Illustration*. London, John Murray with the V & A Museum.

Whitfood, M. (ed.) *The Irigaray Reader*. Oxford, Blackwell.

Wilson, Edmund (1988) 'Introduction'. In James.

Wintersberger, Helmut (1994) 'Costs and Benefits: The Economics of Childhood'. In Qvortrup et al.

Wolfram, Sybil (1987) *In-Laws and Outlaws: Kinship and Marriage in England*. London, Croom Helm.

Wood, Diana (ed.) (1994) *The Church and Childhood*, Vol 31 of Studies in Church History. Blackwell, Oxford.

Wrigley, E. A. (1969) *Population and History*. London, Weidenfeld & Nicolson.

Zelitzer, V. A. (1985) *Pricing the Priceless Child. The Changing Social Value of Children*. New York, Basic Books.

Zipes, Jack (1979) *Breaking the Magic Spell*. London, Heinemann.

# INDEX

abuse of children, 1, 9, 31, 75, 79, 94–9, 101, 103, 105, 195
  discovery of in USA, 75
adult, becoming, 3–5
advertising, 7, 8, 112, 115–16, 119, 199–201, 202–3
Agricultural Children's Act, 1873, 67
alcohol, age at which may drink, 4
anus, symbolism of, 181–3
Ariès, 17, 26–9, 70, 117
  critiques of, 28–9
Aristotle, 46–7
Arnold, Thomas, 72

baby battering, 77
Banaro society, 47
Barnardo, Dr, 69
Barthes, Roland, 11
Bastardy Laws Amendment Act, 56
Beckford, Jasmine, 77
Bell, Mary, 9
Bell, Norma, 39
bestiality, 41
Bible, references to, 3, 55, 146, 194
biological determinism, 23
Birke, Lynda, 17
birth weight, low, 32
black children, 33, 143
Blake, William, 128, 153–6

body, 175
  as metaphor of society, 181
  /mind, 185–91
boot camps, 76
Bordo, Susan, 17
bottle feeding, 48
breast feeding, 35, 37, 47
Brontë, Charlotte, 72
Brown, Martin, 38–9
buggery, 180–4
Bulger, James, 4, 8, 10, 39, 76, 78, 93, 145
Burn, James Dawson, 62

Carlile, Kimberley, 77
Carpenter, Mary, 68
cell theory, 83
charities, use of children in advertising, 2, 8, 115–16, 58
child, definition of, 2–7
  versus childhood, 21–2
  development, 24
  labour, 13, 42, 57, 59
  prostitution, 42, 44, 58
  theories of, 12–17
childbirth, 47
childcare professionals, 1, 103–7, 181
ChildLine, 207
Child Support Act, 209

Child Support Agency, 52
childhood, narratives of, 43
childrearing, 29–32
Children Act 1989, 77
children, and animals, 40, 41
    as insurance, 59
    in nineteenth-century France,
        65–6
    sale of, 48
    and work, 57–69, 136–43
    who kill, 8, 39
chimney sweeps, 62, 63, 66, 138–9
circumcision, 75
*civilité*, 186
class, social, 12, 13–14, 33, 36,
        136–43
    and education, 69–74
Cleveland Crisis, 1987, 19, 64, 77,
        137, 180–4, 210
Colwell, Maria, 77
Conservative government, 33, 56,
        58, 59, 145
Conservatives, 22
Coram, Thomas, 54
Criminal Law Amendment Act,
        198
criminal responsibility, age of, 4
Cunningham, Hugh, 18, 143

darkness of children, 8
Darwin, 25, 75
Davin, A., 67
Defoe, Daniel, 60
dependency, 3, 5, 6, 66, 111, 112,
        136–43
de Sade, 157, 176
Descartes, 40
desire, 178–9, 197–201
Dickens, Charles, 48, 63, 68, 164–6
disabled children, 98
Doyle, Roddy, 172
dress, 122–7
Dunblane, 1, 78, 103, 158

Education, 69–74
Elias, Norbert, 186–9
Eliot, George, 73, 128, 166–8
*Émile*, 152
enfranchisement, 4
Erasmus, 187–8
ethnicity, 12
    and poverty, 33–4
European Court for Human
        Rights, 4
Evangelicals, 128, 136
excremental culture, 184

Family, the, 203–4
fathers/stepfathers, 45, 46, 48, 49,
        51, 53, 55, 56, 63, 64, 89, 112,
        136, 183
fertility, declining, 2
Fever, Fred, 105–6
flirtatiousness, 167
food and feeding, 10, 35–6
Foucault, Michel, 9, 14–15, 83,
        190–1, 196
foundings, 54
Freud, Sigmund, 15, 25, 84–6, 107,
        173–4, 176, 178
futurity, 1, 7, 112, 115

Gangs Act, 1867, 67
gender, 12, 14, 27, 167, 177
    and life chances, 34–6
    and violence, 101–3
Goethe, 81, 82, 84

Haeckel's biogenetic law of
        recapitulation, 5, 24–5, 160
Hall, G. S., 24
Hamilton, Thomas, 1, 97–9, 207
Hanway, Jonas, 139
Hendrick, Harry, 11
Héroard, 24
heterosexual relationships, 3, 177
Highfield Junior School, 206

Hillman, James, 156–7
Hispanic children, USA, 33–4
history and childhood, 26–32
Hobley, Frederick, 71
homosexual relationships, 3
Howe, Brian, 39
Hughes, M. V., 36–7

illegitimacy, 46, 53–7
incest, 177
Infant Life Protection Acts, 75
infanticide, in India, 34
infibulation, 75
innocence, 7, 145–53, 158–63, 168–9, 205
interiority, 81–3, 141
Irigaray, Luce, 16, 177

James, Henry, 162, 169–72
Jordanova, Ludmilla, 6, 64
Joseph Rowntree Foundation, 33, 34
Jung, C. G., 15–16, 86–8, 156

Kerenyi, 87
kinship, 47
Klein, Melanie, 16, 91–2
!Kung society, 26, 37–8

Labour Party, 15, 33, 88–90, 176–9, 199
Liberal Reforms 1906–1914, 76
life chances of children, 11, 12, 13–14, 23, 32–8, 45
life expectancies of children, 32–3
literature for children, 141–2
Locke, John, 47, 86
Lyotard, 16

*Maiden Tribute of Modern Babylon*, 198
marriage, 3, 53
Marxism, 13–14, 23, 70

masturbation, 19, 42, 191–7
Mayhew, Henry, 68
meaning of children to adults, 31–2
memories, 2, 99
memory, 6, 82–3, 159, 164
    False Memory Syndrome, 6
*Mignon*, 82
Miller, Alice, 94–6, 100
modernisation, theories of, 28–9, 30, 70
Moore, Hannah, 69
Moore, Thomas, 157
moral panic, 180
mother(s), 48, 51, 52, 54, 56, 89, 91, 101, 179
    single, 53, 55, 56, 57
Muckford George, 59–60
Muslims, 4, 34
myth, 11, 135–7, 143

nation, 12, 143–4
nature, 39–43, 64, 115, 127–8, 151–2, 160–1
    mechanical versus organic, 41–2
nature versus nurture, 22
Newbery, John, 141
Nietzche, 84
Noble Savage, 151, 160
non-adult, 5, 6, 22
non-children, 8, 39
nudity of children, 119–21
Nussbaum, Hedda, 101, 102
Nyinbas, 3

Oedipal crisis, 84, 95
Opies, 163, 197
organicist views, 41–2, 113
Original Sin, *see* St Augustine
orphans, 51, 53
Osgerby, Faith, 73
other/otherness, 6, 63, 99, 174
'ownership', 5, 18, 46–79

*padrone* system, 46
paintings, of children, 28, 113, 117–31
Pan, 194–5
parent(s), 46, 47, 52, 58, 59, 77, 78
 versus the state, 47, 57, 69, 74, 77, 180
parentage, 147
*patria potestas*, law of, 48
Peirce, Charles, 110
 typology of signs, 111
pets, 113, 127–8
photography, 119, 131–5
Piaget, Jean, 25–6, 161–2
'pin down', 104, 105
Plato, 47
poisonous pedagogy, 94–9
Pollock, Linda, 30–1
Poor Law Act, 51
pornography, child, 198
Postman, Neil, 22
postmodernism, 16, 43, 44, 107
poverty, 1, 32–33, 58
power relations, 9, 10, 45
Prevention of Cruelty to Children Act, 75
Preyer, 24
Prince, Mary, 50–1
projection, 90–3, 102, 106
protection, 63, 74, 90–3, 105, 106, 158
Protestantism, 147–9, 198–9
psychohistorians, 30–1
Puritans, 29, 148, 189–90
*putti*, 118

rape, 45
Renaissance art, 120–1
representation, 109–44
repression, 85
reproductive technology, 24, 203
Rich, Adrienne, 101

Ridings school, Halifax, 158
Romantics, 81
Rose, Jacqueline, 142
Rousseau, 23, 150–2

sale of children, 46, 48, 58
Sarajevo, airlift, 1993, 143
Schelling, 84
Schiller, 84
schooling, 27, 65
Schopenhauer, 84
sentimentalisation of childhood, 130–1, 140
sex clinics, 34
sexual abuse, 173–4
 of Virginia Woolf, 37
sexuality, 175–9
Shaftesbury, Lord, 68, 135, 136
Shakespeare, 63, 160
siblings, 36–8, 48, 67, 73
slavery, 5, 16, 22, 33, 47, 49–53
Smith, Emma, 46, 55–6, 57
social construction of childhood, 21–45, 141
South Africa, 34
Soyinka, Wole, 36
St Augustine, idea of Original Sin, 17, 22, 29, 146–8
Steedman, Carolyn, 82
Steinberg, Joel, 101–3
Steinberg, Leo, 120, 121
Street Arabs, 67, 140
Street games, 197
surveillance, 63, 73, 192, 197

*tabula rasa*, child as, 150
Temple, Shirley, 143–4
theories of the child, 12–17
Third World, 4, 11, 13, 16, 32, 33, 44, 57, 58, 116, 184
Thompson, Robert and Jon Venables, 4, 8, 10, 76, 99, 145

Tiedemann, 24
Twain, Mark, 168–9

unconscious, the, 84–90

Venables, Jon and Robert
    Thompson, 4, 8, 10, 76, 99, 145
'video nasties', 27
violence, 8, 27, 101–2

wet-nursing, 47–8
West, Frederick and Rosemary,
    178
Wordsworth, William, 158–61,
    164

Year of the Child, 1994, 3, 205

Zelitzer, 31